# Quotable

"Call unto the way of thy Lord with wisdom and fair exhortation, and reason with them in the better way. Lo! Thy Lord is best aware of him who strayeth from His way, and He is best aware of those who go aright."
- *Quran 16:125*

"Allah increaseth in right guidance those who walk aright, and the good deeds, which endure, are better in thy Lord's sight for reward,.."
- *Quran 19:76*

"The dogmas of the quiet past are inadequate to the stormy present. The occasion is piled high with difficulty, and we must rise with the occasion. As our case is new, so we must think anew and act anew."
- *Abraham Lincoln. Iconic 16th President of the United States.(d. 1865)*

# The Call Of Modernity And Islam

The Quranic phrase *"I take refuge in God"* written in *tughra* form by the Turkish calligrapher Mustafa Rakim (d. 1767).

# Also by Jamal Khwaja

* Living The Quran In Our Times

* Authenticity and Islamic Liberalism

* Five Approaches to Philosophy

* Quest For Islam

* Essays On Cultural Pluralism

*The Vision Of An Unknown Indian Muslim

* Numerous articles and scholarly essays


To learn more about the author, visit

**www.JamalKhwaja.com**
Download free Digital Books, Lectures, Essays and more …

**Cover illustration:**
*The scholarly figures on the cover have been taken from a miniature painting created by the Mughal Emperor Jahangir's artists (dating back to the mid-1600s) They represent the Muslim orthodoxy, with the only non-conformist being the bare-headed dervish seated at the lower left.*

# THE CALL OF MODERNITY AND ISLAM

## A MUSLIM'S JOURNEY INTO THE 21ST CENTURY

**Jamal Khwaja**
Formerly Professor of Philosophy
Aligarh Muslim University

ALHAMD PUBLISHERS, LLC
Los Angeles

**Copyright © by Jamal Khwaja 2014**

*All rights reserved. Copyright under Berne Copyright Convention, Universal Copyright Convention, and Pan American Copyright Convention. No part of this book may be reproduced, stored in a retrieval system, or transmitted in any form or by any means, electronic or mechanical or otherwise, including photocopying and recording, without prior written permission of the publisher, except for the inclusion of brief quotations in a review.*

For permission to reproduce selections from this book contact the Publisher.

**Published and distributed worldwide by ALHAMD Publishers, LLC.**
3131 Roberts Ave, Culver City, CA 90232, USA.
**www.AlhamdPublishers.com**

**Printed and bound in the United States of America**
Book and Jacket Design by Sandeep Sandhu and Raisa Shafiyyullah
Author Photo by Kenny Zepeda

More information about the Author and his works can be found at
www.JamalKhwaja.com
Look for FREE Downloads of Essays & Articles written by the Author.

ISBN: 978-1-935293-81-1 (Hard cover)
ISBN: 978-1-935293-94-1 (Soft cover)
ISBN: 978-1-935293-79-8 (E-pub)
Publisher's SAN #: 857-0132
BISAC Subject Headings: Religion/Islam/Koran & Sacred Writings (REL041000),
and Religion/Philosophy (REL051000)

*In the name of God, Most Beneficent, Most Merciful*

**Dedicated to the memory of :**
*Rabindra Nath Tagore, Jawaharlal Nehru and
Maulana Abul Kalam Azad*

# *Quotable*

"... Lo! Allah verily is guiding those who believe unto a right path."
- *Quran 22:54*

"Delve deep into the Quran, O Muslim true!
So, may Allah endow you with a character new"
- *Muhammad Iqbal. Pre-eminent South Asian Philosopher-Poet (d. 1938)*

"Something needs to change. We can't solve our problems by using the same kind of thinking we used when we created them."
- *Albert Einstein. He is often regarded as the father of modern physics. (d. 1955)*

"The cry for authenticity does not usually reflect a wish to halt the spread of modernity and restore a traditional society that disappeared a long time ago. Rather, it wants the tiger tamed; it seeks a modernity rendered less arbitrary, less vicious, more comprehensible, and above all, more productive of life-styles people would recognize as spiritually as well as materially satisfying."
- *Robert D. Lee. American scholar.*

# Contents

Author's Preface .................................................................. 11

Introduction .................................................................... 15

**Essay 1:**
What is Modernity? ............................................................ 19

**Essay 2:**
What is Religious Fundamentalism? ...................................... 39

**Essay 3:**
The Islamic Vision of Sir Syed ............................................. 55

**Essay 4:**
Religious Pluralism and Islam .............................................. 75

**Essay 5:**
Tolerance and Islam ........................................................... 85

**Essay 6:**
Democracy and Islam ......................................................... 129

**Essay 7:**
The Concept of an Islamic Economic System ......................... 157

**Essay 8:**
Inter-religious Marriage and Islam ........................................ 181

**Essay 9:**
Sex Morality and Islam ....................................................... 191

**Essay 10:**
Modern Penology and Islam ................................................ 203

## Contents

*(Continued)*

**Afterword** ................................................................. 211

**Appendix 1:**
About the Author .............................................. 215

**Appendix 2:**
The Quest For The Meaning of Islam ................ 219

**Index** ................................................................. 287

# Author's Preface

The ten essays that comprise this work were written mainly after the completion of my earlier work, *Quest for Islam*, first published in 1977. Since a single thread runs between them, the essays are being presented in one volume. Out of the ten presented here, three were published in a volume of *Khuda Bakhsh Lectures*, Patna, and two were published in the proceedings of seminars at the *Institute of Advanced Study*, Shimla.

The latter two, *What is Modernity?* and *Modernity and Traditionalism in Islam*, have been abridged and edited by myself to constitute the revised version of *What is Modernity?* as presented here. I am grateful to the authorities of the *Khuda Bakhsh Library* and the *Shimla Institute* for enabling me to put my ideas in writing. I thank the above prestigious institutions.

The seed issues I had in mind when my work *Quest for Islam* was published were three: How should the 'essence' of Islam be defined? Is Islam, essentially, a total code of life? How should a Muslim today understand Islam and what does it mean to be a good/true Muslim in this age of science and mixed societies all over the globe?

A large number of Muslims as well as others are grappling with the above questions. Words and expressions such as 'secularism', 'Islamic fundamentalism', and '*jehaad*' are frequently used in daily discourse without first defining them with some exactitude. This produces not only quite avoidable controversies and perplexity but serious tensions and conflicts within society.

There is a wide-spread assumption in highly educated Muslims as well as Muslim society in general that Islam is the only true religion, and Islam has only one true paradigm or version. I have termed this belief or approach as '*cultural monism*', and the belief or approach that there are plural paths to God and salvation (and also plural paradigms of Islam, as such) as '*cultural pluralism*'.

## Author's Preface to the Second Edition

The proper way to answer the crucial questions I have posed is to look at religions (including Islam) in the light of reliable history rather than as fixed or abstract entities. When one proceeds in this way one finds that all major religions had a more or less 'totalist' character right until the end of the 18th century. Even though contemporary Judaism, Christianity, Hinduism, and Buddhism are now *not* regarded as living 'totalist' codes of conduct, (as is Islam in the self-image and aspiration of numerous Muslims the world over) the past paradigms of all these religions were very similar to the present Islamic one.

Judaism and Christianity in the West underwent a slow internal transformation of their earlier 'totalist' self-image into their present 'existentialist' or 'inspirational' forms. This process started in the early 18th century under the impact of the European Enlightenment. In India the process of internal change in Hinduism was started much earlier by Guru Nanak and Kabir; under the impact of a then forward-looking *Sufi* paradigm of Islam. The advent of British power and Western thought and culture enormously enriched and invigorated the internal growth of Hinduism and the Bengal Renaissance threw up luminaries, like Ram Mohan Roy, Jagdish Chandra Bose, and Tagore *et al*.

I submit that the spiritual Renaissance or Enlightenment is yet to happen in the case of the Muslim community in the Indian subcontinent and other parts of the world. Sir Syed, the Father of the *Aligarh Movement*, was one of the most charismatic figures in Indian and Islamic history ever. He certainly lit a brilliant flame, but I dare say it spread more heat than light in society. He had both clarity and courage, his vision was broad. But his inputs were rather inadequate. His followers could and should have built on the magnificent legacy he had left, but they failed their great benefactor. Muslim intellectuals in general (with very few exceptions) failed to keep pace with Sir Syed, to say nothing of overcoming his inadequacies.

True progress and enlightenment among Muslims will come only when they are fired by the spirit of free enquiry and they develop the moral courage to follow where the argument leads. They must give up their fear and dislike of cultural pluralism. They must look upon inner freedom of thought and expression as an essential part of the Islamic way of life rather than as a Western fashion or fad. No program of simply 'adjusting' or modifying the *shariah* can help Muslims to become integrated and creative individuals in the conditions of the modern age, unless they, after honest and critical inquiry, redefine the essential function of religion (Islam included) in the modern age. No interpretation of the *Quran*, merely in the light of *Hadees* literature, can be satisfactory without making an in-depth sympathetic critical study of modern thought and institutions.

Many Muslim believers hold that real believers do not need any enquiry, reasoning or study of history etc. in addition to the guidance contained in the Quran and the sayings of the Prophet. This approach is highly simplistic and misleading. There is a clear distinction between the infallible '*Word of God*' and the all too human (hence varied and fallible) interpretations of the unchanged *Quranic* texts in modern times due to the ever changing human situation. Without free enquiry and loving tolerance of dissent, no religious, spiritual or intellectual tradition can survive and retain its primal force of conviction due to new ideas and ideals that are bound to emerge in human society.

The essays in the present collection written in a very simple style develop the main argument of my earlier work, *Quest For Islam* and actually apply it (in much greater detail) to varied problems and issues of politics, economics and social ethics in the contemporary human situation.

I hope and trust all readers, Muslim and others alike, will find the contents interesting and illuminating as my approach is critical and sympathetic at the same time, and my purpose is to promote the unity of the human family rather than to convert or to defend any position.

Jamal Khwaja
Aligarh, 2014

*Acknowledgements*

**Note on suggested reading pattern for the work:**
*The explanatory notes at the end of some Essays are meant to develop the theme and the line of the argument in the text. Each note contains some important information or insight. Reading each note along with the text should considerably add to the pleasure and the profit of reading the Essay.*

*Using two bookmarks, one in each section, would make the process effortless. This arrangement aims to serve the requirements of readers who are hard pressed for time as well as readers who can devote more time for pondering highly complex issues.*

# INTRODUCTION

A sociological and critical historical survey of the human condition from primitive times to the present age shows that the human family has developed from very primitive and crude proto-human levels of consciousness or awareness to the present stage of development in every dimension of human life. The term 'modernity', as used in the context of this work, means the underlying basic beliefs, values, attitudes and world outlook that began to take shape and crystallize in Western Europe from the 15th century onwards and attained fairly stable and identifiable contours by the closing years of the 19th century. This set of beliefs, values and attitudes is, of course, still undergoing internal changes due to ever growing human knowledge of nature, clearer insights into the human condition and cumulative human experience based on trial and error. As of today modernity means possessing an open critical mind that demands appropriate evidence or justification before accepting any truth-claim as true or false, unconditional respect for the human person, irrespective of race, region, religion, caste or gender, equality of status, human rights, and opportunity, free enquiry based on deductive reasoning and scientific investigation and verification, tolerance of disagreement, and the sharing and transfer of political power through peaceful means as pre-conditions of human welfare and universal peace.

The term 'modernity', however, must not be equated with 'Westernism'. In fact, the confusion of modernity with imitative 'Westernism' has led to the coining of the expression 'post-modernism' and the several critiques of western modernism. I, therefore, chose for the present work the title 'call of modernity' in place of 'challenge of modernity'. The eastern and southern segment of humanity should learn from the fallacies and follies of the west, but not fail to acknowledge and appreciate the considerable elements of value in western culture.

To date only a small portion, namely the developed world, has imbibed modernity, as defined above. The developing world and the undeveloped world are at various stages on the path to modernization. The process, to my mind, is irreversible, though we are free to retain or not to retain a due sense of proportion in our responses to the challenges of life. The advocates of extreme views, whether of the left or the right variety, may win a few battles here or there, but the war of minds and attitudes will be won by those who think and act freely, clearly, courageously and consistently and stand committed to spirit-centered humanism and inter-faith spirituality.

Inter-faith spirituality is another basic component of modernity in the sphere of religion or religious faith. The pre-modern view was that only one religion or faith led to salvation, or, in other words, only those who spoke one particular language of the spirit or practiced one particular set of sacred rituals could reach the highest level of felicity or salvation. This approach or view may be called the belief in exclusive salvation. But modernity in the religious sphere makes the substance of religious faith as well as the choice of symbols and rituals optional rather than mandatory for attaining success and salvation.

Modernity implies that authenticity of faith and righteous conduct, rather than any particular creed or conceptual formulation, is what matters for attaining salvation. The inner transition of the individual from mandatory religious monism to permissive religious pluralism and even to neutral secular humanism (for some exceptionally 'tough minded souls' as termed by the American sage and thinker, William James) is the crucial mark of modernity. Modernity, by itself, does not imply accepting or rejecting Theism or Atheism.

The Islamic paradigm, which I authentically accept and the concepts and values of modernity do not clash, provided we interpret the Quranic texts in the light of modern semantic analysis. This approach lays stress on the functions rather than the literal grammatical meaning of any verbal communication system. I have argued and illustrated this crucial point in considerable detail while giving extensive quotations from Quranic texts in my work, *Living the Quran in Our Times*. Evidently, Islamic orthodoxy followed a different interpretation of Quranic texts and projected a different paradigm of Islam. However, several great Muslim thinkers, sages, mystics and poets in the classical creative period of Muslin history, explicitly or implicitly, stated views, same or similar to my own authentic Islamic paradigm.

*Introduction*

Ibn Sina, Ibn Zakarriya Razi, al-Beruni, Ibn Rushd, Jalal uddin Rumi, Ibn Khaldun and Sadruddin Shirazi (Mulla Sadr) are a few illustrious creative minds who had the clarity and courage to dissent from the dominant climate of ideas in medieval times. The dominant orthodox sections in medieval times sidelined these creative spirits. Many of them were even persecuted by those in power. Thanks to modern Western scholarship, at its best, those dubbed as heretics by a large number of Muslims in medieval times are being admired and venerated today as great intellectuals, sages, scientists and spiritual leaders cutting across different religious traditions.

Muslims today should distinguish the timeless primary verities and intrinsic values of Islam: faith in one supreme Creator, Day of Final Judgment, ultimate supremacy of good over evil, the establishment of universal justice, truthfulness, compassion, self-knowledge, respect for life, rational altruism, the exemplary and sublime character of the Holy prophet, and so on – from the secondary instrumental rules every religion prescribes for realizing the primary values. Making this distinction and applying it consistently to different problems and issues, as when they arise, is far more important for both success and salvation than unreflective and unconditional adherence to instrumental rules of conduct prescribed in the past when conditions were different and our knowledge of the 'facts of life' was much less than now.

I have thoroughly analyzed and discussed these complex issues in the long introductory chapter of my work, *Quest for Islam*, revised edition, 2010, and also in *Living the Quran in Our Times*. For the convenience of readers of my other essays on related themes in the volumes, The Call of Modernity and Islam, and Essays on Cultural Pluralism, this chapter has been reproduced, in full, as an appendix to The Call of Modernity.

My paper, What is Modernity? was intensively discussed by the distinguished participants at the seminar on Modernity at Shimla and was much applauded. If I were to re-write it now my language, perhaps, would be much simpler and free from academic jargon found in some places in the original paper. But the general thrust would have been the same. I have, therefore, not attempted to polish it any further.

# Essay 1

## What is Modernity?

In this paper I use the word 'modernity' to describe a basic outlook on life and a system of ideas and values that gradually evolved in the West since the Renaissance. Subsequently, I shall try to define or explain what I understand by the expression 'religious modernity'. Towards the close of the essay I shall discuss the relationship between religious modernity and traditionalism. I shall end with a brief statement of my own authentic position with regard to Islamic modernity.

The word 'modernity' is, obviously, derived from the English word, 'modern' (Latin *modo*) meaning 'just now or in current use or fashion'. The word came into general use (perhaps in mid-20th century) much later than the cognate word 'modernism' that was first used by traditional Catholic critics and opponents of the scientific outlook in the last quarter of the 19th century. 'Modernism' then had a pejorative undertone, and denigrated the then rising liberal and scientific outlook of modernized Christians. Though never restricted to the purely religious sphere, the word 'modernism' became associated with the domain of religion. Thus, the word 'modernity' is later as well as more general than 'modernism'.

The adjective 'modern' (in the literal sense) means what is new or current 'now' without specifying the actual coordinates in space and time. Thus, the adjective performs an umbrella function rather than the descriptive. But the noun 'modernity', in contemporary discourse, broadly refers to a predilection for or acceptance of the basic concepts and values of Renaissance and post Renaissance Western Europe in the different spheres of life. Modernity in the generic attitudinal sense may be imitative/reactive, or creative. Imitative modernity may appropriately be termed 'fashionism' and is at bottom a kind of 'inverted traditionalism'. 'Imitative/Reactive modernity' is a more or less sharp and superficial reaction to a situational challenge. Creative modernity, on the other hand, is not a time bound fixed response but the reflective choice of an autonomous human being.

'Creative-responsible modernity' is an authentic response to the ever-changing human situation that demands creative awareness rather than mechanical adaptation. Reactive modernity may prove as futile or barren as static traditionalism. In the final analysis, it is not the fascination for what is contemporary or blind loyalty to the tradition, but the creative quest of value, the ceaseless search for the better, rather than contentment with the good, which is the fountainhead of all progress.

## ANALYSIS OF WESTERN MODERNITY

Every epoch or society has a unique cultural configuration or *gestalt*. This configuration consists of:

**(a)** a conceptual framework or system of ideas to make sense of human experience in general. This conceptual system is woven on the warp and woof of a number of basic concepts.
**(b)** a distinctive value system.
**(c)** a distinctive artistic or aesthetic sensibility.

A full understanding of the culture of an epoch or society requires the understanding of all the above three dimensions of culture: cognitive, ethical and aesthetic; in their dynamic interaction.

Every society has also its own socio-economic structure, including laws, customs, diverse associations and institutions. Marx did pioneering work in showing the impact of the socio-economic structure upon the cultural *gestalt* of a society, that is, its philosophy, ethics, religion and art. The elements of truth in his approach are undeniable, though he, perhaps, under estimated the plastic role of the society's traditional thought-cum-value system in the march of history. The role played by the sentiment of nationalism in Western Europe, and the role being played now by nationalism in the current Sino-Soviet dispute, or the role played by religious sentiments in the socio-political affairs of present-day India, are serious reminders of the qualifications that must be made in classical Marxian theory.

## What is Modernity?

I shall now enumerate and briefly elucidate the basic concepts as well as the values of Western modernity, that is, of modern Western Europe from the Renaissance onwards.

1. Natural or intracosmic causation: This concept is the foundation of the modern conceptual framework. It implies that every event has a cause located within the total system of events rather than outside the system, and that this total system is an interrelated cosmos having stable patterns of events. This concept does not entail any particular monistic theory of causation constructed on the basis of particular models; say the model of mechanistic physics, quantum mechanics, biological evolution, or human teleological action, etc. All monistic theories result from our being gripped by a particular model. The implication of the concept is merely that the causes of events are to be located in the event-nexus rather than in some transnexus, or, in other words, in a supernatural or super-cosmic nexus. This directly suggests the second concept of empirical explanation.

2. Empirical explanation: This concept is the logical completion or progression of the first. If natural causation be universally operative, then knowledge of the interconnections between events becomes no less essential than the mere description of discreet events. Complete knowledge is not merely description but description plus explanation or descriptive explanation. Apart from this intellectual value, explanation is the basis of all control or regulation of events. Control over events presupposes a prior explanatory framework of events. Now if this framework be such that preferred explanations cannot be checked empirically in accordance with clear and previously agreed rules, then they cannot serve as reliable guides to successful human control over events. This does not imply that there are no other types of explanation or modes of interpretation of human experience, or that such modes are inferior or invalid in principle.

Indeed the poetic, metaphysical, religious and mythical interpretations have their own functions and logic, and the model of empirical or scientific explanation is only one of the modes of unifying or organizing human experience into meaningful patterns. Nevertheless the emphasis upon empirical explanation, that is, explanations that are testable through sense perception, is the peculiar and the most striking feature of the modern temper. It was this that fostered the growth of quantitative methods and of observation under controlled conditions, which in turn fostered the contemporary technological society. More than two thousand years ago metaphysical interpretation had displaced magic, myth and ritualistic religion from their dominant place in the 'thought' of cultivated minds. In the modern age metaphysical interpretation has itself been pushed into the background due to the dominant position and prestige gradually acquired by scientific or empirical explanation.

3. Universal evolution: This concept posits variability in the heart of all things. The accumulation of minute variations is the means both of growth and development as well as of decline and destruction. The concept of evolution implies that change is inevitable, and that reality is a dynamic, living and growing cosmos, rather than a static or completed Divine artifact, or an accidental product of the blind dance of atoms.

The conception of evolution combined the theories of chance occurrences and of purposive creation. Different features of the universe evoke both these theories and worldviews. The conceptions of Divine Creation and of chance configuration resulted from a selective rather than a comprehensive concern with the diverse features of the universe. The concept of evolution attempted to interpret the totality of these features in accordance with the principle of economy of assumptions.

To begin with, evolution was applied to organic life. But gradually the concept acquired universal applicability. This brings us to the fourth concept of social causation.

4. Social causation: This concept was implicit in the wider concept of natural or intra-cosmic causation, assuming that the word 'natural' is used not in opposition to 'social', but in the sense of 'intra-cosmic' as opposed to 'extra-cosmic'. But this concept was made explicit only in the last century, when social phenomena came to be viewed, as much subject to laws as were physical phenomena. Marx has undoubtedly given a powerful impetus to sociology through his concept of historical or sociological materialism. But social causes are highly complex and the contemporary multi-dimensional approach to social causation is definitely an improvement upon Marxian economic determinism.

5. Relativism: This is being used in a very wide sense, which would include positivism and Kant's 'phenomenalism', no less than Einstein's conception of relativity. The implication of this concept is that pure formal logic or mathematics apart, all factual knowledge is relative to the knower and all evaluation is relative to the ethical norms that are

the faith axioms for the evaluator, just as perception is relative to the human perceptual apparatus. Hence, both physics and metaphysics operate only with ideas and concepts relative to human understanding. This realization played a crucial role in the rapid development of the natural and social sciences in the post Hegelian Western world. The grip or fascination of 'Absolutism' waned, not only in the sphere of knowledge, but in all other spheres of human life and religion, morality, language, art, and so on. The 20th century even led to 'relativity' in the sphere of mathematics in the sense of the creation of non-Euclidean geometries and modern algebra.

6. Dimensional integration: This concept implies that reality is sufficiently complex for any one set of concepts or any mono-dimensional approach to be adequate to a multi-dimensional reality. We must always avoid the fallacy of 'reductive simplism' while describing or explaining things. Human disagreement is very largely the function of mono-dimensional perspectives. Their critical and systematic reintegration dissolves all avoidable and unnecessary controversy and directs the human mind to really fruitful lines of enquiry. It leads to a sense of release or deliverance from the clash of partial perspectives to an irenic all-inclusive approach in all enquiry or investigation. This promotes the growth of all the different dimensions or conceptual systems in the spirit of 'epistemic co-existence' and co-operation, that is, dimensional integration. Thus this concept supplements the concept of epistemic relativity, and the two in fact are jointly responsible for the rapid growth of positively verifiable and quantitative sciences in the 19th and 20th centuries.

The above concepts are not exhaustive, though, I believe, they constitute the core of the Western conceptual framework. There is nothing rigid about this scheme, since the basic concepts can be separated or combined according to one's choice and sense of aesthetic elegance. Thus, for example, one could posit 'Naturalism' and 'Universal Causation' separately as two basic concepts instead of combining them into the concept of 'Natural or intra-cosmic Causation', as I have done. The interplay of these concepts generates the worldview, and their analysis helps to crystallize this worldview or total perspective.

I now turn to the basic values of Western modernity. The following list is again illustrative rather than exhaustive. But I believe it includes the core values.

1. Life-affirmation or this-worldliness: This does not mean hedonism or the pursuit of pleasure, though happiness is one of the elements of life-affirmation. This does not exclude belief in life after death. All that this value implies is that this life is important and must be lived as the good life for its own sake and not merely as a preparation for salvation in the hereafter. The emphasis is on the fullness of life and self-realization rather than on renunciation and salvation. This may be called the typical Greco-Roman ethos, as distinct from the Judeo-Christian ethos of West Europe in the pre-Renaissance era.

2. Affluence: This implies giving high importance to the external conditions or socio-economic soil of man's growth and activities. It may be called the typical American ethos, which is only a development of the West European value of 'decent living'. Affluence is not necessarily connected with life-affirmation, but life-affirmation tends to generate affluence through technological progress.

3. Humanistic love and dignity of the individual: Humanistic love is love and respect for the human essence or the person as such independently of the various accidents of his birth, like religion, race, region, language or status etc. The dignity of the individual is a corollary of humanistic love. This love transcends the loyalty to fragmentary groups like the tribe, nation, or church, though it is not incompatible with sincere patriotism or a sense of emotional identification with an ideological group.

Democracy as a way of life and as a political form or institution is a corollary of the dignity of the individual.

4. Spiritual autonomy: This value is closely related to the dignity of the individual. It means that the individual must be inwardly free or self legislative. His commitment must be to his own higher self or the God within him rather than to any external Authority. The conception of the sovereignty of the people is nothing but individual spiritual autonomy writ large. This inner freedom again is not incompatible with religious belief as such, though obviously it is incompatible with all authoritarian religious systems.

5. Polymorphous equality: This is a very recent extension of the value of humanistic love and dignity of the individual. It may be said to be a new dimension added to the merely political equality of voting (or the maxim of one man, one vote) as posited by classical democracy. It means that equality must be polymorphous or multi-dimensional rather than mono-dimensional,

that is, confined to a particular area of life. Thus, there should be equality of opportunity in every walk of life for every individual irrespective of sex, as far as is humanly possible. The ultimate criterion or essence of social justice is seen to lie precisely in the degree of equality of opportunity generated in society. Equality of opportunity must not be confused with literal or bare equality. It is not incompatible with gradations in status, power or wealth. All that it entails is that such gradation should be earned and not inherited. They should be the reward of individual effort under conditions of polymorphous equality, rather than the antecedent gifts of the accidents of birth. It will be seen that no traditional religion has practiced or even preached such polymorphous equality, though some religions have given greater importance to equality, than have others. Socialism is itself partly a means to the realization of the equality of opportunity.

6. Dynamism: This value is a corollary of the theoretical concepts of natural and social causation. Since reality is 'Becoming' rather than 'Being', malleable rather than immutable, it calls for the ethic of action rather than of resignation. Not only must nature be controlled, but also disease, poverty and other social evils must be abolished through planned and systematic effort. Mere contemplation of virtue without the life of action is futile.

7. Ceaseless creativity of values: By virtue of spiritual autonomy inherited values must be conserved, as well as new ones should be created by man. A dynamic, self-critical and perennially open value system is more desirable than a closed and static one. Values grow, and our insight into them matures and new levels or dimensions emerge even in the case of basic values like love, justice, equality, etc. Thus no particular value system can be accepted as final.

## SCALE AND DEGREES OF MODERNITY

On the basis of the above concepts and values we may construct a scale of modernity and can measure the degrees of the modernity of a person, society or epoch. The advantage of such a scale lies in the consideration that the concept of modernity is not simple or atomic, but complex and multi-dimensional. Consequently, an individual or society may be modern in one respect or facet, and medieval or ancient in some other, or more modern in some and less modern in other respects. Moreover, these concepts and values are not the unique features of the modern age in the chronological sense. With the help of this scale of modernity we can make a more accurate and concrete assessment of the qualitative modernity of cultures or societies, irrespective of their chronological or temporal modernity.

When we judge an epoch or society as being modernist or medieval, we obviously refer to its dominant or preponderant character. There is no implication of the total absence of concepts and values contrary to the dominant thought-cum-value system.

## WHAT IS RELIGIOUS MODERNITY?

The following are the essential features of religious modernity and they jointly and severally constitute its essential features:

**(1)** Stress on the fully integrated human personality as distinguished from a fragmented or compartmentalized one. This integration takes into account all the dimensions of human experience like reason, feeling, and morality without suppressing any basic existential or personality need.

**(2)** Distinction between religious experience and its conceptual interpretation.

**(3)** Distinction between the essential core of religious faith and the concrete social, cultural and political *gestalt* of the religious group concerned.

**(4)** Distinction between salvation in the sense of continuous spiritual growth and in the sense of the 'saving' of souls in life after death.

**(5)** Distinction between intrinsic and instrumental values.

**(6)** Stress on the cultivation of basic spirituality rather than any one of its diverse forms as represented by particular religions.

**(7)** Emphasis on spiritual autonomy and the reconciliation of any possible conflict with religious authority.

**(8)** Emphasis on ceaseless creativity of values and extra dimensional progress, as distinguished from the conservation of values and intra-dimensional progress. In other words, the stress is on creative fidelity rather than mechanical conformity to the past.

**(9)** Authenticity/authentic being as an individual's undistorted awareness of or insight into one's depth feelings, attitudes and responses to one's own situation and existence as a whole. In practice to be authentic means to excel in the Buddhist value, *'vipasna'*.

The above-mentioned nine points sum up the essential features of religious modernity in the West and are more or less self-explanatory. I shall however, comment on the first three points and the ninth point which are foundational:

The first feature of dimensional integration of personality is a much more inclusive and richer concept than rationalism. Full integration includes the cultivation of reason but is not reducible to it. The hallmark of 19th century religious modernity in the West was rationalism, which was a legacy of the previous age of reason and enlightenment in Europe. But this mono-dimensional approach has given way to a multi-dimensional approach.

The second basic feature of religious modernity is the distinction between religious experience and its conceptual interpretation. This distinction applies to all forms of human experience and not merely the religious. Religious modernity emphasizes the significance and role of both experience and interpretation in the religious sphere. But, it insists that the two should not be confused, as is actually the case with most popular conceptions of different religions. Religious experience is *sui generis* and cannot be reduced without remainder to other forms of experience like the aesthetic, the moral and the logical etc. Hence, religious modernity is not synonymous with pure ethicism or humanism, which are attempts to reduce religion to the purely ethical dimensions of human experience.

Religious modernity does not accept humanism or ethical religion as fully adequate, because they fall short of and miss the transcendental/mystical dimension of human experience. Man's growth remains incomplete without the flowering of his potential spirituality or spiritual sense as distinguished from his moral potentiality or moral sense. The distinction between the spiritual and the moral sense is analogous to the distinction between the moral and the aesthetic sense. The quest for the existential interpretation of man's experience is a deeply engrained human personality need. Like religious experience, this quest is also *sui generis* and different from the quest of scientific explanation. Mere descriptive knowledge and scientific explanation do not fully satisfy man's yearning for an existential interpretation or significance of the human situation within the total cosmic context. This interpretation, however, is a distinct activity from the original and primary religious experience of man as such. Most religious persons do not make any distinction between religious experience and its interpretation. Consequently, they suppose that the denial of their particular interpretation amounts to a denial of the experience as such. Moreover, they are not aware of the essential relativity of all interpretation to socio-cultural space-time. In other words the popular traditionalist believers of different religions remain unaware of:

(a) the distinction between experience and interpretation, and

(b) the organic connection of the interpretation with the socio-cultural conditions and the inherited conceptual framework of the society in which a particular religion grows.

The systematic conceptual interpretation of religious experience is essential and indispensable. The supposed self sufficiency of mere morality or even religious experience is a romantic illusion born of difficulties or rather man's despair at arriving at a final and universally acceptable conceptual interpretation of the human situation.

Sober religious modernists in the West like Whitehead (d. 1947), Bergson (d. 1941), Hocking (d. 1966), Tillich (d. 1965), Niebuhr (d. 1971), Marcel (d. 1973) and Buber (d. 1965) *et al*, thus do not reject a metaphysical or philosophical theology, as superfluous, but attempt to reconstruct the basic religious concepts of the Christian or Jewish tradition. Their aim is to remove the conceptual difficulties that flow from the traditional meaning given to such concepts as 'God', 'Son of God', 'creation', 'revelation', 'prophecy', 'providence', 'grace', and so on. All creative interpreters of the different religious traditions have always attempted such re-construction. But the distinguishing feature of modern and contemporary religious reconstruction is that it must be done under the umbrella of science and the scientific method.

The third foundational feature of religious modernity concerns the distinction between the essential core and the concrete *gestalt* of a religion. This distinction has been suggested and developed as a result of the growth of sociology of religion on the one hand, and the phenomenology of religion on the other. The sociology of religion shows that all religious traditions have socio-economic determinants as well as dimensions. The phenomenology, of religion, on the other hand, draws our attention to the nature of the essential core of the total religious *gestalt*. This core consists of a thought-cum-value system in organic interaction with the general conceptual framework prevalent in the parent society in which the religion originates. This thought system is the same as the conceptual interpretation mentioned above.

The value system underlies concrete rules, regulations and precepts of a particular religion and should not be equated with these concrete rules. The thought system and the value system jointly entail the precept system of a particular religion and give meaning to its symbolic life. The concrete *gestalt* of a religion, on the other hand, is influenced by the concrete conceptual and social soil in which the religion grows. The concrete personality or *gestalt* of different religions, however, includes a system of institutions over and above the thought-cum-value system, even as a living organism has secondary qualities distinct from its essential attributes.

The practical significance of this apparently academic distinction is crucial. Once this distinction is conceptually registered, we are at once liberated, as it were, from an emotional fixation upon a particular cultural *gestalt* whether Islamic, Christian or Hindu. The confusion between the pure essence and the accidents of its concrete exemplification in social space-time is removed. The 'Idea of Islam', or the 'Idea of Hinduism/Buddhism', in the Platonic sense, generates both conceptual space and an inner freedom of movement without thereby repudiating the concrete *gestalt* of these religions. The possibility of conflict between loyalty to the past and aspirations for the future is reconciled. As a member of the kingdom of ceaseless growth, man is liberated from enslavement to the past as distinguished from a creative fidelity to his religious tradition.

The ninth value of religious modernity, 'authenticity' is, perhaps, the most crucial and foundational of all. It is extremely significant that this value, in some form or other, is regarded as the key value in all religious traditions of the human family. It is the life breath, the essence of spirituality, since, in practical terms, it means that the individual has inner clarity and courage to face whatever lies in the depths of his inmost being.

The foregoing analysis of Western religious modernity should also throw into relief the profile of its contrary, that is, religious traditionalism. But the difference between the two is a matter of degrees, rather than of kind.

# Relationship Between Modernity And Traditionalism

The creation of new values and the conservation of the old that have stood the test of time are both equally necessary. In fact they depend upon each other. The creation of new values pre-supposes a valuational base or support. Similarly, the effective maintenance of this base demands awareness of the subtle changes in the nuances and rhythms of human experience. Eternal and intelligent vigilance is the price of keeping old values alive in the condition of dynamic interaction with the environment rather than as showpieces in the museum of man's heritage.

Creativity ever spun man to go ahead in the realm of values and to yearn for the better rather than be content with the good. The function of tradition on the other hand is to strike a note of caution, lest the pace of change increase to the point of giving diminishing returns. The function of tradition is not the stoppage of growth but only the regulation of the speed of growth. The conservative approach, thus, has its own function in the economy of human progress, provided it does not over reach itself.

Creativity and conservation should therefore dovetail into and supplement each other. Without creativity conservation leads to fossilization, while without conservation, creativity leads to irresponsible experimentation. While such adventures in the realm of art and literature may not be injurious, they could prove catastrophic in the realm of moral and social relationships. The new sex morality of Western Europe and America, according to which the game of sex may be played between any two willing parties without any mutual obligation arising there from, has played havoc with the spiritual growth of the contemporary Western man. It appears to me that the west is gradually realizing this and that a more balanced interpretation of sex is in the process of crystallization. Similarly the limitations of different movements like nationalism, capitalism, socialism, and scientism are being acknowledged. Humanity would have been spared countless tears, had human judgment been more balanced and well informed. But man is neither a mathematician nor a fly in the fly bottle, or a rat in a maze. He is an honest evaluator who commits errors of evaluation. He blunders and pays the penalty in the course of time and gradually forges ahead.

It is precisely man's continual blundering that grips the imagination of the champions of the traditional interpretation of Divine Revelation. They constantly reiterate man's incapacity to regulate his own affairs and point out that the only way open to man is the complete submission to the word of God and the example of His Prophet. These persons are, however, not aware of the different meanings of submission to God. They accept only one conceptual model or meaning, namely the model of the dutiful son or subject submitting himself completely to the will of the authoritarian father or king who acts through his agent.

Similarly the traditionalists do not realize that their concept of revelation is based on the conceptual model of human communication through the spoken language. This model generates its own conceptual difficulties, which the traditionalists tend to ignore in the interest of preserving the integrity of their faith. This evasion of conceptual difficulties has, however, very harmful consequences, though apparently it may serve to keep the faith alive. This type of conceptual pain killing, as it were, leaves man with no intellectual motivation to explore other possible conceptual models for the interpretation of the Prophet's religious or mystical experience of which the Quran is the concrete product. Thus the traditionalist Islamic approach remains unconvincing to the mind alive to the complexities of the human situation.

Those individuals whose conceptual framework has kept pace with the continual developments in the natural and social sciences of the modern West have outgrown the conceptual clothes or models, which appealed to medieval man whether Muslim, Hindu or Christian. These are the people who yearn for a new language and idiom for the articulation of their own authentic religious experience. It appears to me, however, that the Islamic tradition is not a monolithic mausoleum but a garden where a hundred flowers have bloomed, and may still bloom. While getting depressed at the arid deserts of extreme orthodoxy, rigid conservatism and intolerance in the 1400 year old journey of Islam, we must not lose sight of the magnificent mountains and deep rivers that also greet and cheer the traveler. I refer to such liberal intellectuals as al-Farabi (d. 1950), Ibn Sina (d. 1037), al-Ghazzali (d. 1111), Ibn-Rushd (d. 1198), Ibn Khaldun (d. 1406), Rumi (d. 1273), Ibn-Arabi(d. 1240), Khayyam (d. 1131), and al-Biruni (d. 1048), *et al*. Islamic modernists or those who may reject the Islamic tradition outright, unnecessarily deprive themselves of the resources that ought to have been judiciously harnessed for the continuing cultural growth of the Muslim community, instead of being ignored or forgotten.

Every age must look afresh and reinterpret its heritage of concepts and values. The task of revaluation and reconstruction of the Islamic thought-cum-value system will ever remain incomplete as long as man continues to grow and exercise the privilege and the duty of the ceaseless creativity of values.

In the context of Indian Islam such a fresh look by Indian Muslim intellectuals is absolutely essential for giving enlightenment and guidance to the common Muslim who stands totally baffled and perplexed by the antagonistic pulls of theocracy and democracy, clericalism, and secularism, traditionalism and modernity. The average Indian Muslim is more or less a split personality and must be helped to integrate himself. There can be no doubt that the integration should be oriented towards modernity rather than traditionalism. Like, it or not, the human family, as a whole is steadily moving in this direction. The angularities and imbalances that are inevitably generated in different societies are in the process of being corrected, although this process is bound to take a fairly long time to be completed. Different religions are at different stages of modernization, and within the same religion, different groups are likewise at different stages. Even within these groups individual differences obviously exist. But the push of science and the pull of the values of modernity are definitely working to the advantage of modernization.

The need of the age is an authentic dialogue between Islamic modernists and traditionalists. The spirit of polemics only generates mutual resistance in both the quarters helping neither the cause of modernity nor the cause of traditionalism. Unfortunately, many Muslim modernists and traditionalists have a genius for giving offence to each other through various devices. The traditionalist is prone to lament over the opportunism and disloyalty on the part of the modernist. The modernist, on the other hand, is irritated at the fixation or rather fossilization of the conservative or traditionalist mind. The way out of this unfortunate predicament lies in greater tolerance and an authentic dialogue between modernity and traditionalism. The outcome of such a dialogue, to my mind, should be the reconciliation between the two through the liberating concept of 'cultural emergents' that combine continuity with change. The effective promotion of this approach is much more difficult than the downright denunciation of modernism or traditionalism, just as, in a very important sense, living the good life is much more difficult than rejecting life through suicide.

The study of the history of other religions is very useful for a deeper insight into our own religion. It is always easier to detect the psychological defense mechanisms and motives of self-interest, or confusion of ideas and inner contradiction in the case of others than in one's own. The same applies to groups. The limitations of other religions are much more easily grasped than those of one's own. Consequently a critical sociological survey of other religions helps us in a better understanding of the stages and laws of growth of our own culture or religion, its strength and its limitations. This comparative sociology of religions tends to dissolve our natural ethnocentricity and group self-conceit. Self-conceit prompts us to treat our own religion as a class by itself, and hence exempt from sociological laws that apply only to religions other than our own. Having outgrown this natural ethnocentricity and 'group snobbery', if I may call it, we are in a much better position to appreciate the points of excellence of our own religion and its unique contribution in the economy of the human family at large. Moreover, the realization of the variegated changes wrought by time in the fabric of the religious tradition sets our creative imagination at work. Fresh visions are stirred that make us forward-looking, and growth oriented as distinguished from backward looking and tradition oriented.

Creative growth, however, implies the conservation of the values of the past. Cultural borrowing from others is one of the means of such growth. Early Islam was conspicuous for its spirit of assimilation of Greek, Iranian and Indian cultures. The cross-fertilization of intercultural concepts and values is an ever-recurring world process, though it usually operates at the unconscious level. Its conscious practice, however, does not render it any the least objectionable.

Cultural assimilation need not be confused with imitation or a patchwork synthesis. At its best, cultural assimilation is neither imitative nor synthetic but creative. It pre-supposes a critical evaluation of the culture of others no less than one's own. It is precisely this creative fusion that leads to 'cultural emergents'.

The basic ingredients of the different world religions are essentially the same, namely a thought-cum-value system, a precept system and an institutional system that is certainly an organic part of the total cultural *gestalt* but not included in the religious core. Provided the genius of a particular religion has been grasped, its basic nuclear content can be preserved and cherished in the midst of a conscious assimilation of other concepts and values without impairing the basic integrity and personality of that religion.

To my mind, the concepts and values of religious modernity (as I have enumerated above) need to be consciously integrated into living Islam together with some basic values of ancient Indian and Chinese spirituality. The value of 'authenticity' as it has emerged in Western Europe, under the joint impact of modern science, linguistic analysis, sociology and psychoanalysis, is a key value (quite irrespective of creedal faith) and is integral to both Western modernity as well as Eastern spirituality at its best.

The contemporary age is the age of spiritual crisis and nihilism. A simple faith, whether in religious or secular values, has become more or less impossible for the sensitive and informed person, unless he first goes through a period of intense self-searching. One is, therefore, sorely tempted to cut short this arduous and long journey in the dark night of the soul in order to reach quickly the haven of faith and certitude. Man is eager to end the painfulness, nay the torture and agony involved in the loss of faith and a naked exposure to a total nihilism. The value of authenticity is an appeal to man not to fall a prey to intellectual dishonesty, self-alienation, and the compartmentalization of his personality, in order to escape doubts or the awareness of conflict between his different attitudes and beliefs.

## Conclusion

There is no unbridgeable chasm between religious modernity and traditionalism. The ideal is to be a growth oriented person rather than be a traditionalist or modernist. The growth oriented approach implies that no one vision can be accepted as final. Ghazzali's great synthesis in the 11th century between the strands of rationalism, mysticism and legalism was a monumental achievement. But no vision or interpretation can be allowed to become static.

The conceptual interpretation of the totality of human experience is a collective and progressive enterprise that should transcend the barriers of region and time, language and religion. The task of interpretation can never be completed. Human experience grows, yielding fresh factual data. This, in its turn, reacts or should react upon the conceptual interpretation in the lap of which the data first confronted man. This dialogue between experience and interpretation (leading at times to the discovery of fresh facts and at others to the formulation of fresh interpretations) is a part of the unending human adventure or man's quest of value. To give only one example of this dialogue, the conquest of poverty and disease and the control of human population have profoundly modified the conception of a personal God. On the other hand, it was the concept of a Supreme and Just Creator that had centuries earlier helped in the emergence of the concepts of cosmos and science. The important thing to note is the organic character of the interpretative framework, which attracts data from every dimension of human experience.

The reconstruction in the meaning of traditional symbols and images takes time. There is a 'conceptual/cultural lag'. Loving tolerance towards tradition oriented persons is absolutely necessary. In this respect, the ancient Chinese and Indian tradition of many sided truth and the ethos of creedal tolerance is highly useful. Linguistic analysis as practiced by modern analytical philosophers is also very illuminating. These philosophers hold that different philosophical theories arise because they select different facts for emphasis. Hence the important thing is not the acceptance or rejection of any theory or verbal formulation but rather the full awareness of the complexity of the situation concerned. Provided this complexity is grasped, any formulation may be retained. This principle may aptly be called the 'principle of formulational tolerance'. This principle together with the concept of conceptual lag should help our modernists in carrying out an authentic and fruitful dialogue with the traditionalists, as recommended above.

The principle of 'formulational tolerance' is also a notable feature of Islamic mysticism or *Sufism*. The well-known story of *Moses and the Shepherd*, in the *Mathnawi* of Maulana Rumi (d. 1273), is perhaps the most striking and pregnant recommendation for the acceptance of this principle. Indeed, Rumi goes on to say that the violation of this principle leads one to 'conceptual idolatry', that is, the worship of one's conception of God, rather than of God Himself.

Earlier still, both Ghazzali and Ibn Rushd had posited the principle of 'formulational pluralism': truth must be communicated to suit the mental level of the hearer. This concept releases us from the monopolistic grip of traditional formulations as well as the jargon of all interpretative system: Marxism, Positivism, Idealism, Theism, Vedanta, or what not.

Every thought and value system has limitations which must be acknowledged and overcome. This applies to every historical individual and epoch, including Prophet Muhammad ﷺ. To accept this however, in no way, compromises the absolute sincerity, integrity and status of the Prophet, in the light of clear Quranic texts that affirm that God alone is all Powerful, all Knowing and Infallible.

The quest of growth must not however blind us to the power of the symbols and images of a tradition. These symbols must be retained and at the same time they must be reconstructed. If the symbols are discarded, the new ideas and values have no legs to stand upon, or no vessels to be poured into. If on the other hand, the symbols are retained, it becomes very difficult to make them first absorb or assimilate and then convey the new ideas and values in question. The symbols cast their shadows and tend to obscure and distort the fresh stirrings of the human soul. Moreover, even if this difficulty be overcome, there is another dilemma. If the symbols are retained in their traditional sense, the reformer is heard but barely understood by the group, which does not move forward or towards the vision of the leader. If the leader retains the symbols but deconstructs and revises their operational meaning or practical significance, those members of the group who have no reason to feel dissatisfied with the traditional interpretation of the symbols actively oppose and resist the reformer's interpretation of basic concepts and values.

Every creative individual, therefore, has to solve this predicament. The fear of the charge of hypocrisy should not deprive him of the advantages of his membership of a living church or tradition (provided he feels an emotional involvement with the tradition). To my mind, if the many elements of value in the tradition genuinely inspire and motivate the reformer he should go ahead with the task of revising and deepening the tradition rather than breaking away from it. The charge of hypocrisy, after all, is not more serious or demoralizing than the charge of *Kufr* or apostasy that was in vogue in both medieval Christianity and Islam.

The charge of hypocrisy will be valid only if the individual distorts his authentic meanings in order to get an audience. But, if the recommended reconstruction of the operational meaning or function of the traditional symbols are not concealed but fully and frankly acknowledged, then using them to promote the inner spiritual growth of the community can never be regarded as hypocrisy. Indeed this is the only way to promote the peaceful and harmonious growth of the human spirit in an ever-changing human situation. Buddha, Socrates, Christ, Prophet Muhammad ﷺ and Gandhi, and (in an important sense) even Marx, all followed this basic ethical principle or maxim.

# Essay 2

## What Is Religious Fundamentalism?

The expression '*religious fundamentalism*' first came into common use in approximately 1920 in the USA as the name of a vigorous Christian movement to oppose Christian liberalism, which had earlier swept the Western world from the mid-19th century onwards. The fundamentalist's looked upon the ongoing wave of liberal Christianity as a grave dilution of the very essentials or fundamentals of the Christian faith, as they saw it. They aimed to restore the said fundamentals to their central position in the Christian belief system. They also desired that religion should function as the rock bottom foundation of all human activity instead of being regarded merely as one of the players on the human scene, as it were.

The Steward brothers in the USA published several religious tracts on Christian fundamentalism between 1910 and 1915. The Five Points of Fundamentalism were inerrancy of the Bible, virgin birth of Jesus, supernatural atonement, physical resurrection of Jesus, and authenticity of Gospel miracles. To these might also be added the acceptance of the Bible in the literal sense. The fundamentalist movement reached a climax in USA in 1925 when its leaders prosecuted a Biology teacher on the charge that his teaching Darwin's theory of evolution to school children was an anti-Christian activity which came under a local legal ban. The prosecution attempt, however, failed.

The fundamentalist movement in the New World was a very late and minor attack on Christian liberalism relative to the much earlier counter-attack by the Catholic Church in the last quarter of the 19th century. Pope Pious IX enumerated and condemned sixty-nine propositions of modernism. Pope Leo XIII warned against 'Higher Criticism' of the Bible in order to check the growing trend among liberal and rationalist Christian circles to question the dogma of the literal truth and the authenticity of the gospels. Pope Pious X banned 'modernist' religious literature. By 1910 some modernist Catholics were excommunicated from the Church.

Christian liberalism (which was rather pejoratively called Christian 'modernism' by the Orthodox Church circles) was the mature fruit of the great liberal rational upsurge or 'Enlightenment' which had spread in Western Europe before and after the French Revolution of 1789. This had led to a liberal and permissive approach to institutional Christianity among the educated and rising upper middle classes in the entire West. No longer was religion supposed to dominate and legislate for every sphere of human activity and no longer did the writ of religion run supreme over the state.

Thus, the new economic thinking ceased to respect the traditional doctrine of the Church that interest on sums lent to others was sinful. Likewise, the new political thinking was premised on the rights of man rather than obedience to a king, as the shadow of God, or to the Pope, as the *Vicar of Christ*. The new world view affirmed that man was born to fashion nature and society after the ideals he freely cherished rather than to prepare for the hereafter, according to a rigid total code of conduct, that free enquiry, tolerance and compassion for others was the right and desirable response to cultural, religious and racial plurality found in human society, rather than the objective of universal conversion to the one true religion of Christianity. God, certainly, had not been dethroned or executed except for a brief period immediately after the French Revolution. But in the emerging value system of the 'Enlightenment' the belief in the fatherhood of God had become optional, while the brotherhood of man, the supremacy of reason and the tolerance of dissent the corner-stone of the new secular as well as Christian thinking.

The towering liberal thinkers who had ushered in the 'Enlightenment': Locke (d. 1704) and Hume (d. 1776) in England, Rousseau (d. 1778) and Voltaire (d. 1778) in France, Kant (d. 1804) and Hegel (d. 1831), Goethe (d. 1832) and Schiller (d. 1805) in Germany, among others; were neither materialists nor atheists, nor were they Christians in the traditional sense. They held on to Christianity or rather to Christian Deism, in their own way, remaining highly sensitive to the order and beauty as well as the chaos and sordidness of the universe. They also remained deeply committed to the spiritual and moral values of Christianity. In other words, they had 'liberated' Christianity from the stranglehold of theology and canon law but did not repudiate the basic 'Idea of the Holy' and the sense of inscrutable mystery underlying the universe. This constituted the nucleus of the liberal Christianity, as distinct from the traditional version of Christianity, both Catholic and Protestant.

To sum up, religious liberalism does not reject the function and the power of religion to nurse, purify and elevate the human spirit; it merely rejects the iron grip of religious authoritarianism on every aspect of human life. Religious liberalism, thus, stresses the crucial importance of cultivating the spiritual dimension of life along with other human concerns or needs: material, social, intellectual and aesthetic. Religious fundamentalism stresses the crucial importance of having faith in the infallibility of some scripture or person and of unquestioning obedience or submission to the said authority.

It is pertinent to point out that while the prefix 'liberal' is quite illuminating in the literal sense, the other prefix 'fundamentalist' is rather ambivalent. It illuminates but at the same time it also misleads those who may not be aware of how the term 'fundamentalism' became current coin. The word 'fundamental' means, as we all know, the essential part of a larger totality or whole. In this sense the 'fundamentals' of any religion, system of thought or discipline would mean the basic or essential core of the said religion or thought system. In this sense, therefore, all those Christians who stick to the essentials (as they see them) of the Christian faith but reject the secondary or tertiary detailed interpretations and institutions of the Church could be said to be 'fundamentalist Christians' with much greater justification than those Christians who do not bother to separate the essentials or fundamentals of Christianity from Christianity in the concrete historical sense.

The actual usage of the word 'fundamental Christianity', however, is quite different. The actual use stipulates that a 'fundamentalist Christian' is one who accepts the fundamental importance and supreme authority of a religious authority in every walk of life and rejects the view that there may be some spheres of human activity where independent reasoning and spiritual autonomy may be more desirable, rather necessary for the pursuit of truth and human welfare.

In view of the established usage it is, perhaps, better to stick to it rather than to question or disapprove the appellation 'fundamentalist' in the context of Islam or any other religion. After all the word 'fundamentalism' is also used in a broadly similar, though not exactly parallel sense, in the contexts of say, economics, agriculture, industry, and various branches of knowledge. Thus, we could say, quite justifiably, that Marx stood for economic fundamentalism, Freud for sexual fundamentalism, Comte, the great French thinker of mid-19th century, for ethical fundamentalism, while the Western civilization, in general, stands for industrial fundamentalism.

## Religious Fundamentalism Today

Today one hears a lot about Islamic fundamentalism, but hardly about the fundamentalist versions of other religions. The reason for this is not any prejudice or hostility against Islam or the Muslims, as the latter generally tend to believe. The plain fact is that while religious fundamentalism has practically withered away or is merely peripheral in major religions, other than Islam, fundamentalist thinking remains fairly strong and vigorous in Muslim societies.

The ongoing struggle of Muslim countries to free themselves from the iron grip of Western political and economic domination also goes to reinforce fundamentalist thinking among Muslims. The search for national or regional self-assertion and dignity of the 'Muslim David' against the 'Western Goliath' often takes the form of or seeks inspiration from religious fundamentalism tinged by Messianic hopes of the eventual triumph of Islam in the world at large. The life situation of other large religious groups of the human family being quite otherwise they gravitate to other patterns of religious response or behavior.

Western Europe and America were the first Christian societies to outgrow the religious fundamentalism of the medieval era. As is well known, the USA was the first major state based on the principle that religion was a personal matter of the citizens of the American state which, as a state, did not profess any particular religion, but respected and guaranteed the freedom of conscience of all its citizens. The idea of a secular state, thus, never repudiated the validity of different religious faiths professed by its citizens as autonomous individuals. Hinduism soon followed the modern Western example.

As we all know, the people of medieval India were predominantly Hindu, but the country was under Muslim hegemony for several centuries. It is utterly false and misleading to view this historical reality as a picture of Hindu-Muslim confrontation, or of Hindu enslavement under Muslim tyranny. The basic truth is that extended Muslim hegemony and religious, social and cultural interaction between the two major segments of the population worked, slowly and silently, to a pragmatic separation of the spheres of politics and religion. In other words, the modern principle of separation of politics and religion came to prevail in practice, due to the peculiarities of the medieval Indian situation, without the word 'secularism' or the terms 'liberalism' and 'fundamentalism' coming into use. In effect, the rules and the elite (both Hindu and Muslim) functioned 'as if' religion was a matter of personal faith, while politics was centered on loyalty to the sovereign, quite irrespective of his religion. Though the Muslim *ulema* in general, in the name of Islamic fundamentalism, disapproved of this pragmatic separation, the *Sufis*, in general, preferred the path of religious 'quietism' and practical indifference to the state.

This was the scenario in which the *Battle of Plassey* in 1757 paved the way for British political supremacy and the resultant social and cultural interaction between the triumphant West and the decaying East. This interaction gradually led to the emergence of modern Hindu liberalism, to begin with, and subsequently, of modern Indian territorial nationalism, secular democracy and the struggle for liberation from British colonialism. Islamic liberalism in the modern sense, emerged approximately a century later, in the thinking of Sir Syed (d. 1898), Ghalib (d. 1869), Salar Jung (d. 1887), and Badruddin Tyabji (d. 1906) *et al.*

However, this approach could not adequately develop and get consolidated in Muslim thinking. For various reasons, which need not be elaborated here, the struggle against colonialism led to unresolved internal differences between different sections of Indian opinion over the sharing of power after independence. This resulted in the partition of the country in 1947 as the price for the transfer of power from the British.

Of late Hindu fundamentalism is trying to assert itself against the much more powerful and well established liberal versions of modern Hinduism which fructified first in late 18th century Bengal and, subsequently, in different parts of the land. So far Hindu fundamentalism in India is merely an emerging trend rather than an established pattern of Hindu response. In this case also the real but rather hidden players on the contemporary Indian scene are political and economic factors, rather than simple religious piety. In view of the enormous internal divisions and clashing interests of Indian society and the Hindu family itself a monolithic fundamentalist response does not at all appear likely. The sound and fury of some militant Hindu fundamentalists seems to have unnerved liberal sections, both Hindu and Muslim. However, my perception is that if those who are genuinely committed to secular democracy (and I believe they are quite large in numbers) carry on their work on right lines secular democracy, as enshrined in the constitution of India, will prevail.

## Religious Fundamentalism and Secular Democracy

The central point or purpose of this section is to articulate the following insight: Though there is a basic conflict between religious fundamentalism and humanistic secular democracy there is no conflict between religion, as 'spiritualized morality and faith in the Unseen', and secularism. This insight is very simple and fruitful, but many conventionally religious persons, especially among the Muslims, are apt to miss this crucial truth.

It is a rather common tacit assumption that the separation of politics from religion amounts to politics without any moral or ethical constraints. Many of those who oppose separating or de-linking politics from religion disapprove of, in real terms, the idea of amoral politics rather than of secular politics as such. However, they are hardly aware of this confusion in their thinking.

The plain fact of the matter is that the principled separation of politics from religion entails neither the rejection nor the devaluation of religion and of morality. What the modern principle of separation does is merely to say that the proper jurisdiction of religion be restricted to the sphere of the moral and the spiritual dimensions of life. Religious liberalism accepts the principle of separation, while religious fundamentalism affirms that the jurisdiction of religion is total.

If we accept the principle of separation no conflict will ever arise between science and religion, or between reason and revelation and faith, or between secularism and spiritualism. In the domain of sense perception and empirical explanation, which jointly comprise factual knowledge, we ought to accept the exclusive authority and methodology of science; in the domain of spirituality and morality we ought to accept as final the inner authority of our authentic creative conscience or of some spiritual leader of our own choice, as the case may be. Likewise, in the domain of logic or deductive reasoning we may accept the authority of the analytical intellect, while in the domain of the metaphysical interpretation of the mystery of the universe we may accept our own conceptual picture or existential insight, or the insights provided by some preceptor or guide. Yet again, in the domain of polity we may accept the authority of reversible secular legislation, subject to continuing democratic review, in the light of actual experience;

while in the domain of art and culture we may accept the authority of our own aesthetic preferences of taste. In short, we can live harmoniously on different planes which will not clash, provided we do not seek to bring them all under the total jurisdiction of one single authority, be it religion, philosophy, logic, science or art.

## ISLAMIC FUNDAMENTALISM

I would like to round off the above conceptual analysis of religious fundamentalism with some specific remarks on Islamic fundamentalism in both theory and practice.

Sizeable sections of Muslims in different parts of the world still gravitate to the pre-modern fundamentalist approach to religion. Liberal Muslim intellectuals or leaders are apt to be criticized or denounced as opportunists rather than as honest seekers of truth, as they see it. A very large number of conventional Muslims are still in the grip of the rather facile assumption that there is only one model or paradigm of true Islam; their own conception. All other versions are looked upon as heresies. There is no developed concept of the tolerance of dissent and of plural interpretations of the Islamic creed itself. The traditional version of Islamic tolerance is restricted to acceptance of plural schools of jurisprudence and the prohibition of forcible conversion to Islam; the traditional version or concept does not include the dimension of the unfettered 'freedom of conscience' as a basic human right. The '*Fear of Freedom*', as beautifully put by Erich Fromm, still grips the Muslim mind. This fear leads to their distrust of democracy in the present, their nostalgia for the golden period of Islamic piety in the past, and their yearning for a future Messiah.

Muslim believers are generally inclined to hold that other religions may allow the separation of politics and religion since their scriptures or founders have not provided complete and detailed guidance for life as a totality. Since, however, this is, precisely, what the Prophet of Islam has done, it is said that Muslims have the religious obligation to bring the totality of life under the jurisdiction of religion. Many non-Muslim scholars also appear to endorse this view, despite the fact that several eminent Islamic liberals have unequivocally rejected this approach.

Indeed, it is incorrect to hold that among the various world religions Islam, alone, prescribes a complete way of life in addition to the prescribed code of spiritual discipline, prayer, and fasting, etcetera. The plain fact is that up to the closing years of the 18th century every world religion aspired to regulate every sphere of the life of its followers; food, dress, entertainment, laws of marriage, inheritance and punishment for crimes, methods of governance and trade practices, etc. It is quite immaterial whether these directives were contained in the principal scripture or in the ancillary regulations of the various religions, since they all claimed to be sacrosanct and authoritative.

What really differentiates Islam from other religions is the very early unification of church and state in the career of Islam while this process took centuries to get completed in the case of other religions. The union of church and state in Islam had been affected in the last few years of the Prophet's life at Medina. On the other hand, this union was achieved after centuries had lapsed in the case of Buddhism, under Ashoke, and of Christianity, under Constantine. Though the career of Hinduism refuses to conform to any usual slot the *Brahmanic* religion also proffered to be a complete guide or way of life for the faithful. However, the peculiar historical feature of Islam has definitely led Muslims and others also to believe that Islam alone teaches the organic unity of the spiritual and the worldly, or of the sacred and secular aspects of life.

The protagonists of Islamic fundamentalism, further, hold that the ever-changing human situation does not pose any difficulty in accepting that the Islamic canon law (*shariah*) is applicable in every walk of life. The reason given is that the Islamic doctrine itself authorizes the Muslim scholar jurists (*ulema*) to reinterpret, modify and develop the *shariah* to meet new needs and changed situations in the course of time. This is the position, which Iqbal and Mawdudi have adopted, though it would be unfair to bracket the two of them on the scale of religious fundamentalism.

The above mentioned line of thinking, certainly, does help Muslim society to meet the challenges of an ever changing human situation, and is, therefore, a definite improvement upon the extremely rigid and stagnant views held by some Islamic fundamentalists of the old school. Nevertheless, the qualified liberal content of the approaches of Iqbal and Mawdudi will not suffice to meet the requirements of Muslims in the modern age. Their approaches do not question the underlying traditional assumption about the jurisdiction of religion. In other words, these approaches remain rooted in the traditional paradigm of religion as a total code of conduct rather than as 'spiritualized morality'. Consequently, the above approaches do not enable genuine Muslim believers inwardly to accept the modern idea of the separation of politics and religion, and its corollary that this separation does not, necessarily, lead to totally unprincipled or amoral politics.

The approaches of Iqbal and Mawdudi may work (up to a point) in purely or, predominantly, Muslim societies, but they will just break down in plural societies, which, as we know, are the general rule in the modern scientific and technological age. However, even in Muslim societies composed of different Muslim sects or denominations intra-Islamic tensions and conflicts are bound to arise when the spheres of politics and religion are not clearly demarcated.

Educated Muslims today are faced with a deep spiritual crisis. They are confused as to what is the true face of their cherished religion. The middle of the road or qualified liberal position of Iqbal and Mawdudi evokes somewhat less resistance than does the modern idea of separation of religion and state. It is true that Muslims in India today vociferously proclaim the virtues of secularism. But I, respectfully, submit that very few among the Muslim advocates of secularism have a sound and consistent vision or world view which could effectively support their rather superficial secularism.

The Islamic paradigm held by Iqbal and Mawdudi or the rulers in Iran, Libya and Saudi Arabia will not suffice for the present age. What the Muslims need today is an informed and honest questioning (based on the history, sociology and philosophy of religion) of the traditional idea of the function and jurisdiction of religions, including Islam. This questioning will, perhaps, reveal that the Islamic approaches of Sir Syed and Azad are more relevant and fruitful than those of others. This, however, is not to say that their positions require no amendments or inner growth. In the final analysis, the growth of new ideas and values and the ceaseless flowering of new dimensions within them is the only way to arrive at complete truth, which, however, recedes even as we just manage to catch a glimpse.

# Religious Predicament of Muslims Today

The predicament of Muslims in the modern age is that their religious tradition stands for the unity of religion and state, while the modern mind stands for the separation of religion and state. The Islamic tradition is that Islam is not merely a spiritual discipline, but a complete way of life, including a polity (*shariah*). Though not inspired like the Quran, the *shariah* is deemed as all embracing and sacrosanct. Only the *ulema* are empowered to modify it according to a definite procedure. But it would be absurd to claim or expect that the *shariah* should be binding on the Parliament of a sovereign secular state. Muslims in general hold that a sovereign secular democratic state is bound to fall headlong into 'Satanic' politics and the amoral pursuit of power. In other words, they equate the separation of religion from politics with immoral politics. They honestly tend to hold that the secular approach to politics destroys or erodes true Islam which is a seamless and complete map of conduct according to Divine guidance. This is the spiritual predicament of traditional Muslims all over the world including the followers of Mawdudi's school of Islamic thought that is, relatively, liberal, but falls short of the fully integrated and spiritualized religious sensibility of the modern mind.

Western educated Muslims in general, and, particularly, those belonging to plural societies are, increasingly, becoming aware of this predicament. But they lack the moral courage and the credentials to question the validity of the time honoured traditional approach and the exclusive authority of the *ulema* in such matters. Another reason why the educated Muslim laity is reluctant to assert itself is the lack of proper grounding in religious learning and the Arabic language. These perplexed believers silently wait for the day when the *ulema*, on their own, will take the initiative to revise or redefine the proper scope of the *shariah*.

The *ulema*, hardly aware of the complex issues of modernity (understandably) suffer and, unconsciously, go on the defensive when confronted with the immense gap between medieval learning and the much more developed natural and social sciences in the modern age. I submit, in all humility, they, in the best interests of all concerned, should ponder on the full implications of four basic truths:

**(a)** granted that all Muslim believers must accept the Quranic text as infallible, no human interpretation of the text can claim to be infallibly true;

**(b)** interpretation, in some form or other, necessarily, enters into all efforts at understanding the Quranic text;

**(c)** the proper understanding of any communication involves a frame of reference within which the 'addressee' interprets the words or expressions used in the original communication;

**(d)** the frame of reference as well as the concrete meanings or usages of words necessarily change in the course of time. These truths apply to all communications or languages including the 'Word of God'.

It follows that whosoever interprets the Quran, whether one be an Arabic speaking lay person or scholar, necessarily, interprets the Scripture relative to one's own set of Arabic usage and understanding of the context of the communication. The *ulema* are entitled to the utmost respect because they know the language and are also better informed of the history and context of the revealed contents. But this could hardly justify them to suppress the spiritual autonomy of other believers to reinterpret the Scripture. This was the stand of Martin Luther when he challenged the Pope's claim to be infallible.

Gandhiji took the same stand when he redefined Hinduism and purged it of much that was dear to orthodox Hindus. Muslims face a similar challenge and are called upon to define the quintessence of Islam in the modern age. Some *Sufi* versions of Islam have done so already. However, this task is a continuing one. The right direction for Muslims in the modern age is the critical redefining of the proper scope or jurisdiction of the *shariah*, and the dynamic cultivation of the 'essence' of Islamic faith and spirituality. Sir Syed and Azad strongly recommended this, while Iqbal did the same. Mawdudi merely recommended making adjustments in the polity of the *shariah*. This was his idea of combining modernity and tradition. He stood for a reformed and dynamic *shariah* but he just did not or could not appreciate the scope and spirit of religious liberalism, under the impact of the scientific revolution and European Enlightenment in the 18th and 19th centuries. Mawdudi was, certainly, not a supporter of terrorism or Islamic extremism. However, one can say that they are the illegitimate and unwanted children of Mawdudi's earnest quest for Islamic resurgence without his having acquired a critical but sympathetic insight into the concepts and values of liberal religious modernity.

The indirect impact of the Aligarh Movement did produce some eminent liberal Indian Muslims, like Badruddin Tyabji (d. 1906), Amir Ali, Yusuf Ali (d. 1953), Iqbal (d. 1938), and Azad (d. 1958) *et al*. However, with the solitary exception of Azad, in his later mature phase, none of these luminaries addressed themselves critically (unlike the great Sir Syed) to the crucial issue of the essential nature and function of religion in the modern age. For all his vast range of learning and his poetic genius Iqbal reiterated that Islam was an organic unity of the spiritual and the mundane in a manner that indirectly perpetuated the hold of *'shariah'* as a seamless all embracing code of conduct. Abul Kalam Azad showed greater awareness and willingness to face this issue in a consistent and realistic spirit though his accessibility to Western thought was considerably less than that of Iqbal. However, Azad's more insightful and realistic approach was overshadowed by the charisma of Iqbal's immortal poetry.

Iqbal's poetic genius and wide exposure to modern European thought and culture had given him an international reputation. His impact upon the Indian Muslim educated classes was almost as great as that of Tagore on the liberal Indian mind as a whole. But Iqbal became many things for many people, stimulating and inspiring Muslim politicians, journalists, theologians and intellectuals alike, including some non-Muslim circles as well. Iqbal's Islamic outlook was liberal and dynamic and contained powerful elements of modern religious existentialism. He, following Sir Syed, made a laudable attempt actually to *'reconstruct religious thought in Islam'*. He also strongly pleaded for reconstructing the traditional corpus of the *shariah*. A young and bright *urdu* journalist, Abul Ala Mawdudi, responded though he was hardly gifted to understand and appreciate the creative genius of the poet philosopher. Indeed, Iqbal's insight into the human situation was incomparably wider, deeper and far more logically penetrating than that of Mawdudi, who was, essentially, a modern incarnation of the *Deobandi* approach to Islam. However, political factors just before and after the partition in 1947 pushed Mawdudi into ever growing prominence. Iqbal's eloquent and philosophically backed stress that Islam stood for the organic unity of the mundane and the spiritual greatly helped Mawdudi in expanding his influence among Indian Muslims. At a deeper conceptual level the two towering modern Indian religious thinkers, Iqbal and Azad, were religious existentialists, but they started to drift in different paths from the early thirties of the 20th century. This was a long period of political disillusionment and ideological confusion in the Indian subcontinent after the failure of the Gandhian vision and promise of Hindu-Muslim unity in a free India. Iqbal's religious existentialism and radical plea for reconstructing religious thought in Islam gradually yielded to the rather simplistic approach of

Mawdudi that the mere 'adjustment' of the *shariah* was the panacea for the ills of the modern age.

The Western educated Indian Muslims whose intellectual *Mecca* was the Aligarh Muslim University were seduced, as it were, by Mawdudi's catchy phrase *'God's sovereignty'* and Iqbal's eloquent expression *'the organic union of the spiritual and the mundane'* as the differentia of Islam. They then deduced that Islam was incompatible with modern secular democracy, and were unfortunately propelled into accepting the monstrosity of the two-nation theory as the justification for the creation of a separate and sovereign homeland for the Muslims of India. What is happening in the homeland is the virtual banishment of the dream of Iqbal, Jinnah *et al* and the virtual strangulation of the spirit of the religious existentialism of both Iqbal and Azad at the altar of the movement for the Islamization of the polity of Pakistan.

## RELIGIOUS FUNDAMENTALISM AS A MINDSET

The expression 'Islamic Fundamentalism' irritates many Muslim quarters. I have the least desire to hurt Muslim co-religionists and will gladly abjure the use of this term. But the point is that some other expression will be required to designate a definite attitude or approach to religion or to a religious mindset clearly different from the mindset designated as 'religious liberalism'.

The term 'religious fundamentalism' was first used in the late 19th century to pinpoint the distinction between the new liberal version of Christianity and the dominant Catholic Church. The term 'fundamentalism' was gradually extended to contexts other than religion. Thus it became meaningful to say that Karl Marx was an 'economic fundamentalist', or that Freud, a 'sexual fundamentalist', because Marx' primary stress was upon economic factors and Freud's stress was upon sex in their basic thinking.

The word 'fundamentalism' is quite useful in the above sense. But it is also used to refer to the roots or essence of a thought or value system. Thus, one refers to the 'fundamentals' of Marxism or, for that matter, to 'the fundamentals' of Philosophy/ Economics/ Mechanics, and so on. Now, it is one thing to be committed to the 'fundamentals' of any religion, be it Islam or what not; it is an entirely different thing to be a 'religious fundamentalist'. Sir Syed, Iqbal, and Azad were all committed to the fundamentals of Islam, but they were far from being 'Islamic fundamentalists' in the technical sense which first emerged in the late 19th century.

In the technical sense 'religious fundamentalism' means that religion is the final and supreme lever for controlling and directing the course of life in all its myriad aspects or dimensions. In this sense, Christianity, Buddhism, and modern Hinduism have all abdicated this claim in modern times. However, some schools of Islam and Islamic political quarters still wield this claim as an ideology as well as vigorous practical politics. The expression 'Islamic fundamentalism' is thus quite current, while one hardly hears of Christian or Hindu fundamentalists. Unfortunately, some sections among the vast Hindu population of India are now being powerfully attracted to '*Vedic* Fundamentalism'. It seems to me that this is a passing phase.

What are the fundamentals of Islam? For the best answer to this question I would rather turn to Sir Syed and Azad and (to a lesser degree) to Iqbal. The case of Jinnah is unique. For the major part of his life he stood for the fundamentals of Islam, and vigorously opposed Islamic fundamentalism, in the technical sense. But the trials, tribulations and temptations of politics made him drift into the direction of 'Muslim separatism' without his turning into a religious fundamentalist. The case of Azad is just the reverse. To begin with, he was a sort of religious fundamentalist but he flowered into an outstanding religious liberal.

The essence of Islamic fundamentalism is to stress the seamless unity of religion and politics as the twin sides of Islam. The essence of Islamic liberalism (as well as of all religious liberalism) is the proper demarcation of the function and sphere of religion. The present day Islamic militants go a step further and turn into '*Islamic Naxalites*', as it were. Dividing the human family into '*the party of God*' and '*the party of the Devil*', they outrun the, relatively, sober views of Mawdudi. Pakistan is now bearing the brunt of their violent irrationalism in the name of 'true Islam'. The vision of Islamic moderation and liberalism projected by Iqbal, Ayub and Musharraf will have to face and overcome immense obstacles due to the aberrations and blunders of the past regimes.

The dominant *Sunni* Islam combines belief in pure Monotheism with the belief that the long line of Divine messengers finally culminated in Prophet Muhammad ﷺ. Though the Islamic formula of faith, '*There is no god except God; Muhammad is His Messenger*' does not specifically refer to the finality of Prophet Muhammad ﷺ, the Quranic text describes him as the '*seal of the prophets*'. His being the last and final prophet of God has been an integral part of the faith since its very inception. The different sects that arose within historical Islam did add some supplementary beliefs relating to the special status or function of some very exalted person or persons. These new dimensions of the parent stem of faith were (understandably) resisted and strongly opposed by the general body of the Muslims, yet, the innovators, eventually, managed to retain their Islamic identity. The only exception is the position, to date, of the *Ahmadi* Muslims in Pakistan and Saudi Arabia,

The Pakistan government, has, officially declared the *Ahmadi* sect of Muslims as a non-Muslim religious minority group in Pakistan, along with Christians, Hindus and others. The Saudi Arab government also treats the *Ahmadi* Muslims as non-Muslims. Even Iqbal, for all his Islamic liberalism, had cast serious doubts, and implicitly, if not explicitly, rejected the Islamic identity of the *Ahmadi* Muslims. Without entering into a detailed discussion of this issue, I must, in all humility, express my strong regret and disagreement with this approach.

I hold that the heart of the Islamic faith does not lie in any particular interpretation of any Quranic verse or verses or any theory of the nature and mechanics of revelation. The essence of the Islamic faith in God and His messenger is rooted in and flows from the belief in the absolute veracity of the historical Muhammad ﷺ, who, at a particular point of time in his life, made the claim that he had received a Divine communication and command to proclaim the truth about the unseen. The heart of this belief does not entail any additional belief relating to the exact nature of the Spirit or of God and the mode of revelation. Nor can such transcendental beliefs ever be made transparently clear. All such beliefs are secondary conceptual elaborations that form the stuff of Theology. The essence of Islam is the simple faith enshrined in the simple Islamic creedal formula, rather than in any particular metaphysical or theological formulation of the nature of God and the exact mode of Quranic revelation.

The simple fact is that truth claims having a 'transcendental component' can never be made transparently clear in ordinary language or 'proved' as true or false. Thus, beliefs relating to God, Divine attributes, Divine creation, Divine revelation, Day of Judgment, heaven and hell etc. are all 'condemned' to be ever 'opaque', and cannot but carry within themselves the seeds of plural interpretations.

All theories of revelation are secondary interpretations of the primary faith in the absolute veracity and authenticity of a person of flesh and blood who lived, worked and died in Arabia in the sixth/seventh century. Every theory flows from a set of presuppositions or background assumptions, and theories are bound to differ from age to age, and even from person to person, according to one's conceptual framework and range of awareness.

Modern Muslims should welcome the growing influence and progress of the inter-faith movement initiated by liberal Christians and Vedantic Hindus in the West. The pure Quranic teachings, free from the gloss of medieval interpretations, support and proclaim the same. The Prophet also desired to establish a spiritual commonwealth of Muslims, Jews and Christians when he initiated the *Covenant of Medina*, though his vision, then, could not be consummated due to *Realpolitik* of the time. Perhaps, the time is approaching when liberal Muslims, along with the rest of the great human family all over the world, will embrace the spirit of the Prophet's approach of interfaith and international cooperation.

All who accept the veracity of Prophet Muhammad ﷺ and hold the Quran as the supreme mystery of faith and, furthermore, identify themselves with the Islamic community and desire to be so identified by others must be accepted as Muslim believers, irrespective of any internal diversity in creedal or legal matters. If some fresh dimensions emerge in the primal stem of the Islamic faith (enshrined in the *kalimah*) this (to my mind) is not a valid or sufficient ground for discriminating, persecuting or expelling the person or persons concerned from the Islamic community. My submission or recommendation to this effect, however, presupposes the spirit of mutual respect and tolerance from all sides concerned. In short, there is no alternative to the unqualified acceptance of plural interpretations of all religious creeds, of inter-religious as well as intra-religious tolerance, indeed, of full tolerance of even those who may not profess any religion or creed at all, provided they do not commit any violence against others.

# Essay 3

## The Islamic Vision Of Sir Syed

### Introduction

Three theses concerning religion are now generally accepted by all enlightened students as well as practicing followers of different religions:

**(a)** every religion is rooted in man's existential response to the mystery of the universe,

**(b)** every religion is a nuclear core of relatively abstract ontological convictions or dogmas, and basic ethical values embedded in a concrete and extensive peripheral system of beliefs, laws, institutions, customs and folklore, and,

**(c)** the nuclear core rather than the peripheral beliefs and institutions constitute the stable identity and vital breath of the religion. Great religious thinkers attempt, from time to time, to distil the nuclear essence of a religious tradition from the tangled web of the socio-cultural environment of the religion concerned. Ram Mohan Roy (d. 1833), Vivekananda (d. 1902), Aurobindo (d. 1950), Tagore (d. 1941), Gandhiji (d. 1948) and others performed this vital task for the Hindu tradition, while Tolstoy (d. 1910), Inge, Neibhur (d. 1971), Tillich (d. 1965) and others for the Christian. More than a century ago Sir Syed (d. 1898) did the same for Islam in a comprehensive and systematic manner.

Sir Syed was not a professionally trained philosopher, social scientist or historian. But his extraordinarily sharp intellect, intuitive insight and commonsense, and, above all, his intellectual honesty and moral courage enabled him to accept the above-mentioned theses. Taking his authentic faith in Islam as his point of departure Sir Syed proceeded to distil the nuclear core of Islam from its concrete historical forms in the past as well as in his own milieu. Indeed, Sir Syed himself adhered to the ideas of his Muslim milieu until he was about 45, though he had already come under the influence of the great philosophical theologian of Islam in the 18th century, Shah Waliullah (d. 1762) of Delhi. It is instructive to recall that in his early phase Sir Syed criticized, in writing, the Copernican theory. Sir Syed also thought that Islam demanded complete adherence to the example of the Prophet in every walk and detail of life. However, in his mature phase Sir Syed outgrew this approach without rejecting the core concepts and values of Islam. Those who were unable to appreciate the growth in his ideas charged the great man of having abandoned Islam or distorting it for ulterior motives. In reality, Sir Syed remained rooted, as ever, in the eternal verities of Islam but he became open to the scientific humanism of the modern age. Half a century later Abul Kalam Azad went through a similar intellectual and spiritual development and had to face similar charges.

It is tragic that numerous contemporaries of Sir Syed failed to appreciate the genius of the person who they hailed as their leader and savior after the debacle of 1857. It is a continuing tragedy that the study and research on Sir Syed's writings on Islam are almost a taboo in the very university, which is looked upon as the embodiment of the great leader's vision and dedicated concern for the Muslims. Till very recently no collected works of Sir Syed had been published in the subcontinent with the sole exception of the laudable but incomplete 16 volume work, edited by Muhammad Ismail Panipati of Pakistan.

When Sir Syed's Urdu journal, *Tehzeebul Akhlaaq*, dating back to the late 19th century was re-started by the authorities of the Aligarh Muslim University in the eighties of the 20th century there was no attempt to capture the spirit and the basic thrust of Sir Syed's thought and outlook. Only the name of the famous journal and its cover design and format were retained. Iqbal's lectures on the *Reconstruction of Religious Thought in Islam* (first published in the thirties of the 20th century), on the other hand, have been printed several times in the Indian subcontinent. This has happened even though Iqbal was very brief and allusive in his treatment of religious and theological themes in Islam while Sir Syed did the opposite. Perhaps, the magic of Iqbal's Urdu and Persian poetry made him rather immune from attack from the orthodox *ulema*, while Sir Syed's simple and candid style attracted bitter criticism. The situation has not changed even after the lapse of a century.

It is perhaps ironical that those very admirers of Sir Syed who celebrate Sir Syed's birth anniversary with much aplomb every year systematically ignore his great contribution to the evolution of Islamic liberalism in the Indian subcontinent. Till very recently his works were deliberately excluded from the syllabus of theological studies at the *Aligarh Muslim University*. The *ulema* still dismiss his writings on Islam as encroachments upon their own jurisdiction. Many sober and highly educated university people honestly hold that the curtain of silence that has been lying on the religious views and writings of a great statesman and social reformer should not be lifted at all. The great man should be honored but not read or discussed since any widespread discussion of his religious ideas would, in their honest opinion, open the floodgates of heretical ideas among the younger generation. These persons do not realize that the above approach is highly negative and reprehensible. Surface religious conformity and evasion of truth produce spiritual alienation and unending inner conflict, not genuine faith and felicity. Clarity, candor and conviction are writ large on every line of the voluminous writings of Sir Syed on Islam and they are far more voluminous than those of Iqbal or Abul Kalam Azad. The time is now ripe for their critical re-evaluation.

## 1. The Sociology of Religion

Every religion is related to a wider social and cultural environment comprising myths, ancient collective memories, tales, anecdotes, proverbs, jokes, folklore, customs, superstitions, images or stereotyped concepts of various out-groups and so on. All these elements are enmeshed or intertwined with the basic spiritual dogmas, moral values and convictions of the group. The average believer does not separate the above ingredients of his religious tradition. Nor does he bother to distil the nuclear core of the cultural manifold in which he lives, moves and has his being. The ingredients hang together to form an integrated cultural pattern.

The guardians of the group tradition are apt to frown upon any actual or intended departure from the approved total pattern, as if the repudiation of even a small portion were a serious lapse from rectitude. However, one or a few religious leaders are given a measure of discretionary authority to innovate a little under changed conditions. No society can manage to exist as an island in the vast cultural ocean of the human family. Interaction (both peaceful and violent) between different segments and wings of the human family is the normal socio-cultural mechanism for change and innovation in human affairs. Both the victors and the losers in the ongoing struggle for power change and learn from each other. At times the currents and cross currents of change are so powerful that the values and institutions of the weak and stagnating group become totally incapacitated to cope with the far reaching consequences of interaction. Under such conditions one or two creative and dedicated souls from within the tradition may feel called upon to examine afresh their cherished concepts and values in the light of the fresh knowledge, insights and experience in the onward march of history. Thus human ideas, values and institutions develop and spread. The flame of progress sometimes flickers, grows dim and even dies out at particular time and place, but the light never entirely disappears from human society, if we view it as a single family of diverse races, religions and cultures. The dusk of culture in one wing of the human family is followed by a fresh dawn in some other.

The early Muslims borrowed from the Greeks and Romans, Iranians, Egyptians, Chinese and Indians and also enriched the family treasure house of human culture and civilization. All impartial historians of ideas and culture agree that the Islamic vision of the early Muslim savants represents a creative advance on the pagan, Jewish and Christian thought and institutions. The early Muslims dominated the others not only in the field of battle but also in the fields of natural science, astronomy, mathematics, medicine, surgery, geography, history, Historiography, logic, metaphysics, literature, music, painting, architecture, statecraft, navigation, agriculture, horticulture, and so on. What the Egyptians, Iranians, Greeks, Indians, and Chinese had done at different times by way of contributing to the ever-incomplete story of man's creativity the early Muslims did in the medieval times.

The Western races took up the creative role in the modern era. The keynote of the modern era is the scientific paradigm of knowledge – empirical investigation, framing of tentative verifiable hypotheses or conceptual models for unifying, predicting and controlling the sequence of events here and now. In the above paradigm there is no room for myths, purposive explanations, cosmic moral order, Divine creation, Providence, life after death, angels or the devil, since such concepts are not verifiable in the scientific sense. Though no scientist denies or could, possibly, deny the importance of moral, spiritual and aesthetic values for the harmonious development of the individual and of society, yet the scientific temper of the modern age has bred extreme permissiveness and even indifference to belief or lack of belief in myths, miracles, all speculative theories, astrology, and the like, for the same reason. To the extent extraordinary or paranormal phenomena admit of controlled observation or statistical treatment many leading scientists and thinkers concede their relevance and importance for arriving at a rational and balanced worldview. Otherwise, all unverifiable explanations, which are empirically barren or neutral (devoid of operational significance), are looked upon as hangovers of the pre-scientific stage of human thought.

The scientific revolution started in the 17th century and its impact on religion came to be felt, in a big way after the lapse of more than a century. Earlier the Renaissance and the Reformation had already prepared the mental soil of the West for cultivating inner freedom and rational enquiry instead of the medieval emphasis on faith and the concern for salvation through dogma and miracle. The German Protestant thinker of the 20th century, Bultmann, has called the gradual process of distilling the lasting core beliefs and values of a developed cultural tradition the 'demythologization' of religion. Bultmann dealt with Christianity, but his concept has a universal and timeless relevance. Indeed, Islam, as preached by the Prophet in its pristine form at Mecca, was itself a demythologized version of the two principal semitic traditions of the region. In course of time Islam itself built a mythology of its own out of its semitic roots. Much earlier, Buddha had demythologized *Brahmanism*, but later Buddhism also spun out its own myths and miracles out of its Indian roots. The same happened in the case of Guru Nanak.

It is in the light of the above framework of ideas that Sir Syed's contribution to Islamic thought should be examined. His authentic faith in Islamic monotheism implying that the Quran was the revealed 'Word of God', his sharp and perceptive mind which clearly grasped that the success of the Western powers all over the world was based upon superior scientific knowledge, technology and administrative skill, his genuine admiration for British democracy, his intense concern for the rehabilitation of his uprooted fellow Indians after the debacle of 1857 led him to reflect on the proper concept of religion in general and Islam in particular. He put forward a program of education comprising:

**(a)** the study of Western philosophy, natural and social sciences, and

**(b)** formulation of a demythologized approach to Islam based on the Quranic texts and to prune the Islamic tradition from all its semitic or other cultural accretions during the course of time.

In fact, Sir Syed had the same approach to Hinduism, but obviously he was not qualified to speak on the subject. Moreover, he felt that Hindu religious and social reformers had already undertaken this crucial task with very good results.

## 2. SIR SYED'S ISLAMIC LIBERALISM

Sir Syed remained firmly rooted, as ever, in the essentials of the Islamic faith. However, he reconstructed some of its basic concepts as philosophical theologians routinely do to keep the faith alive and relevant to the needs of the believers in an ever changing and evolving human situation. Sir Syed took up the following main themes:

**(a)** the traditional belief concerning the mode of Divine revelation through the mediation of the angel, *Jibreel* (Gabriel), or the *Roohul-Quddus* (Holy Spirit),

**(b)** the traditional belief that the prophets of God, (including Prophet Muhammad ﷺ) performed miracles,

**(c)** God sometimes permits nature to depart from its course,

**(d)** the occult powers of the *Sufi* saints,

**(e)** the over-riding authority and infallibility of Quranic texts in all matters including natural science,

**(f)** the basic principles of Quranic exegesis,

**(g)** the status of *Hadees*, and,

**(h)** the proper jurisdiction and scope of religion. I shall deal with the above themes in the given order.

**(a)** The traditional view is that God revealed Quranic verses piece meal through the agency of the angel, Gabriel, who used to appear before the Prophet sometimes as an angel (visible only to the Prophet) and sometimes in human form visible to others also. Gabriel, according to the traditional view, used to recite the verses, which got imprinted on the Prophet's consciousness and retained in his memory without effort or error. At his first convenience the Prophet dictated the verses to one of his several scribes and also indicated the sequence and chapter in which they were to be placed. The traditional view, or rather, views go into much greater details, which need not be mentioned, in the present context. The crucial point is that all of them are human projections or interpretations of abstract and almost bare Quranic references to the mode of revelation. And Sir Syed gradually became unwilling to accept any human interpretation as infallible or as having any divinely sanctioned binding power upon the believer. According to Sir Syed, the reference in the Quran to the Holy Spirit does not warrant the inference that Gabriel is an external being or the acceptance of any other belief about the concrete mode of Divine revelation. This is essentially a mystery or miracle indicative of Divine creativity and power.

Sir Syed holds that the Quranic name, *Jibreel* (Gabriel) or expression, (*Roohul-Quddus*) 'Holy Spirit' and which refer to the mysterious agency of God's revelation of the Quranic text refer to God's gift of prophecy to some 'Divinely elected' human messengers of the Creator. Sir Syed holds this gift to be the highest level of divinely endowed gifts to created beings. These gifts are 'potential talents' which develop and mature with the passage of time and they include music, poetry, mathematics, creative imagination etc. Human beings become creative in the course of time through interacting with others. Their 'artifacts' remain imperfect because they are all the 'work of humans'. However, the natural world, being the 'Work of God' and the Quranic text, being the 'Word of God' are perfect.

In other words, Sir Syed made a distinction between the belief that the Quran is 'The word of God' and the belief in the traditional conception or understanding of how the "Divine Word' was revealed to fully human messengers of God. Sir Syed, thus, fully retained his faith in the Divine Source of revelation but rejected conventional views concerning the modus operandi of the revelatory process. He boldly said that the conventional views on this matter reflected semitic myths or folklore and anthropomorphic conceptualizing of the contents of Divine revelation to provide a platform for rightly guided human decision-making and action.

Sir Syed holds that God inspires and guides created beings, high and low, from the meanest insect, bird or animal to man himself through a spiritual mechanism of internal guidance (in the form of instinct, intuition, vision, audition etc. that is most appropriate to the level of the created being. Thus, the terms 'Gabriel' or Holy Spirit do not refer to some external being or agent, but to the higher prophetic talent or genius vouchsafed by God to the prophets, among whom, Muhammad ﷺ occupies the highest rank.

Sir Syed's theory of revelation is basically similar to the views of classical Muslim thinkers and savants; Ibn Sina, Ibn Rushd, Ibn Khaldun *et al*. It is also adumbrated in the writings of Waliullah and Abul Kalam Azad.

**(b)** Sir Syed held that the universe had been created by the all powerful God who, in His wisdom, endowed His creation with specific attributes or fixed patterns of behavior, apart, of course from the freedom vouchsafed to human beings to choose between good and evil. Nature thus behaves in a uniform/manner, not because of any laws inherent in nature without reference to God's will, but precisely because nature is the 'Work of God'. Science is the systematic empirical study of the work of God, and far from being opposed to religion, it makes mankind aware of the wonders and beauties of the 'the Work of God' just, as 'the Word of God' makes man aware of what is right and what is wrong in the sphere of human conduct.

Sir Syed's approach thus far is the same as that of theism, in general, according to which, there is no conflict between the scientific postulate of causal uniformity of nature and the religious belief in the omnipotence of God and His power to change the so called laws of nature at His sweet will. But having said so, Sir Syed holds that even though God's omnipotence implies His power to permit miracles He does not, as a matter of fact, indulge in miracle making. In other words, though miracles are logically possible there is no sufficient evidence that miracles take place. He holds that genuine faith in God does not imply faith in miracles. Nor does the occurrence of a so called miracle prove the existence of God, since what is prima facie a miracle or violation of the expected and usual pattern of events may, in reality, be in accordance with, as yet, laws unknown to humans at present.

Sir Syed is of the view that belief in miracles is a part of the folklore and the anthropomorphic thinking of early man when the scientific paradigm of knowledge was hardly possible. We feel amused at the miraculous elements in the folklore of others, but we rejoice at our own. And we hardly notice our double standards. The moment, however, somebody demands proof from us we fall back upon blind faith that we are right and the other wrong.

The source of Sir Syed's approach to miracles was not merely his intellectual honesty and scientific attitude but the significant fact that the Quran itself repeatedly declares the Prophet's inability to work any miracle in support of his claim to be a prophet when his opponents or skeptics demanded him to produce any miracle to support his claims. It seems that Sir Syed argued that if Prophet Muhammad ﷺ did not have the 'gift of the miraculous', how could earlier prophets have had this gift? He presumed that the followers and posterity of the earlier prophets wrongfully attributed miraculous powers to their holy figures because of early man's fascination for the miraculous. However, according to Sir Syed, the true miracles are the myriad processes of nature in all its breathtaking majesty and glory, and it is to them that the Quran repeatedly draws our attention. The regular motions of the heavenly bodies, the rhythms of night and day, life and death, growth and decay, the blowing of the winds, the songs of the birds, and so on and so forth, proclaim the power and the glory of the Creator. No need is, thus, left for believing in pseudo-miracles purporting to violate the laws of nature or rather the permanent pattern of behavior God has ordained for His creation.

Sir Syed's line of argument appears to be valid if we confine ourselves to pre-Quranic scriptures. But his approach breaks down when one finds that the Quran itself relates several miracles performed by previous prophets. Sir Syed could not argue that the Quranic statements were false. He, therefore, was compelled to infer that Quranic reports of such miracles in reality refer to popular beliefs rather than to facts. This line of argument, to my mind, appears quite convincing in several Quranic narratives. Many of the Quranic texts that have been traditionally interpreted in supernatural terms could, possibly have been interpreted (with great plausibility) in an entirely natural and normal sense by a reader or hearer who looked at the world with bare eyes without any colored lens. Sir Syed points out several Quranic verses that can be so interpreted, and explains how supernatural interpretations came to be placed upon them. But this is not always the case. His painstaking and, to my mind, honest efforts break down and fail to convince us.

**(c)** Sir Syed, however, is not on such weak ground in the case of petitionary prayer to God. As is well known, all religions, including Islam, hold that God, as the loving Father and all powerful Sustainer of all creation, grants the sincere prefers of the faithful and the elect, without any hindrance from the laws of nature. Sir Syed holds that this belief also suffers from the anthropomorphic fallacy. The real function of prayer is not magical manipulation of reality by supernatural causation, but rather the giving of solace, heightening of morale and of human creativity. In this sense God always answers man's sincere prayers. Sir Syed's scientific approach is thus quite compatible with his belief that prayer to God, though not a magical tool, is an effective source of Divine help.

**(d)** In keeping with his scientific attitude Sir Syed also distinguishes genuine spiritualism and Sufi culture from superstitious beliefs and practices which in the course of time had come to be grafted upon the real thing. He followed Jalaluddin Rumi's claim that he had *'kept the kernel of the Quran and thrown away the bones to the dogs'*. He rejected talismans, lengthy liturgical recitations, or a life-negating fatalism and stood for the gospel of rational action and spiritual prayer.

**(e)** There is no contradiction between the laws of nature as established by science and the statements found in the Quran. Seeming contradictions arise because of human misinterpretations of the language of scripture due to one reason or other, projection of false or misleading notions current in the milieu upon the 'Word of God'. But the contradiction vanishes if the text is interpreted in the right way. Sir Syed holds that no human interpretation of the 'Word of God' or for that matter, no scientific theory can claim to be final because of human limitations. If and when new facts come to our notice requiring revision of scientific theories presently held the Quranic text will also be found to yield fresh meanings in harmony with the facts newly discovered. This is a unique feature or the miracle of the 'Word of God': its remarkable plasticity which allows fresh dimensions or connotations to emerge on the canvas of the Arabic text without any ulterior apologetic twisting of the standard meanings and uses of Arabic words and expressions.

**(f)** Sir Syed was highly dissatisfied with classical works of Quranic exegesis despite the enormous learning and scholarship of their learned writers. He held that their voluminous commentaries on the Quran were based on reported sayings of the Prophet, Biblical stories and Greek philosophical notions. The truth of all these was itself questionable. Sir Syed pointed out the various sources of error in the proper understanding of the Quranic text: relying on the literal sense of the words without understanding the situational context of the revelation, confusion of meanings, anthropomorphic interpretations of Divine attributes and so on. He could not complete his monumental commentary on the Quran, nor could he do full justice to the principles of Quranic exegesis. However, his long article on the basic principles of Quranic exegesis remains extremely illuminating.

**(g)** Sir Syed adopted a very balanced approach to the status of *Hadees*. He did not blindly accept the judgment of the two top *Sunni* Muslim authorities, Imam Bukhari and Imam Muslim as to which reports were authentic and which were not. Nor was his approach one of wholesale rejection of all *Hadees* literature. Sir Syed held that despite their great learning, piety and labors the judgment of Muslim divines cannot be accepted as infallible and binding upon the faithful. One could never be sure that the reports, adjudged as absolutely authentic, were really so because the process of their collection and evaluation started some two hundred years after the Prophet's passing away. The great scholars did formulate and apply rigorous criteria for determining the degrees of authenticity of reports, but this labor and their methodology could create only a presumption but never certainty about what the Prophet said or did, quite unlike the quality and degree of certainty pertaining to the authenticity of the Quranic text.

Sir Syed also holds that the Prophet never claimed that his judgment was infallible in worldly matters. Indeed, the Prophet used to consult his colleagues or followers and often heeded their advice. Sir Syed also makes a distinction between purely religious/spiritual issues and social or political and other worldly matters and holds that no preferences of the Prophet in the latter case could be deemed binding in an ever-changing world. There is nothing Islamic about purely social customs, proper names, style of living and dressing and so on, that prevailed in the time of the Prophet or were even retained by the Prophet himself. Neither these purely social matters nor even otherworldly issues of politics, economics, administration and scientific enquiry come under the jurisdiction of religion so long as no Quranic injunction is violated.

Sir Syed, thus, considerably reduced the scope of the *shariah* to purely moral and spiritual matters, and repudiated the view of many present day protagonists of Islamic renewal and revival that the proper scope of religion extends to each and every sphere of human life.

Sir Syed's approach, therefore, is far more radical than that of Iqbal who merely wanted the *shariah* to remain flexible and dynamic but did not question the scope of the *shariah* as Sir Syed did. Despite his far greater access to and command of modern thought and Western literature Iqbal could not appreciate Sir Syed's radicalism in the above matter. To my mind, Iqbal erred in extolling Mawdudi's project of revision and Islamizing of politics and economics as a substitute for Sir Syed's project of separating matters of polity from matters of spirituality and religion. This put the clock back, somewhat like what Aurangzeb did, some two hundred years earlier, in relation to Akbar's project of establishing 'functional secularism' under Mughal rule.

Iqbal's basic approach to religious faith was existentialist, and in this sense, his insight into the nature of religious truth was deeper and clearer than Sir Syed's rather outdated (pre-Kantian) rationalistic natural theology of Locke, Paley *et al* that pure reason could prove the existence and unity of the supreme Creator (*Allah* of Islam) and also the universe as the 'work of God' and the Quran as the 'word of God'. Yet, Sir Syed's rather groping and blurred vision of 'functional secularism' was a wiser step in the right direction as compared to the much more sophisticated and learned thesis of Iqbal that Islam stood for the organic unity of the spiritual and the mundane. Abul Kalam Azad's vision combined the truth of religious existentialism and the pragmatic necessity of democratic secularism in the modern world, but Azad's voice was lost in the din and dust of the politics of the Jinnah era.

**(h)** Sir Syed really stood for the separation of religion from the state, though the words 'secularism', or the expressions, 'Islamic state' and 'sovereignty of God' did not occur in his writings. He generally adopted a secular approach on both Indian and international issues. His clear and unambiguous rejection of Pan-Islamism earned him and his close supporters in the Aligarh movement the bitter criticism of Jamaluddin Afghani who was then the foremost champion of Pan-Islamism. Sir Syed looked upon the violent conflicts and wars in the Balkan region of Europe as a political confrontation between Balkan nationalism and Turkish imperial interests, not as a holy war between the Crescent and the Cross. Sir Syed also rejected the concept of '*Khilafat*' as an integral part of the Islamic faith, though he accepted the idea of Muslim brotherhood. However his idea of Muslim fraternity did not exclude his idea of Hindu-Muslim fraternity. He called the Hindus and the Muslims the two eyes of the bride that was

India: the common beloved motherland which nourished all her children without any discrimination. He even said that all those who lived in and belonged to India were Hindus in the political sense. It is, however, true that some of his perceptions and political prescriptions differed from those of the Congress leaders who were demanding the immediate introduction of advanced political reforms.

He felt apprehensive that Muslims, as an educationally backward group, in an extremely heterogeneous society that was fast being transformed by the English educated class of *'Bengali Babus'* may become totally marginalized and feel like aliens in a world they just could not relate with. Whether these fears were reasonable or not, they were natural and understandable at that period of Indian history, and it would be an over-simplification to say that Sir Syed's reservations were patently groundless. It must, however, be conceded that while Sir Syed had very clear and consistent ideas on Islamic liberalism he lacked a clear and consistent modern political philosophy. Consequently, he was subject to conflicting pulls and pushes in his political responses. His references to *'Bengali Babus'*, Hindu domination, the character of the lower classes (both Hindu and Muslims), reflect the limitations and prejudices of his feudal milieu, which he could not transcend as adequately as he had outgrown traditional Muslim theology. The documented controversy between the two Muslims giants of the age, Sir Syed and Badruddin Tyabbji, on the question of Muslim participation in Congress politics shows the latter's approach was far more integrated and far sighted. In any case, Sir Syed was not the father of the idea of partitioning the Indian subcontinent.

The plain fact of the matter is that Sir Syed belongs to the galaxy of early Indian liberals; Hindu, Muslim and Parsi; who all hailed British rule as a Divine dispensation for the welfare of the world at large. Some traces of this approach had survived in the vision of the great Gokhle and Gandhi himself, though Tilak was always a tough-minded realist. Indeed, it was the tragedy of *Jallianwala Bagh* that transformed 'Mr. Gandhi' into 'Mahatma Gandhi', but Sir Syed had already been dead and gone two decades before this transformation. Perhaps, Jawaharlal's verdict on Sir Syed is the most balanced and valid of all the assessments made of the strengths and weakness of a truly great Indian.

Several critics accuse Sir Syed of being non-secular; others charge him as having reduced Islam merely to a system of prayers, fasting etc. on account of his separating politics form religion. According to these critics (influenced by Abul Ala Mawdudi), Islam is a complete code of conduct for life as a totality without any separation between the church and the state. This line of thinking totally misrepresents or distorts the issue. No sane Muslim asserts that mere prayer, fasting and pilgrimage etc. suffice to make a person a good Muslim. The performance of external acts of religious discipline must be supplemented by a high quality of individual and social life and the proper fulfillment of one's obligations and duties at all levels. And surely, Sir Syed never neglected these aspects. Indeed, he laid the greatest stress upon these matters. He never said or implied what he is charged with, namely, that merely praying five times and fasting for one month etc. suffices to be a good Muslim. He also never said that to be a good Muslim, one need not bother about the pursuit of individual morality and social justice. All that Sir Syed said was that such matters fall in the realm of rational and free democratic discussion rather than in the domain of the *shariah*. The principled separation of religion and politics, by no means, implies separating morality or ethical principles from politics or public life. The Quran is concerned with faith in the Unseen, spirituality and wisdom, not with scientific knowledge, economics or administration. These latter should be left to democratic decision-making in the light of the moral principles of the Quran. The polity and administrative culture of independent Arab, Iranian, Turkish or other states in classical period of Muslim dominance has no normative religious significance for Muslims, according to the thinking of Sir Syed. He stood for an open mind, free enquiry and tolerance of dissent and totally rejected the language of heresy, apostasy and hatred of out-groups.

## 3. LIMITATIONS OF SIR SYED'S APPROACH TO ISLAM

Sir Syed accomplished his mature work on Islamic Liberalism in the mid-19th century when the remarkable creative contribution of such intellectual giants as Darwin (d. 1882), Marx (d. 1883) and Freud (d. 1939) had yet to make their full impact upon the modern mind. Sir Syed remained in the intellectual company of rationalistic theologians; the Mutazalite theologians among the Muslim academics, and Descartes (d. 1650), Locke (d. 1704), and Paley (d. 1805) *et al* among the moderns (who, broadly speaking, claimed that reason could prove Theism), rather than in the company of the *Sufis* and of Pascal (d. 1662), Hume (d. 1776), Kant (d. 1804), and Schleiermacher (d. 1834)*et al* who never accepted the claims or pretensions of human reason to conclusively prove the truths of religion and theology. Today, it is the latter who stand vindicated, since the modern theologians and religious thinkers all have seen through the fallacies and limitations of medieval rationalistic theology, Muslim, Christian or Jewish. The existentialist approach to religious truth as initiated by the Danish Christian theologian, Kierkegaard (d. 1855) has carried the day. Sir Syed, however, continued to operate in the framework of pre-Kantian thought. Sir Syed's key concepts: 'the Work of God', 'The Word of God', his concern to remove the seeming contradictions between the two, do not satisfy the intellectual difficulties or problems posed by several factors: the presence of unmerited pain and evil in the world, the tortuous path of trial and error in the course of biological evolution, the culture-bound limitations in the conceptual framework of all lawgivers (including divinely inspired prophets) that necessitate continual revision and growth of the believer's heritage of moral and spiritual values, and finally, the disturbing feature of conscientious objection to some portion of scripture.

Sir Syed, to my mind, had successfully addressed the difficulties found in popular views of how God revealed the Quran through the angel, Gabriel, but his critical approach does not help us to reconcile the contradiction between the Quranic truth-claim that Divine wrath caused natural calamities or that God's messengers performed miracles, on the one hand, and the scientific law of uniform causality in nature, on the other.

Sir Syed had rightfully broken the shell of unexamined dogma, anthropomorphic thinking, myths, miracles, and folklore. He had shown how many intellectual difficulties arose, due to wrong interpretations of Quranic texts rather than any inherent contradictions in the text itself. However, Sir Syed did not realize that equal stress upon the authority of reason and faith in any external authority (deemed as infallible) is untenable. This approach, inevitably, leads to inner tension and conflict, since it pushes the individual into the arms of Freudian 'rationalization' of an externally given truth, rather than Socratic free enquiry and going where the argument leads. Sir Syed saw the danger and the fallacy of allegorical interpretation (taweel) of Quranic texts, but he did not see the danger and fallacy of apologetical interpretation when one tried to give equal authority to human reason and faith in any external authority whatsoever. Thus Sir Syed's reconciliation between reason and revelation breaks down if and when the seed of 'conscientious objection' begins to sprout in the depth consciousness of the believer who regards the Quran as the infallible 'Word of God'. Since, however, Sir Syed did not hold the 'word of the Prophet' was also infallible just like 'the Word of God', Sir Syed's approach leaves a way open for honest dissent in spite of sincerely venerating the Prophet. In this sense, Sir Syed's rational approach to Islam is a half-way and shaky compromise between faith and reason without affirming either full human autonomy or extolling existentialist faith without the seal of human reason.

**2.** Another serious limitation of Sir Syed's outlook is his inadequate background knowledge of modern history and social sciences as well as of ancient Indian and Chinese thought and culture. Precisely due to this limitation Sir Syed could not develop a mature sociological approach to the issues of Indian politics and economics. He could not envision the long-term future of India after the end of British imperialism in the context of an ever-evolving world order.

Sir Syed was fascinated by British democracy and welcomed it to India. At the same time he was apprehensive of the success of the principle of adult territorial franchise, of the one-man-one-vote type, in caste ridden India. The liberal Western educated Hindus in general, understandably, were optimistic about the eventual success of the Western secular democratic model. But the Muslims liberals were not so confident. And to be fair to them and to Sir Syed, their apprehensions and reservations were justified in view of the simple arithmetic of democratic politics. They could not easily visualize that the game of democratic politics was supposed to be played, not by simple monolithic groups of Hindus or Muslims, but by the complex play of group-interests and ideals giving ample scope to all to exercise power in a secular democracy. What was needed was an act of faith in secular democracy. Such faith requires a profound grasp of modern history and social sciences. Perhaps, Sir Syed lacked this grasp, though as a genuine religious liberal, he was extremely friendly to all Indians who warmly reciprocated his affectionate sentiments and trust. Indeed, this was the general pattern of social relations in the entire medieval era of Indian history.

Though Sir Syed made an intensive study of the Bible and sought to remove mutual misunderstandings and ignorance of each other's basic beliefs and values as a mean of promoting inter-religious harmony and human brotherhood, Sir Syed's knowledge of Indian thought and culture was too limited to make him into a prophet of an integrated humanism to accommodate the diverse spiritual traditions of the human family. In other words, Sir Syed's Islamic vision, broad and truly liberal as it was, did not have the range and depth required to make the appeal universal and timeless. Indeed, even the Muslims of India could not cherish his politics for long. Sir Syed's contemporaries (including some of his closest associates) barely understood his religious genius, while many seized upon his limitations. This hampered the general acceptability of his religious approach.

The *Khilafat* agitation weakened the appeal of Sir Syed's religious liberalism and political moderation. Sir Syed had refused, on principle, to give a religious complexion to the Balkan problem, which remained a burning international issue throughout the 19th century. The leaders of the *Khilafat* movement deliberately combined religion with politics, but Sir Syed, in keeping with his genuine Islamic liberalism, had consistently kept politics and religion apart. The *Khilafat* leaders repudiated an essential plank of Sir Syed's Islamic liberalism. A large majority of the *Khilafat* leadership entertained the traditional view that Islam stood for the organic unity of religion and politics and that Sir Syed and his school had been indifferent to true Islam.

The *Khilafat* movement, as we know, fizzled out by the mid-twenties. It was followed by petty political squabbles in the environment of tough competition in the face of extremely limited opportunities for a steadily growing educated and ambitious middle class among both Hindus and Muslims. This was quite enough to create ideologies that would help and favor one's chances in the competition for jobs and economic gains. This was good soil for strengthening the appeal of the ideas of group solidarity and reservation quotas for different groups. Iqbal's poetry stressing Muslim identity and solidarity and his philosophical affirmation of the organic unity of religion and politics in Islam, the revivalist slogans in some Hindu quarters, the requirements of British imperial interests all conspired to add to the already mighty obstacles in the way of Islamic liberalism and secular humanism. Gradually there arose the fateful demand for the partition of the country. It is really a 'historical irony' that the person who won the battle for Pakistan had been a renowned commander of the Indian liberal secular brigade right till 1936.

The bends and turns in the meandering stream of history, however, must not blind us to the direction of its flow. The direction is determined by several factors – technological, geographical, economic, political, apart, of course, from the felt desires and wishes and efforts of human agents. Indian Muslims of my generation who had entered the golden threshold of adulthood just before India and Pakistan won freedom in 1947 and had also been touched by Gandhiji's vision of Hindu-Muslim unity and Abul Kalam Azad's vision of the essential unity all religions will ever be haunted by Sir Syed's metaphor of Hindus and Muslims being the two eyes of the Indian bride. Alas! the metaphor could not survive the onslaught of short term politics.

## 4. Sir Syed and the Future

Different religions, till very recently, have been cultural islands without any bridges due to difficulties of communication and of transportation. The communication revolutions of the modern age have greatly changed the human situation. The ease of cross-cultural communications has initiated a chain process of dialogue between different wings of the human family. This dialogue is, progressively, revealing the significant similarities in the basic human needs, aspirations, fears, hopes, strengths, weakness of men and women, and also how different religious traditions satisfy them. Their significant differences are also becoming more accurately understood, thereby reducing the film of prejudice or misunderstanding that clouds our vision. The rigid shell of ethno-centricity is in the process of being broken by humanity in search of truth and universal peace.

The movement of inter-religious or cross-cultural dialogue and understanding, however, is not without resistance and opposition, which is as understandable as the process of dialogue. The resistance is partly due to cultural inertia, partly to fear of the unknown, and partly to a perceived threat to the vested interest of the religious high command. They honestly fear that religion is in danger, though what is really endangered is their own stagnant version of religion.

These facts inevitably slow down the rate of the emerging religion of the spirit born out of honest enquiry and the concern to know the full truth without fear or favor. History shows that every age has a set of special needs and aspirations which demand fulfillment. Any religion or theological system that tends to frustrate these situational needs fails to retain an authentic grip over its adherents or win over fresh hearts and minds to its message. The dominant 'situational need' (*zeitgeist*) prevails over all obstacles and challenges to its movement even as a powerful surging flood sweeps over the surface of the earth. The *zeitgeist* is not a spirit or ghost in the socio-economic machine. Nor do socio-economic forces work blindly like electro-magnetic fields or lines of force. The *zeitgeist* may be likened to the ever-evolving nuclear core of the perennial human quest for value and perfection (by virtue of the Divine spark within the human). The world, however, is not perfectible and its polarities of good and evil, joy and suffering, harmony and strife ever persist. The *zeitgeist* remains ever pregnant with new life and with new promises, but the perfect fruit thus never grown upon the tree of human ideals and aspirations. The temporal fruit remains, sweet and bitter, nutritive yet somewhat toxic, an advance yet an arrest of the quest for value.

Likewise, the perfection claimed to be present in any particular Divine revelation is like a new life ever in the womb of the ceaseless human quest for value. The truths of revelation may be perfect at the abstract level but when we interpret or try to apply them to the concrete human situation at any point of time they cannot but become time bound and provisional. If we treat them as final or closed they lose their power to inspire and create new forms of value. When one ignores the above motioned complexity of the human situation and either accepts truths of reason or of revelation, as absolute, or regards all values to be totally relative to the various stages of human development one falls into the trap of one-sided ideologies. Another error of one-sided thinking arises when we expect that the course of history always follows the demands of pure truth or justice without being deflected by negative or evil influences of human hubris and the struggle for power.

This struggle between ideals and interests goes on quite independently of all religions or ideologies. Individuals and groups cannot help using ideals as strategic reinforcements in the struggle for power. In other words, the human search for inner peace and self-respect in combination with one's interests move individuals and groups to choose as they do. The different interpretations of Islam or of other basic thought patters and value systems are subject to this analysis of the human situation.

The Islamic vision and value system, as an open and ever growing response to the mystery of the universe, has been distilled, time and again from its rigid shell of time bound beliefs and codes of morality, thanks to the efforts of savants such as Ibn Sina (d. 1037), Ibn Rushd (d. 1198), Al-Beruni (d. 1048), Ibn Khaldun (d. 1406), Ibn Arabi (d. 1240), Fariduddin Attar (d. 1221), Jalaluddin Rumi (d. 1273), Hafiz (d. 1390) and others. Sir Syed also attempted to distil the nuclear essence of Islam in the framework of modern thought, as he understood it. It is high time, instead of merely glorifying his contribution to the educational and political advancement of the Muslims of the subcontinent, his admirers make Sir Syed's Islamic liberalism the starting point for their fresh thinking on the meaning of Islam in the modern age.

# Essay 4

## Religious Pluralism And Islam

In this essay I shall seek to answer:

**(A)** How did the rise and development in the West of modern thought and science gradually transform the view that religion was a complete code of conduct for every sphere of life, and further that there was only one true or right path to success and salvation?

**(B)** Why is it so imperative that Muslims properly understand the dynamics of the above transformation of Western religious consciousness? To date, Muslim reformer and religious leaders are busy either with apologetics or the task of 'adjusting' the *shariah* to meet fresh situations as and when they arise.

### (I)

The remarkable progress of the natural and social sciences during the modern age has enormously increased the range of human choice in dealing with nature and society. Humans can now control population growth, conquer disease and poverty, make deserts bloom and even colonize the moon. Likewise, the advent of secular democracy has empowered democratic societies and governments to redefine the scope and function of organized religion and to demarcate the jurisdiction of church and state after a long and bitter confrontation between the two prior to the Protestant Reformation in Western Europe in the 16th century. The emergence in the next two centuries of the idea of universal human rights and pure morality based on reason rather than revelation, on the one hand, and the idea of universal causality in the domains of both nature and society, on the other, led to the West European Enlightenment and the rise of liberal religion and the spiritual humanist movement in the West. Locke, Hume, Spinoza, Rousseau, Voltaire, Kant, Schiller, Goethe, Hegel are among the architects of this second Renaissance in Western Europe.

All the above ideas, ideals and movements of conceptual reconstruction and reform combined to give a new face to Christianity in Western Europe. Islamic countries in West Asia and North Africa were in decline and had lost the creativity and élan of early Islam. Mughal culture retained its creativity a little longer, but it too came to an inglorious end almost immediately after the death of Aurangzeb in 1707.

Until the end of the 18th century the function of all major religions was to supply a complete map of the good life to their followers in all spheres of human activity. The idea that Islam alone provides complete guidance, therefore, is a half-truth, since right until the end of the 18th century social and legal regulations and casuistry were integral to all religions, not merely to Islam. The full truth of the matter is this: The spiritual seed or nucleus of other major world religions took a rather long time to mature and develop into state or state-like establishments wielding total power over the individual and society. Every spiritual vision tends to generate its own distinctive web or organization of ideals, institutions and interests in the long run. As we all know, the spiritual vision of Buddhism took several centuries to 'crystallize' into a state presided over by Ashoke, the emperor. The spiritual vision of Jesus also took several centuries to flower into the Holy Roman Empire. In the modern era the vision of the creators of the European Enlightenment also took a long time to flower into the sovereign liberal democracies of Europe and America, and the scientific socialist vision of Karl Marx to develop into the Soviet Union of Socialist Republics. In contrast, the seed of the spiritual faith which, Prophet Muhammad ﷺ proclaimed at Mecca, fast blossomed at Medina, into a polymorphous establishment of 'church-state' under his charismatic leadership. Perhaps, it was the deep and sincere faith of the earliest Muslim disciples and believers that Muhammad ﷺ (though very much a human like unto themselves) was also a messenger, directly guided through piecemeal revelations (*wahee*) that was the sociological cause of the unprecedented rapid emergence of the Islamic church-state. This happened some six hundred years after Jesus and some twelve hundred years after Buddha. The speed of the crystallization process of vision into social reality remains a marvel to date.

Western Europe was the first to question this hegemony of religion over society, thanks to the great minds of the West mentioned above. As British power and Western thought reached India the Islamic and Hindu establishments (that had long co-existed in a spirit of mutual accommodation) found themselves in total disarray. The British rulers had no agenda to convert the population, but cultural and religious interaction was unavoidable.

What actually happened was that some charismatic and creative minds among the Hindus in Bengal and the Pune-Mumbai region emerged on the scene, and this paved the way for their cultural dialogue with the West. Due to a combination of political and social reasons the Muslim establishment (that had long enjoyed a position of dominance in medieval India) failed to participate in the new setup and thus got isolated from their rising and forward looking Hindu brothers. As a result the Hindu religious mindset became far more open and receptive to modern ideas and ideals than the Muslim. The English educated classes among Hindus began to appreciate the principled separation of the church and the state, based on a well considered delimitation of the proper scope and function of religion; the keystone of modern secular democracy and of the constitution of America. The Muslim mindset remained more or less stagnant, and they sincerely and passionately clung to the medieval idea of Islam as a complete revealed code of conduct for every sphere of life. This holds good of the Muslims in general all over the world to date. In fact the belief that Islam will not remain Islam or survive as a distinct religion if Muslims were to discard the 'organic unity' of religion and state is the crux of the spiritual crisis of Muslims in the age of modernity. Even the great Muslim philosopher poet of the modern age, Iqbal subscribed to the idea of a seamless unity of church and state in the very concept of Islam while (according to him) no such unity was involved in the basic idea of Christianity or other religions.

The gradual transformation in the West of medieval Christianity into its modern American or European version has been well described by such eminent cultural historians and philosophers as Briffault, Butterfield, Whitehead (d. 1947), Russell (d. 1970), Bernal and others. Those who favor this change think this was a happy growth of the enduring Christian tradition, but those, not in favor, regard it as a degeneration of Christianity. It is obvious that all orthodox religious believers, no matter what their religion, will lament if the scope and jurisdiction of their religion suffers a loss.

The success story of the natural sciences was written by such giants as Copernicus (d. 1543) and Galileo (d. 1642) in the field of Astronomy, Leibniz (d. 1716), Newton (d. 1727) and Einstein (d. 1955) in the field of Mathematics and Physics, and Darwin (d. 1882) in the field of Biology, and so on.

Social sciences emerged much later. The crucial point for our purpose is the phenomenal growth in the human quest or passion for accurate and quantitative observation, experimentation, explanation through verifiable hypotheses and the formulation of general laws governing natural phenomena but accepting them only when they are confirmed through agreed methods rather than by reference to Divine Will or abstract reasoning. This approach greatly weakened belief in miracles, increased human self-reliance, promoted medical research and the discovery or invention of new therapies.

The next major application of the law of natural causation was Adam Smith's (d. 1790) pioneering and seminal work, *The Wealth of Nations*. 'Theoretical Economics and General Sociology' thus took birth. The full flowering of other social sciences like Anthropology, Philology, Linguistics, and of scientific History soon followed in the next century. The next stage was the revolution in industrial technology. All these developments liberated the human mind from the natural ethnocentricity of the human species.

The most fruitful concept in the remarkable growth of philosophy and science in the 19th century was the idea of slow growth or 'evolution' of all existence, rather than its instant creation. Hegel used this key idea in a logical or speculative manner to show how the interconnectedness of all that exists; Darwin used it in a scientific manner to explain the slow development of the totality of organic species from some simple living source. Marx used the same idea to explain the evolution of human society and the growth of various institutions and social formations from its earliest beginnings to the present after passing through several clearly demarcated stages, like primitive communism, tribalism, mercantilism, feudalism, capitalism, etc. In other words, Adam Smith (d. 1790), Darwin (d. 1882), Hegel (d. 1831) and Marx (d. 1883) all held that every event or structure, be it material, biological or social is a process in time and has ascertainable causes. If we want to control events we must understand their cause or causes and behave accordingly rather than depend on prayer or faith in some supernatural agency to grant success.

Other philosophical developments were:

**(a)** the rise of Pragmatism in America and Philosophical Analysis in Britain. The movements gave us the crucial insight that there are several types of truth-claims and there are different ways to test them rather than one single way of natural science, and,

**(b)** the rise of religious and non-religious existentialism.

According to the existentialist approach, religious faith is not the product of logical or rational thinking or scientific experimentation, but an inner and compelling response to the mystery of 'Being'. It is the most vital form of subjectivity and the deepest and highest form of existential response to the mystery of existence as such. But the subjectivity of religious truth is not like the subjectivity of a taste for coffee cold, or for coffee hot. It is subjective in the sense in which deep personal love or commitment to moral values is qualitatively different from an objective judgment, 'this table is three feet high'.

The combined effect of all the above philosophical and scientific developments was to create a strong dislike for the pure rationalistic approach of philosophical theists and theologians (such as Aquinas, Descartes, Locke, and others) who strongly claimed that their own religious truth-claims could be proved, but not those made by others. The great German thinker, Kant, had already come to this conclusion and rejected the pure rationalistic defense of Theism and the so-called proofs of God's existence. It is crucially important to point out that what Kant rejected was the 'proofs of God' and not faith in God or religious faith as such. However, some hundred years after Kant's death in 1803 the Communist followers of Marx actually banished God from their universe. But what they abolished was faith in God but not commitment to a new value system called 'socialist values'. From a functional point of view they created a new religion whose formula of faith was, '*There is no God but Marx is the last Prophet*'. It is quite another matter that Marx himself had said that he was not a Marxist. In the final analysis all the historical facts mentioned above generated what has been called 'new wave' religious thinking in the contemporary West.

If the scientific revolution of the 18th century led to new conception of nature, the sociological revolution of the 19th to a new conception of social phenomena and change, the analytical and existentialist revolutions in Western philosophy and the Communist revolution of the early 20th century have led to a radical shift in religious thinking. There is now very little chance that the human family would or could reverse the further progress of the existentialist approach to religion in the broad sense. Believers will go the wrong way and land themselves in total frustration if they attempt to restore the old type of religious polemics or apologetics. Religious truth cannot be proved or confirmed by experiments or argumentation. The believer must learn to look within the depths of one's own being and have the moral courage to face the verdict or voice of his liberated conscience.

Religion, in the above sense of an integrated authentic response to the mystery of the cosmos, like morality, art, and power structures is indispensable for humans. This view of religion is not the degeneration of the major religious traditions of the human family but a consummation of the dream of a united fellowship of religions. This approach is not due to forced surrender of the lawful territory of religion at the point of the whip of science, the imitation of some dominant temporal authority or trend of the times, or some fear or lure of gain, but a voluntary and principled abdication of a claim that has clearly become untenable at the point where humanity now stands.

This spiritual revolution of the 20th century, however, is not new if we just pause for a moment to see, in retrospect, the past of the human family. Illumined souls in all ages and climes have always been religious existentialists without having studied any philosophy, sociology or science. Great mystics, sages and poets have always found several paths leading to God. The important thing is not to talk about the path but to travel on the path. They have always preferred the 'eloquence of silence' to the 'power of argumentation'. To give unconditional love to all and pray for their welfare, rather than to convert or 'save souls' has been their principal passion.

I cannot help referring to the following anecdote in the *Sufi* poetry of Fariduddin Attar. God once asked angel Gabriel to bring the most sincere lover of God to the Divine presence. The angel could not decide whom to bring, and implored the Lord to identify the person. When Gabriel reached the indicated person and spot what he found was a person engaged in deep and reverent worship of his chosen idol. God informed the perplexed angel what the idol worshipper was worshipping was God, as such, though his vision was blurred.

Jalaluddin Rumi's anecdote of *Moses and the shepherd* makes the same point. The Persian poet, Nazeeri, points out the same truth when he says that what the moth craves is the flame, whether the candle burns in the *Kaaba* at Mecca or in some temple elsewhere. Persian and Urdu poetry overflow with such ideas and sentiments. However, it remains true that Islamic orthodoxy has always disapproved of such charming anecdotes for their permissiveness and (implied) scant respect for the *shariah*. It is also true that all semitic religions including Islam (as it is commonly understood), entertain the concept of exclusive salvation. But the Quran itself does not give a clear support to this belief. The *Aryan* religions, on the other hand, view salvation as the final release from the cycle of repeated births and deaths. This approach does not require adherence to any dogma as such. In this sense, creedal pluralism is native to Hindu religious thought, though it has some other limitations.

## (II)

Let us now ask what role can Islam play in the modern world? Should Muslims today in the age of global mixed secular societies and cultural pluralism all over the world:

**(a)** stick to the medieval approach of cultural monism and the 'totalistic' function of religion as held by classical Muslim theologians, jurists and the overwhelming body of Muslims themselves, quite content with a minimum of 'adjustments' in the *shariah*, or should Muslims,

**(b)** engage in 'affirmative action' to develop the basic concepts and values of the Quran and the teachings of Prophet Muhammad ﷺ as the call of their Islamic identity, as such, be they citizens of Islamic states or of non-Islamic ones?

As we all know, Islamic orthodoxy holds that all non-Muslims (no matter what their quality of life and character) would burn in hell, while all Muslims (no matter what their quality of life and character) would, eventually, glory in heaven. Such views not only hurt modern religious and spiritual sensibility but also do not find clear support from the Quran. Such interpretations of Islam, to my mind, will gradually wither away despite their present strong hold on the Muslim mind till today.

Cultural monism was more or less unavoidable until very recent times due to obvious difficulties of communication and transportation. However, the rapidly emerging modern global internationalism is fast eroding the natural ethnocentricity of human groups all over a much shrunken world. Cultural monism, lack of intercommunication and what the American philosopher psycho-analyst, Erich Fromm, aptly calls the 'fear of freedom' jointly lead to self-alienation as well as intergroup alienation. When this happens different believers begin to crave for compensatory substitutes of some sort or other.

The authentic believer, on the other hand, (no matter what his values) remains self-integrated and socially integrated and experiences an inner joy and contentment. Such a person cherishes inner freedom for himself as well as all others. He respects others even when they are sincerely committed to other beliefs or values. He knows that no religious truth-claims or dogmas can be proved, but the bliss of an inner conviction courses through his spiritual arteries. However, unlike the religious monist, he does not hold that all other paths other than his own, lead into the wilderness. He has a permissive approach to different sects or denominations within his larger religious community and also to other religious groups in general. He is more or less completely free from the basic in-group/ out-group dichotomy. This is the essence of religious pluralism.

Religious pluralism implies that faith, like true love, wells forth from the depths of the human being even as water gushes forth from a perennial spring. Faith provides anchorage and stability to the vulnerable and brittle human individual ever weighed down by frustration, guilt and dread. This is also the function of a philosophical worldview, as the German thinker, Karl Jaspers (d. 1969) holds. Philosophical faith, according to Jaspers, springs from critical enquiry, while religious faith is assimilated with the mother's milk followed by social indoctrination. Philosophy and religion both function as 'attitudinal anchors'; natural sciences accurately describe and connect natural phenomena and empower us to control and manipulate the course of events; history and social sciences do the same for society; art and literature please and great art also edifies and illuminates the human condition; morality is an inner censor that regulates human conduct; legal codes check and control interpersonal and intergroup transactions and actions. But, all said and done, only philosophy and religion address the residual mystery whether the great chain of being and becoming is, after all, a cosmos or a chaos.

In other words, only religion or philosophy tap the sense of wonder that overwhelms us when one attempts to make a choice one way or the other. Thus, even when a person is a sincere and conscientious 'atheist' but does not reject values such as truth, goodness, love, compassion, justice, equity, beauty and so on and, in fact, actively strives to promote them (according to his own lights) he must command our respect Honest difference of opinions or of religious convictions should not stand in the way of friendly relations or dealing between persons who value and practice integrity of character.

Numerous Muslim believers honestly hold that if Islam is really true and if they are true believers in Islam, other religions must be false and it is one's Islamic duty to bring them into the fold of the one and only true religion. Such Muslims also honestly think that by trying to convert or 'revert' non-Muslims they act in the best interests of others in this life as well as life after death, rather than for any personal gains as such. Such self-perceived Muslim benefactors of humanity do not realize that their mission, however altruistic and sincere it might be, is misconceived and rather irrational for the following reason: religious truth-claims or convictions can neither be proved nor disproved by logical force and argumentation. If this be the case the real reason or reasons behind conversions (that do take place) must lie not in the head but rather in the human heart, as it were.

I respectfully submit that the core of the Islamic or the Christian faith is not violated at all, whether one believes in life after death in the semitic sense of one single rebirth after the end of terrestrial history, or whether one is pulled to the Aryan concept of repeated rebirths in the continuing cycle of life ending in death. The reason is that such dogmas just do not admit of any proof, yet the basic function of both beliefs is exactly the same – the maximization of righteousness and virtue and the elimination or avoidance of evil and vice.

The same remark applies to other basic religious concepts. To my mind, therefore, religious truth-claims are, strikingly, closer to aesthetic and ethical value judgments rather than to factual truth-claims of science or ordinary perception. Very obviously, they are totally different from logical or mathematical truth-claims. Hence, plural religious convictions just do not present any problem or difficulty that arises when one person asserts '*p*' and somebody else asserts '*non-p*', provided social peace remains inviolate. This is the essence of religious pluralism and it is very compatible with Islam in its literal sense.

The theoretical and practical thrust of the above discussion is this: One can have a sincere and deep conviction that the truth-claim of religion '*X*' or '*Y*' is true and also an honest aspiration for and active commitment to the core values of the religious tradition without the additional belief that other religious convictions are false and, therefore, should be displaced from human society. This religious pluralism is the seed that produces the tree of a grand 'fellowship of faiths'. This is the paradigm of tolerance that the global human society needs today. The idea of cultural monism, like the other ideas of monarchy, male dominance, race or caste supremacy, white man's burden, chosen people or language, etc. are all echoes and shadows of the past, not the call of the future. And the Quran fully supports this paradigm of Islam, no matter what the classical interpreters or custodians of the tradition, in their own wisdom, may have projected in the past.

# Essay 5

## Tolerance And Islam

### Introduction

Analyzing the concept of tolerance is the job of the philosopher, while describing the rule of tolerance in the history of Islam is the task of the historian. The historical question itself comprises two distinct issues:

(a) what are the ideals or teachings concerning tolerance in the scriptures and the writings of theologians, jurists and saints, and

b) how far have these ideals and teachings been practiced at different points of time? To confuse the above two issues, (as is not uncommon even in highly educated quarters), leads to futile controversy.

In the following pages I wish to:

(a) give a philosophical analysis of the concept of tolerance, as understood in the modern sense of the term,

(b) give a historical review of the idea and practice of tolerance in history,

(c) give a critical analysis of tolerance, as understood in classical Islamic thought derived from the Quran, and finally,

(d) describe how tolerance was actually practiced by Muslims in the Islamic world with special reference to medieval India.

## THE CONCEPT OF TOLERANCE

The original use of the word 'tolerance' referred to tolerance of metals, of gold and silver coins, of bridges to bear stress, and of the capacity of a person to bear pain or suffering, physical and mental, that is, the capacity for endurance. These uses of the word were gradually extended, perhaps, in the 17th and 18th centuries, to the use, which concerns us here. A standard English dictionary defines tolerance as 'the disposition to tolerate or allow the existence of beliefs, practices or habits differing from one's own, now often freedom from bigotry, sympathetic understanding of others' beliefs etc., without acceptance of them.'

The diverse uses or meanings of any word show the futility of picking upon 'the' meaning or essence of a concept. Instead, we must make a contextual analysis of the different uses of a word or expression. This analysis may well be supplemented by a conceptual analysis of the core use of the word in a particular context. This core use should then be distinguished from cognate or related concepts to avoid confusion.

Contextual analysis means translating the analysandum into expressions, which are simpler, clearer and conform to natural or ordinary usage rather than to the specialized usage or language of philosophers or scientists.

Let us now attempt a contextual analysis of the statement, 'Ahmad is a tolerant person'. Most of us would agree on the following contextual analyses, which are illustrative rather than exhaustive:

**(a)** Ahmad tries to understand the other's point of view with sympathy.

**(b)** Ahmad does not believe that those who differ from him are dishonest, ill motivated or perverse, unless there be clear evidence for this.

**(c)** Ahmad realizes that beliefs, attitudes or approaches other than his own could possibly be right or justifiable.

**(d)** Ahmad realizes that value judgments can never be proved conclusively, so that disagreement among different persons is unavoidable.

**(e)** Ahmad does not allow his differences with others to cloud his judgment concerning their good points, or to make him hostile to them.

**(f)** Ahmad factually befriends or is ever willing to befriend those who honestly differ from him but are decent persons.

**(g)** Ahmad believes that the inherent dignity of a human being should be respected irrespective of race, religion, politics or gender.

It may be added that tolerance has several dimensions and degrees. Thus a person may be tolerant in one sense, or with regard to a particular dimension, but not with regard to others. Again, he may be tolerant up to a particular degree but not beyond that. To give two striking examples, the British philosopher, John Locke, who was the father of the movement of religious tolerance in 17th century England, was not prepared to tolerate atheists. Madan Mohan Malaviya, a great Indian nationalist, freedom fighter, and colleague of Gandhiji, could not tolerate *non-Brahmans* at his dining table.

In view of the above fact that tolerance has different dimensions and degrees, no individual or society should be judged to be tolerant or intolerant on an either-or basis. The application of a simple two-dimensional either-or logic would mislead us and would fail to capture the complexity of different situations. The proper course, therefore, is to identify the different elements and degrees of tolerance or intolerance and to grade individuals or societies accordingly.

Let us now distinguish the concept of tolerance from some related or cognate concepts with which it is liable to be confused. A person who is tolerant in religious matters may have profound religious faith and be strongly committed to moral values. Or a tolerant person could be indifferent to religion, or be a septic, yet very respectful of those who are genuinely religious. If a person be both tolerant and courageous, he would say after Voltaire and Mill: *'I do not agree with a word of what you say, but I shall give my life to defend your right to say so'*. A tolerant person need not accept a secular approach to politics, even though a secular approach to politics helps promote religious tolerance. Tolerance may co-exist with religious fundamentalism, provided the latter is of a form which does not involve any discrimination against others on grounds of faith.¹ Since, however, the fundamentalist versions of all religions have some in-built elements of discrimination (in some form or other) the practice of complete tolerance does require a secular approach to politics. However, secularism, as such, is neutral with regard to theism or atheism. Commitment to secularism does not imply any corollary of theism, agnosticism or atheism, but merely the principled separation of religion and politics. This must, however, not be misconstrued as the separation of morality from politics.²

A tolerant person need not be apathetic to persuading others to accept his own views or values, since tolerance is not the same as apathy. However, the concern of a tolerant person for the welfare of others is tempered by humility instead of a hidden desire to dominate others and impose one's own ideas or values, as the absolute truth. Tolerance is not the fear of giving offence, just as it is not the fear of commitment to a particular viewpoint. Tolerance does not conflict at all with spontaneous self-expression and active communication or dialogue, provided mutual goodwill and respect be present. Dialogue helps to promote greater harmony even though it may also bring existing differences into sharper focus. A tolerant person, therefore, need not remain a silent spectator in the face of conflicting truth-claims.

A tolerant person need not appease those who disagree with him. Tolerance is an intrinsic value like love of truth or devotion to duty, while appeasement is a strategy for buying agreement or peace on an ad hoc basis. A tolerant person may be extremely firm and unbending in doing one's duty or in resisting evil. Tolerance may result in self-sacrifice of a martyr, while appeasement seeks the easy way out. The birth of tolerance, however, does not signify the death of genuine faith in one's own cherished tradition. Tolerance merely signifies the willing acceptance of the view that beliefs or convictions, other than one's own, may also inspire goodness and beauty in the depths of the human soul. This approach is quite different from merely tolerating dissenting views which are deemed to be essentially evil or, at least, devoid of any real value. In other words, tolerance, at its best, is not passivity at the follies of others, beyond our power of correction, but rather profound humility in the face of the inscrutable mystery of reality, and of genuine respect for different perspectives and views.

## SOCIAL ROOTS OF TOLERANCE

The individual, as a child, is obviously, culturally conditioned in respect of language, morals, religious convictions, artistic as well as sensory taste, body language and so on. Thus, he speaks not language, in general, but a particular language; he follows not religion and morality, in general, but a particular religion and moral code. Now the crucial feature of the conditioning process is that the individual is, on principle, screened from exposure to other languages, morals, religious convictions and art forms, as if, they were aberrations to be concealed from the tender and innocent mind of the child. In other words, the inbuilt cultural plurality of the human situation has no impact upon the individual. To a considerable extent this is a pedagogic necessity since too many cultural stimuli would, obviously, confuse the child. But the way in which the child is more or less indoctrinated by his parents and teachers almost inevitably leads to the fallacy of cultural 'reification' – the identification of symbols with what is symbolized. This, in effect, means equating particular language forms with the structure of the world itself, particular moral codes with absolute morality itself, particular perspectives of reality with reality itself. In other words, the individual is made to feel, as if, his cultural world alone accurately mirrors or reflects reality, while all other cultural worlds are, more or less, miserable caricatures. Thus what is, really, a model of reality is reified as the reality as such.

The simple truth (which is difficult to learn because of our cultural conditioning) is that while, reality is one, its symbols are many; that the same experience or response can be expressed in a variety of forms or ways. The crucial reason why a particular conceptual model or form appeals to me has much to do with my own cultural conditioning, even if this may not be the only factor. The realization that one's beliefs and convictions would have been very different had one been born in a family professing a different faith shows the essentially contingent character or complexion of one's beliefs system. This realization ought to fill one with humility as well as empathy for other traditions.[3]

What social factors promote or retard the prospects of tolerance? It seems mixed racial, ethnic, language and culture subgroups within a larger territorial unit play the dual role of generating tension and conflict within the group, yet facilitate the eventual growth of tolerance. The greater the area of inner differentiation within a large and complex society, the greater the chance of conflict as also the greater the need of mutual understanding and accommodation to prevent the disintegration of the society into smaller warring subgroups. If the internal unity of the society, as a whole, be a crucial survival value for most members composing the large group, the will to preserve its unity will generate tolerance and mutual accommodation of diverse points of view. Since, however, the needs and interests of individuals and of subgroups often clash with each other, and also with the society, as a whole, they may adopt strategies calculated to promote their own limited interests at the cost of the long-term interest of the society as a whole.

The appeal of tolerance is relatively greater for those individuals and sections, which enjoy high status or power and possess material means enough for sustaining their dominance. A few highly evolved and sensitive souls may, however, reach the level of pure morality transcending individual or group-interests.

## INTELLECTUAL ROOTS OF TOLERANCE

Awareness of plural truth-claims and a measure of existential perplexity are the essential conditions of tolerance. Empathy and respect for the individual who may hold different views from one's own intensify one's existential perplexity and also of genuine humility, specially, when a person who is held in high esteem (due to his or her moral integrity and status) hold views contrary to one's own convictions. Though differences in sensory taste are well tolerated irresolvable differences over moral or religious issues do lead to inner perplexity and anxiety.[4]

The simple knowledge that the 'milieu' plays a tremendous role in shaping one's ideas, values and convictions, and the further knowledge that these ideas or values are not logically or scientifically demonstrable give a further boost to tolerance. In short, tolerance of diverse views is the only proper response to cultural plurality.

## THE IDEA AND PRACTICE OF TOLERANCE IN ANCIENT AND MEDIEVAL PERIODS

The idea of religious tolerance was understood and practiced in China, India, Greece and Rome in the ancient period. The religious and philosophical approach of the ancients was that there were many roads to salvation and the individual should be free to take any road one liked.[5] The Emperor Asoka (d. app. 235 BC) stood for tolerance, not merely in the sense of tolerating religious dissent, but in the higher sense of respecting plural convictions or faiths other than his own. The classical Hindu concept of *'Isht Devata'* (choice of deity) also reflected the same basic approach. Unfortunately, the *Sanatana Dharma* of India was vitiated by intolerance in the shape of the most heinous forms of caste taboos and prohibitions on social intercourse. There was no concept of the dignity and equality of the individual, irrespective of caste.[6]

The freedom of thought and tolerance prevailing in ancient Greece and Rome was free from caste discrimination, though there were rigid class distinctions and a strongly entrenched system of slavery. The populace was ever attracted to myth and ritual, connected with religious beliefs, while philosophers loved abstract reasoning. Neither the conflict between myth and reason nor the wide variety of myths and philosophical theories led to any rancor or intolerance of dissent in the pre-Christian era. It appears that the rise of semitic Monotheism and the denunciation of idol worship in Palestine then under Roman occupation created a new psychology or attitude, both among the monotheists themselves and the pagans or the worshippers of tribal deities. The Jewish prophets proclaimed the destruction of Roman glory and political supremacy because the people did not worship the one true Lord of the whole universe. The Jewish prophets held that all those who did not worship the one Lord of the world were wicked people and deserved dire punishment.

However, the Jews, and later the Christians were treated as too insignificant a minority to be taken seriously by the mighty Romans.[7] The emperor Domitian (d. 96), however, thought that the other-worldly concern and the repudiation of Roman gods was a potential danger to Roman solidarity; but he was not intolerant to the Christians. Emperor Trajan (d. 117) was the first to ban the propagation of the new religion, as it was totally opposed to the Roman creed. The Christians were subjected to mild suppression, which however, became intensified under the reigns of Decius (d. 251) and Valerian (d. 260). Numerous Christians became martyrs, though, according to modern historical research, the tales of their savage persecution are myths or exaggerated. At last, better sense came to prevail, and Emperor Constantine (d. 337) inaugurated the era of religious toleration, vide the

Edicts of Milan of 311 and 313. Around 321 Constantine himself embraced Christianity and made it the state religion of the now 'Holy Roman Empire'. This was indeed a turning point in world history.

The Christian subjects of the Roman Empire had been eulogizing the virtues of tolerance for the past two hundred years. But no sooner did Christianity become the official religion of the empire; the Christians started to eulogize the necessity of saving the souls of non-Christians, even by force, if necessary. They came to believe that if people refused to convert to the one true faith and died without being baptized they would suffer everlasting damnation in hell. Therefore their death at the point of the sword was a lesser evil for them. It is said that St. Augustine (d. 430) interpreted the words of the gospel, *'Compel them to come in'* in this sense.

The emperor Julian the Apostate (d. 363) stopped the persecution of heretics and pagans at the hands of the Christians who now ran the Roman Empire. But it was a stillborn move. Emperor Theodosius I (d. 395) resumed the policy of persecuting pagans and heretics. This state of affairs continued until the end of the sixth century.[8]

A new era dawned in world history with the advent of Prophet Muhammad's ﷺ mission in the early seventh century. Islam, though a continuation of the semitic tradition of Monotheism, rejected the dogma of exclusive salvation and welcomed Jews, Christians and all others into its rapidly expanding territories.

The political expansion of the Arab-Islamic state in the regions adjoining Arabia proper took place at the point of the sword (as all political expansions have done in history), but not Islam, as a religious faith. The truth is that the political hegemony of Islam, on the basis of an almost unceasing chain of military victories against the then super powers, created the social psychological space for the eventual peaceful conversion of the non-Muslim subjects of the Islamic commonwealth due to a combination of social, psychological, cultural, and political factors. Islam ushered in a plural society based upon tolerance, though the tolerance was not perfect and fell short of the modern concept of tolerance. Inter-religious co-existence and tolerance prevailed for four centuries in the territories of Islam until they were attacked by the Christian crusaders at the fag end of the 11th century. These crusades continued, with interruptions, for almost the next three centuries.

Impartial Western scholars of repute have pointed out that the defenders of the Cross unleashed a reign of terror, not only against the Muslims and Jews, but also the local Christians of the areas 'liberated' by the crusaders and ruled by them for approximately eighty years. Eventually the crusaders were thrown back by the legendary heroism and inspiring leadership of Sultan Salahuddin (Saladin the Great) in the early 13th century.[9] Immediately afterwards, or almost at the same time, the Islamic world had to face the terrible fury of the Mongol hordes leading to the almost total destruction of Baghdad in 1258. Though Iran recovered after approximately, two hundred years, under the great Safavids, who ushered in the golden age of Persian culture and Islamic humanism, the Arabs could not recover. In fact, they regressed into a state of utter political, economic and cultural decline, lasting until the beginning of the present century.

Turning to the story of Christian militancy in the struggle for political power, Pope Innocent III, at the end of the 12th century, embarked upon the policy of penalizing Christian kings who the Pope adjudged as heterodox. The most tragic victims of this policy were the Count of Toulouse and the Albigeios community in France. Pope Innocent III set the precedent that the Pope had the right to coerce a Christian ruler in matters, both temporal and religious, on the principle of the supremacy of the spiritual over temporal power.

Shortly afterwards Pope Gregory IX initiated the idea of the Inquisition, which idea was put into practice by Pope Innocent IV in 1252. Going far beyond the punishment of heretics, the objective of the Inquisition was to pry into the inmost depths of the human soul to punish the minutest doubt or deviation from the dogmas of the Church.[10] The work of the Inquisition was supervised directly by the Pope over the head of the Bishops who had no say in the secret workings of a super investigative net-work throughout the Christian lands. The most ruthless agency of this Papal tyranny was the Spanish Inquisition which concerned itself not merely with Christian heretics but also with the persecution of Spanish Muslims.

In 1556 Philip II decreed that Muslims should abandon *'at once their language, worship, institutions and manner of life'*. The final order of expulsion was given by Philip III in 1609, and more than three million Muslims were executed or banished from Spain. Not less tragic than the persecution of heretics was the persecution of women dubbed as witches in medieval Europe. As late as 1484 Pope Innocent VIII said in a Bull that plague and storms were the work of witches.[11]

## THE IDEA AND PRACTICE OF TOLERANCE IN THE MODERN AGE

The capture of Constantinople by the Turks in the mid-15th century and the final collapse of the Eastern wing of the Roman Empire (Byzantium) is another turning point in world history. Christian scholars, who were exclusive custodians of the Greek classics in the original, migrated to the Italian mainland, which was the seat of the Pope and an integral part of Western Europe. Till that time Western Church fathers, scholastic thinkers and writers were not acquainted with the full range of Greek thought and culture, their attention being focused on translated versions of some selected writings of Aristotle and others derived from Arabic sources. The Western mind now, for the first time, came in contact with-the Greek classics in the original. This triggered the great cultural revolution known as the Renaissance.

The independent states of southern Italy became the cradle of the new movement, which, in the course of time, radiated to the whole of Europe and transformed the intellectual, cultural, religious, political and economic climate of the entire Western world. The Renaissance was soon followed by movements of religious reform in several Christian communities by Wycliffe (d. 1384), Hus (d. 1415) and Martin Luther (d. 1546). Luther's Reformation proved to be the most effective and durable, but Luther was far from being a consistent champion of freedom of conscience. Having succeeded in repudiating papal authority, in the name of liberty of conscience, Luther tried to impose his own conscience on others with the help of force. He declared Anabaptist Christians as heretics who should be put to the sword. Likewise, Calvin (d. 1564) of Switzerland, the other outstanding Protestant reformer of the age, substituted his own brand of religious and political authoritarian ism in place of the Pope. Calvin stood for the organic unity of the church and the state, that is, the complete fusion of spiritual and worldly power in the manner of Islamic fundamentalism today. He is generally accused of the execution of the great Spanish religious liberal, Servetus, in 1553.

The real protagonists of Christian liberalism and religious tolerance were the Italian pioneers of the Unitarian version of Christianity – Sozzini (known as Socinus in English speaking countries), Castellio and others in the second half of the 16th century. These honest and brave souls were hunted out of Rome and fled to Switzerland, Transylvania and Poland to escape the wrath of Calvin. Eventually, they took refuge in Germany, Holland, England, and finally, in the New England state of the America. The Unitarians rejected the dogma of Trinity, but held Jesus to be the perfect man and the exemplar for all times. Though Sozzini did not affirm the separation of church and state, he stood for complete tolerance of all views within and without the Church.

It was natural for the Catholic Church to fight back the different reform and liberal Christian movements from Luther to Sozzini. Pope Paul III severely punished free enquiry in religion and science. The most tragic episode was the burning of the great scientist and thinker, Bruno of Italy, in 1600. The massacre of French Protestants had earlier taken place on St. Bartholomew's Day, 1572. At least 7000 innocents lost their lives in cold blood. The conscience of France was shocked, and, to make amends, the *Edict of Nantes*, 1598, ensured bare tolerance to the Protestant minority of France for almost the next hundred years. However, in 1676 persecution of Protestant recommenced and this continued until the French Revolution of 1789.[12]

Voltaire's contribution to freedom of conscience and tolerance is well known. Though far from demanding the separation of the church and the state, he championed free enquiry and complete tolerance. His great contemporary, Rousseau (d. 1778) did the same, though he had no place for atheists in public office. The brigade of the French Revolution, retained Catholic Christianity as the 'dominant religion' of the Republic, but gave the right of public office to all French citizens with the exception of Jews. Absolute or unqualified equality of status of all French citizens was established, in theory and practice, only in 1795 when the modern 'principle of separation' between the church and the state was substituted in the French Constitution in place of the earlier 'principle of jurisdiction'. According to the constitution of 1795 'Theo philanthropy' (Divine Love of Humankind) was the new official philosophy or secular religion of the state. This 'Love of Humankind' was claimed to be 'the religion of Socrates, Marcus Aurelius and Cicero', a religion which cut across all religions in the conventional sense. Ironically, Napoleon who claimed to be an atheist and humanist entered into a pact with the Pope in 1801 (*the Concordat*) and re-established the 'principle of jurisdiction', thereby restoring the authority of the Pope over the French constitution. Napoleon thought that 'using the Pope as an instrument' he could control the consciences of men and more easily carry out his plans of empire. *The Concordat* lasted till 1905 when the principle of 'separation' (first applied in 1795) was restored in France.[13]

The story of the birth of religious tolerance in Germany is far more consistent than the French experience, until the advent of Hitler's ideology implying racial as well as religious intolerance of the worst kind in human history. Germany, however, had to go into a incredibly prolonged and tragic baptism of fire and blood in the form of the Thirty Year's war which was occasioned and fed by religious intolerance.[14] The famous Treaty of Westphalia of 1648, which ended the infamous war, stipulated religious tolerance and equality of status to Catholics and Lutherans though not to the Jews and others. Frederick, the Great, after his accession in 1740, extended full tolerance to all, including the Jews, though the principle of 'jurisdiction' was retained and Lutheran Christianity remained the religion of the State. The great emperor, who befriended Voltaire and who had a cosmopolitan outlook, even toyed with the idea of inviting Muslim settlers in his dominion and giving them equal rights. Frederick held that *'every one should be allowed to get to heaven in his own way.'* The outstanding German thinkers, poets and scholars who ushered in the German Enlightenment of the 18th and 19th centuries; Kant, Schiller, Goethe, Hegel, Dilthey, *et al* were all great champions of religious tolerance.

Coming to England, the turning point in the history of religious tolerance in the country dates to the Glorious Revolution of 1688 when Queen Anne and Prince Williams were raised to the English throne after the long period of instability, strife and uncertainty which followed the beheading of King Charles I in 1649. The horrors of the Thirty Year's war brought home to Englishmen, no less than to Germans and others, the utter futility of intolerance, thereby generating a sort of moral revulsion against bigotry. It is significant that the Treaty of Westphalia was signed in 1648, and exactly forty years afterwards, the new English sovereign proclaimed the principle of tolerance in his realm. The British Parliament passed the Act of Toleration in 1689. The philosopher, John Locke of Oxford, published in the same year his first Letter Concerning Toleration. Locke had great influence over the thinking of the period. The great philosopher was in favor of the 'principle of separation' between church and state, but this separation, in the strict formal sense, never came about in his own country, even though it eventually came to be implemented in the New World, as we shall shortly see. Interestingly, rather paradoxically, Locke did not extend the principle of tolerance to atheists. Earlier the great English poet, Milton, had strongly championed the liberty of conscience. Milton declared in 1644, '*Give me the liberty to know, to utter, and to argue freely according to conscience, above all other liberties*'.

The *Act of Toleration* of 1689, however, did not bring about complete tolerance in the modern sense of the term. It was only the first beginning of a long process of social and legal changes that eventually culminated in the establishment of full and unqualified tolerance and equality of status in the modern sense. Legal discrimination against the Jews and the Unitarian Christians continued. It is significant that the great physicist and philosopher of Cambridge, Newton (d. 1727) who was strongly drawn to Unitarianism conducted his scholarly research into Christian dogmas in complete secrecy and dared not air his views in the open. These disabilities were not removed until mid-19$^{th}$ century. Disraeli could not have become Prime Minister of England, had he been born a quarter of a century earlier.[15]

I now turn to America, which has given the greatest importance to complete religious tolerance and where the principle of separation between church and state was first applied in the history of mankind. This was done in the city-state of Providence on the eastern cost of the USA. Roger Williams founded the city in the 17th century with a view to securing complete equality and dignity to all its citizens, irrespective of their religion. The Roman Catholic colony of Maryland, established in 1649, also ensured complete toleration, though the state had retained the traditional principle of 'jurisdiction', that is the jurisdiction of Christianity over the state.[16]

The first large modern state, founded on the principle of separation of church and state, is the United States of America. The principle of separation was applied here even earlier than in the case of the French Republic. The secular constitution of the USA was, however, not the work of atheists, agnostics or materialists, but of committed Christians who sincerely and passionately had veered round to the belief that religion was, essentially, a personal matter which should be kept separate from the affairs of state and public issues, and the state, as a public corporation, should have no official religion. This philosophy of the nascent American Republic was the fruit of the sad and the bitter experience of the fanaticism and intolerance prevailing in the countries of the old world. The founding fathers of the American constitution held that the principle of jurisdiction enabled and encouraged one particular religion or sect to use the power and machinery of the state for promoting its own cause at the expense of the non-official sects or denominations. The constitution, therefore, declared the state to be neutral and equidistant from all religions, and every citizen, irrespective of his religion or lack of religion, was guaranteed equal status, as an American citizen. The constituent states of the Federal Union were, however, granted the right to follow the principle of separation or of jurisdiction with respect to their internal matters. The principled separation of the state and the church by the founding fathers of the American constitution reflected the religious maturity of enlightened and sincere Christians who had certainly not repudiated spiritual or moral values, or even institutional religion, provided it did not over-step its proper sphere.[17]

Humankind, however, is still far from the practice of tolerance, at its best, whether it be USA, Europe or other countries of the world. Tolerance, in the sphere of marriage between Catholics and Protestants, still does not come naturally or readily in the Western world, and many sincere Christians are compelled to resort to a civil marriage. The Jews still have their problems of emotional distance or prejudice. In America the Catholics would not readily give full marks to the overwhelming Protestant majority when deciding who should occupy the White House and other such issues. However, the movements of Unification theology, inter-religious dialogue, Human Rights and so on are all contributing to the desired goals.

The recent 'communications revolution' bears the promise of ushering in a multi-cultural global society. Almost every nation or linguistic and religious group, hitherto steeped into an ethnocentric outlook, has been exposed to multi-cultural stimuli and to the knowledge explosion. The tribals of a remote village in India mingle with the folk dancers from USSR, or listen to the music at St. Peter's; a puritanical mullah of a mosque in the interior of Pakistan or Afghanistan watches the temple-dancers of India or Indonesia, and so on. The sheer force of technology has shattered the cultural insularity of the past. Great diversity and disparity certainly characterize the human situation, and there is, as yet, no common language, no common religion, political authority or economic system. Yet, the awareness of cultural plurality is steadily steering the human family in the direction of permissiveness and tolerance in all cultural matters including religious belief or faith. The phenomena of religious fundamentalism, violence-and terrorism does raise fears of an impending catastrophe round the corner. However, in my thinking, though the fundamentalists or terrorists may win the battles, here and there, the humanists are going to win the war.

Secular Humanism, when not equated with atheism, does not destroy genuine religious feeling and spirituality, it merely rejects that form of religion which seeks to regulate the total behavior of the believer and which, furthermore, divides humanity into 'we-they camps' with respect to every sphere of human activity. Religious tolerance, when not equated with indifference, is not the axe, which destroys the tree of faith, but rather the fruit, which grows upon it.

## THE ISLAMIC DOCTRINE OF TOLERANCE

The concept of tolerance in Islam is derived from the Quran and the practice of the Prophet. The reported sayings and doings of the Prophet were put into writing, sorted out and classified a little less than 200 years after his passing away. Meanwhile the different schools of law founded by Abu Hanifa (d. 767), Malik (d. 795), Shafai (d. 820), Hambal (d. 855) and Jafar Sadiq (d. 765) crystallized after the Umayyad Caliphate had been displaced by the Abbasid wing of the Prophet's family. The Umayyad Caliph's who were more self-reliant or independent in their judgment on public matters had adopted a more or less eclectic and pragmatic approach to Islamic polity under the influence of Iranian and Roman ideas, which were adopted to promote the social dominance and economic interests of the Arab ruling class. During this period Islamic piety was focused, more on the five pillars of the religion, rather than on the social aspect of the *shariah*.

The subsequent literary, intellectual and cultural efflorescence in the middle Abbasid period was based on the earlier spadework under the Umayyad Caliphate. This gradually led to the full growth of the *shariah* whose authority became almost indistinguishable from the 'Book' as such. The interpretations of the major jurists, scholars and theologians were made in such a subtle manner that the distinction between the Quranic texts and their interpretation virtually disappeared. This led, in the course of time, to a situation where the inevitable imperfections of fallible individuals and the limitations of the spirit of the age in which they lived came to be projected on the 'Word of God' or the 'Book' as such. The fall of the titular Abbasid Caliphate (1258) at the hands of the Mongol hordes put the last nail in the coffin of the Islamic creativity of the earlier days. The tradition lost, for centuries to come, its inner dynamism and creativity in an ever-changing human situation.

It is, therefore, imperative to make a clear distinction between the Quranic texts, as such, dealing with tolerance (or any other concept or belief for that matter) and its traditional understanding or interpretation. According to the orthodox view, the traditional understanding is based upon the precepts and practice of the Prophet, the pious Caliphs and authoritative jurists. We must, however, realize that, firstly, all natural languages (including Quranic Arabic) are, inevitably, open to diverse interpretations, specially in the case of metaphysical, metaphorical, evaluative and directive uses of language.

Secondly, whenever we act on the basis of a general statement or command, diverse interpretations of the 'real' meaning become unavoidable. In other words, the principle of plural interpretations is an in-built feature of the Quran no less than of other scriptures or of language in general. Therefore, while Muslim believers must much respect the traditional interpretation of the Quranic texts no individual, school or system can rightly claim absoluteness or finality in an ever-changing human situation. The inevitable growth or movement of thought will inevitably and rightly suggest fresh interpretations of the scripture of Islam as of other religions.

Coming to the subject of tolerance, the Quran abounds in verses that prescribe tolerance of a high order, though the texts also contain some injunctions, which, prima-facie, negate the spirit of humanistic love and tolerance. However, contextual enquiry and careful textual scrutiny of the relevant verses, scattered in different parts of the Quran, show, beyond any doubt, that these injunctions were temporary regulations during the state of war or belligerency rather than basic maxims of conduct.

I shall now first cite some Quranic texts, which prescribe tolerance, inter-religious harmony, and the essential oneness of all religions.

*(Quran: Al-Baqarah, 2:256)*
*There is no compulsion in religion. The right direction is henceforth distinct from error.*

*(Quran: al-Kafirun, 109:6)*
*Unto you your religion, and unto me my religion.*

*(al-Imran, 3:84)*
*Say (o Muhammad): We believe in Allah and that which is re-*

vealed unto us and that which was revealed unto Abraham and Ishmael and Isaac and Jacob and the tribes, and that which was vouchsafed unto Moses and Jesus and the Prophets from their Lord. We make no distinction between any of them, and unto Him we have surrendered,

(Quran: al-Baqarah, 2:136)
Say (O Muslims): We believe in Allah and that which is revealed unto us and that which was revealed unto Abraham and Ishmael and Isaac, and Jacob, and the tribes and that which Moses and Jesus received, and that which the Prophets received from their Lord. We make no distinction between any of them, and unto Him we have surrendered. Lo: those who disbelieve in Allah and His messengers, and seek to make distinction between Allah and his messengers, and say: We believe in some and disbelieve in others, and seek to choose a way in between ; Such are disbelievers in truth; and for disbelievers We prepare a shameful doom.

(Quran: an-Nisa, 4:150-152)
But those who believe in Allah and His messengers and make no distinction between any of them, unto them, Allah will give their wages; and Allah was ever Forgiving, Merciful

(Quran: al-Baqarah, 2 :285)
The Messenger believeth in that which hath been revealed unto Him from his Lord and (so do) the believers. Each one believeth in Allah and His angels and His scriptures and His messengers—we make no distinction between any of His messengers—and they say; we hear, and we obey. (Grant us) Thy forgiveness, our Lord! Unto Thee is the Journeying.

(Quran: al-Mumin, 40:78)
Verily We sent messengers before thee, among them those of whom we have told thee, and some of whom We have not told thee; and it was not given to any messenger that he should bring a portent save by Allah's leave, but when Allah's commandment cometh, (the cause) is judged aright, and the followers of vanity will then be lost.

*(Quran: al-Baqarah, 2:62)*
*Lo: those who believe (in that which is revealed unto thee, Muhammad) and those who are Jews, and Christians, and Sabaeans —whoever believeth in Allah and the Last Day and doth right — surely their reward is with their Lord, and there shall no fear come upon them neither shall they grieve.*

*(Quran: al-Ma'ida, 5:69)*
*Lo : those who believe and those who are Jews, and Sabaeans, and Christians — whosoever believeth in Allah and the Last Day and doeth right — there shall no fear come upon them neither shall they grieve.*

*(Quran: al-Ma'idah, 5:48)*
*And unto thee have We revealed the Scripture with the truth, confirming whatever Scripture was before it and a watcher over it. So judge between them by that which Allah hath revealed and follow not their desires away from the truth which hath come unto thee. For each We have appointed a divine law and a traced-out way. Had Allah willed He could have made you one community. But that He may try you by that which He hath given you (He hath made you as ye are). So vie one with another in good works. Unto Allah ye will all return, and He will then inform you of that wherein ye differ,*

*(Quran: al-An'am, 6:108, 109)*
*Had Allah willed, they had not been idolatrous? We nave not sent thee as a keeper over them, nor art thou responsible for them. Revile not those unto whom they pray beside Allah lest they wrongfully revile Allah through ignorance. Thus unto every nation have We made their deed seem fair. Then unto their Lord is their return, and He will tell them what they used to do.*

*(Quran: Jonah, 10:100, 101)*
*And if thy Lord willed, all who are in the earth would have believed together. Wouldst thou (Muhammad) compel men until they are believers?*

*It is not for any soul to believe save by the permission of Allah. He hath set uncleanness upon those who have no sense.*

*(Quran: Jonah, 10:109)*
*Say: O mankind: Now hath the Truth from your Lord come unto you. So whosoever is guided, is guided only for (the good of) his soul, and whosoever erreth, erreth only against it. And I am not a warder over you.*

*(Quran: al-Anbiya, 21:92-94)*
*Lo:this your religion, is one religion, and I am your Lord, so worship me. And they have broken their religion (into fragments) among them, (yet) all are returning unto Us.*
*Then whoso doth good works and is a believer, there will be no rejection of his effort. Lo! We record (it) for him.*

*(Quran: an-Nur, 24:54)*
*Say: Obey Allah and obey the messenger. But if ye turn away, then (it is) for him (to do) only that wherewith he hath been charged, and for you (to do) only that wherewith ye have been charged. If ye obey him, ye will go aright. But the messenger hath no other charge than to convey (the message) plainly.*

*(Quran: al-Ghashiyah, 88:21, 22)*
*Remind them; for thou art but a remembrancer, Thou art not at all a warder over them.*

*(Quran: al-Baqarah, 2 : III, 112)*
*And they say: None entereth Paradise unless he be a Jew or Christian. These are their own desires. Say: Bring your proof (of what ye state) if ye are truthful. Nay, but whosoever surrendereth his purpose to Allah while doing good, his reward is with his Lord; and there shall no fear come upon them nor shall they grieve.*

*(Quran: al-Baqarah, 2:113)*
*And the Jews say the Christians follow nothing (true), and the Christians say the Jews follow nothing (true); yet both are readers*

of the Scripture. Even thus speak those who know not. Allah will judge between them on the Day of Resurrection concerning that wherein they differ.

*(Quran: al-Maidah 5:18)*
The Jews and Christians say: We are sons of Allah and loved ones. Say: why then doth He chastise you for your sins? Nay, ye are but mortals of his creating. He forgiveth whom He will, and chastiseth whom He will. Allah's is the Sovereignty of the heavens and the earth and all that is between them, and unto Him is the journeying.

*(Quran: al-Hajj 22 :34)*
And for every nation have We appointed a ritual, that they may mention the name of Allah over the beast or cattle that He hath given them for food; and your God is one God, therefore surrender unto Him. And give good tidings (O Muhammad) to the humble.

*(al-Hajj, 22 :67)*
Unto each nation have we given sacred rites which they are to perform; so let them not dispute with thee of the matter, but summon thou unto thy Lord. Lo! Thou indeed followest right guidance.

*(al-Maidah, 5:68)*
Say: O people of the Scripture! Ye have naught (of guidance) till ye observe the Torah and the Gospel and that which was revealed unto you from your Lord. That which is revealed unto thee (Muhammad) from thy Lord is certain to increase the contumacy and disbelief of many of them. But grieve not for the disbelieving folk.

*(al-Ma'idah, 5:47)*
Let the People of the Gospel judge by that which Allah hath revealed therein. Whoso judgeth not by that which Allah hath revealed, such are evil-livers.

*(Ha-Mm, 41:43 )*
Naught is said unto thee (Muhammad) save what was said unto the messengers before thee. Lo: thy Lord is owner of forgiveness, and owner (also) of dire punishment.

*(al-An'am, 6:161)*
*Whoso bringeth a good deed will receive tenfoid the like thereof, while whose bringeth an ill deed will be awarded but the like thereof, and they will not be wronged.*

*(al-Imran, 3:199)*
*And Lo! of the People of the Scripture there are some who believe in Allah and that which is revealed unto you and that which was revealed unto them, humbling themselves before Allah. They purchase not a trifling gain at the price of the revelations of Allah. Verily their reward is with their Lord, and lo! Allah is swift to take account.*

*(al-Mai'da, 5:83)*
*When they listen to that which hath been revealed unto the messenger, thou seest their eyes overflow with tears, because of their recognition of the Truth. They say Our Lord, we believe. Inscribe us as among the witnesses.*

*(al-Qasas, 28:52-53)*
*Those unto whom we gave the Scripture before it, they believe in it. And when it is recited unto them, they say: we believe in it. Lo! It is the Truth from our Lord. Lo! even before it we were of those who surrender (unto Him).*

Here are those Quranic verses which, prima facie, contradict the spirit of Humanism but which are not contrary to the spirit of tolerance when their historical context is understood:

*(Quran: al-Imran, 3:28 )*

*Let not the believers take disbelievers for their friends in preference to believers. Whoso doeth that hath no connection with Allah, unless (it be) that ye but guard yourselves against them, taking (as it were) security. Allah biddeth you beware (only) of Himself. Unto Allah is the journeying.*

*(Quran: al-Imran, 3:118 )*
O ye who believe! Take not for intimates others than your own folk, who would spare no pains to ruin you; they love to hamper you. Hatred is revealed by (the utterance of) their mouths, but that which their breasts hide is greater. We have made plain for you the revelations if ye will understand.

*(Quran: an-Nisa, 4:139)*
Those who choose disbelievers for their friends instead of believers, do they look for power at their hands? Lo! all power appertaineth to Allah.

*(Quran: an-Nisa, 4:89 )*
They long that ye should disbelieve even as they disbelieve, that ye may be upon a level (with them). So choose not friends from them till they forsake their homes in the way of Allah; if they turn back (to enmity) then take them and kill them wherever ye find them, and choose no friend nor helper among them.

*(Quran: an-Nisa, 4:144 )*
O ye who believe! Choose not disbelievers for (your) friends in place of believers. Would ye give Allah a clear warrant against you?

*(Quran: al-Maidah, 5:51)*
O ye who believe! Take not the Jews and Christians for friends. They are friends one to another. He among you who taketh them for friends is (one) of them. Lo! Allah guideth not wrongdoing folk.

*(Quran: al-Maidah, 5:57)*
O ye who believe! Choose not for friends such of those who received the Scripture before you, and of the disbelievers, as make a jest and sport bf your religion. But keep your duty to Allah if ye are true believers.

*(Quran: af-Bara'at. 9:23)*
O ye who believe! Choose not your fathers nor your brethren for friends if they take pleasure in disbelief rather than faith. Whoso

*of you taketh them for friends, such are wrongdoers.*

(Quran: al-Bara'at, 9:5)
Then, when the sacred months have passed, slay the idolaters wherever ye find them, and take them (captive), and besiege them, and prepare for them each ambush. But if they repent and establish worship and pay the poor-due, then leave their way free. Lo! Allah is Forgiving, Merciful.

(Quran: al-Mumtahanah, 60:7-9)
It may be that Allah will ordain love between you and those of them with whom ye are at enmity. Allah is Mighty, and Allah is Forgiving, Merciful.

*Allah forbiddeth you not those who warred not against you on account of religion and drove you not out from your homes, that ye should show them kindness and deal justly with them. Lo! Allah loveth the just dealers.*

*Allah forbiddeth you only those who warred against you on account of religion and have driven you out from your homes and helped to drive you out, that ye make friends of them-- (All) such are wrong-doers.*

(Quran: al- Bara'at, 9:28)
O ye who believe! The idolaters only are unclean. So let them not come near the Inviolable Place of Worship after this their year. If ye fear poverty (from the loss of their merchandise) Allah shall preserve you of His bounty if He will. Lo! Allah is knower, Wise.

(Quran: al-Taubah, 9:33)
He it is who hath sent His messenger with the guidance, and the Religion of Truth, that He may cause it to prevail over all religion, however much the idolaters may be averse.

*(Quran: Al- Imran, 3:85)*
*And whoso seeketh as religion other than the Surrender (to Allah), it will not be accepted from him, and he will be a loser in the Hereafter.*

The above set of Quranic texts have a different thrust from the previous set that stressed the values of tolerance, peace and universal harmony. Nevertheless, the fact remains that the grim sternness and severity of the injunctions concerned reflect the extreme danger and risk faced by the nascent Islamic movement at the time the verses were revealed. As said earlier, these verses are, essentially, war time safety precautions and regulations for Muslims, not the basic values and virtues of normal human social intercourse and relationships.

A comparative study of the Quranic texts, in the light of the situational context of the revelation, confirms the view that humanistic love and tolerance are the fundamental directive principles of the Quran, while mistrust of non-Muslims, social exclusiveness and harshness towards non-believers were merely temporary rules or security measures during the state of belligerency.

## TOLERANCE AND APOSTASY IN THE QURAN

Apostasy or religious defection from one faith to another or to total disbelief was a great sin in pre-Islamic times, and was punishable by death both in Judaism and Christianity. Islamic canon law (*shariah*) did the same, even though the Quranic texts, as such, relating to apostasy did not prescribe this extreme penalty. The relevant Quranic texts are as follows:

*(an-Nisa, 4:137)*
*Lo! those who believe, then disbelieve and then (again) believe, then disbelieve, and then increase in disbelief, Allah will never pardon them, nor will He guide them unto a way.*

*(al-Maidah, 5:54)*
*O ye who believe! whoso of you becometh a renegade from his religion, (know that in his stead) Allah will bring a people whom He loveth and who love Him, humble toward believers, stern toward disbelievers, striving in the way of Allah, and fearing not the blame of any blamer. Such is the grace of Allah which He giveth unto whom He will. Allah is All-Embracing, All-Knowing.*

The above verses, read in conjunction with the clear and categorical Quranic text, (2:256) by no means validate the pre-Islamic penalty for apostasy. Yet the classical Islamic jurists did so. Perhaps, they reasoned that the Quranic text (2:256) *'there is no compulsion in religion'* prohibits Muslims to convert others to Islam by force, but does not permit a Muslim to renounce Islam. Should a Muslim do so he becomes guilty of apostasy that is a heinous sin that God never pardons. The apostate should, therefore, be executed.

In other words, while use of force for conversion to Islam is prohibited, use of force is lawful for preventing a Muslim believer from defecting to some other faith or sheer paganism. Thus, Islamic jurists of all schools declare that once a person accepts Islam, he forfeits the freedom to repudiate his allegiance to Islam. Should he do so, he attracts the death penalty. But there appears to be absolutely no warrant for this extreme view in the relevant verses of the Quran.

Apostasy became a major issue after the death of the Prophet when some Arab chieftains who had earlier accepted the Prophet's call to Islam decided to repudiate Islam or the authority of the successor to the Prophet. It seems that two logically distinct issues, namely, repudiation of the Islamic creed proclaimed by the Prophet, and repudiation of the political authority or supremacy of the successor to the Prophet got intertwined in the historical developments after the passing away of Prophet Muhammad ﷺ.

In other words, the ideas of 'religious defection' and of rebellion got mixed in the Islamic response to behavior of the 'false prophets' after the passing away of Prophet Muhammad ﷺ. As we all know, all societies or states mete out the death penalty to anybody who challenges the power of the supreme authority at any point of time. The earliest Islamic establishment did the same without making any distinction (valid and essential for the modern mind) between political loyalty and religious faith, or between the matters of inner autonomous faith and the matter of loyalty to the sovereign. Perhaps, at that critical juncture the successors to the Prophet had no time and patience to go into the distinction between the freedom of conscience and loyalty or obedience to the ruler.[18]

## THE STATUS OF NON-MUSLIMS IN THE ISLAMIC STATE

According to the Islamic doctrine of religious tolerance conquered territories ipso facto become parts of '*the land of Islam*' (*darul Islam*). Those inhabitants who lay down arms, but are not willing to embrace Islam were entitled to full protection of life, property, honor and freedom of belief in and practice of their religion, and the carrying on of their normal means of livelihood, provided they paid '*jizya*', a special discriminatory tax on an annual per capita basis. Women, children, the aged and the infirm were exempted.

The concept of the '*jizya*' was taken from the ancient practice in Iran and fully harmonized with the spirit of the times. The Islamic rationale for adopting this practice was that it was a substitute tax for '*zakaat*', which was a Quranic obligation upon Muslims alone. The defense of the Islamic state against external attack was also obligatory upon the Muslims but optional for the '*dhimmis*'. The protected non-Muslims (*dhimmis*) had the option to seek exemption from '*jizya*' by simply offering to participate in the joint defense of the Islamic state against external attack.

It is significant that without the '*jizya*' the economic liability of the Muslims actually exceeded that of the '*dhimmis*'. In fact the '*jizya*' was a device to keep both Muslim believers and the rest of the peaceful citizens on par in purely economic terms. Moreover, the Islamic establishment actually protected the '*dhimmis*' against the land hunger of the Muslims themselves. In short, in actual practice, the '*jizya*' was not a penal tax but merely a more or less functional substitute tax for non-Muslim citizens, who, by definition, could not attract all the rights and obligations associated with Islam, but wished to continue living in lands that had become a part of 'the land of Islam'.[19]

Unfortunately, some prejudiced historical writings have created a false impression that the '*dhimmis*' were subjected to several humiliating disabilities, as mentioned in the so called *'Compact of Omar'*, the second pious Caliph. Modern research (thanks to the labors of reputed Western scholars, no less than Muslims themselves) has exploded the myth. What happened was that Omar II (d. 702), the Umayyad Caliph, who came on the scene more than half a century after the pious Caliph Omar did put some restrictions upon the *'dhimmis'*, and, subsequently, some jurists also adopted a discriminatory approach against non-Muslims. But even Omar II did not issue any 'Compact' at all, and he should not be held responsible for some really objectionable views and practices of much later jurists in medieval times in India and elsewhere. These doctrines are much later developments and have no place in the Quran, and the practice of the Prophet and the pious Caliphs.[20]

## RESPECT FOR PLACES OF WORSHIP

The Islamic doctrine of tolerance categorically prohibits desecrating any place of worship, or forcibly using it for Islamic worship. However, the Prophet did remove the idols from the *Kaaba* at Mecca on the ground that the *Kaaba* was, originally, a mosque built by Abraham. The Prophet viewed the 'cleansing' of the *Kaaba* from idols as the restoration of a monotheistic place of worship to its original status.

This is a solitary instance of the Prophet having removed or destroyed idols from a place of worship under the control of non-Muslims for several centuries. Syria was conquered during the caliphate of Abu Bakr. Iraq, Iran and Egypt during the caliphate of Omar, and Khurasan during that of Usman. No expansion took place during the caliphate of Ali. During this entire period of about thirty years no place of worship belonging to non-Muslims was desecrated, nor any icon destroyed or any encouragement given to iconoclasm.

## PERMISSIBILITY OF INTER-RELIGIOUS MARRIAGE

A unique feature of the Islamic doctrine of tolerance is that Islam permits inter-religious marriage, when no other religion does so. The Islamic tradition permits marriage between Muslim men and non-Muslim women belonging to the 'people of the Book' (*ahl-e-kitab*). Muslim women are, however, not permitted to marry non-Muslim men. The *'people of the book'* meant, in practice, only the Jews and the Christians, to begin with. Later on the Zoroastrians of Iran, and the Hindus of Sind were also included for a brief period.[21]

## DARUL ISLAM & DARUL HARB (LANDS OF ISLAM & LANDS OF WAR)

The Islamic doctrine of tolerance presupposes the division of the world into the land of Islam and of non-Islam, and the duty of Muslim believers to transform the entire world into the land of Islam. The traditional Islamic doctrine affirms a state of continuing conflict between Islam and non-Islam. However, there is room, on a temporary basis, for a transitory truce, no-war pacts, or treaties of mutual aid. Islamic jurists were the first to frame a code of conduct for Muslim participants in war and also for Muslims living in the land of non-Islam.[22]

## ISLAMIC TOLERANCE IN PRACTICE

The Prophet had brought about the political unification of the Arab tribes shortly before his death. This great achievement represented the combined victory of Arab nationalism over centrifugal tribalism, as also of Islam as the revised version of ancient Judaism and Christianity. The, hitherto, camel-drivers, petty traders and desert freebooters emerged from the backwaters of history onto the world-stage. The almost unbroken chain of military victories against the then super-powers, inevitably, fostered a new self-image of the emerging Arab elite. In this self-image were inextricably mixed Arab nationalism and faith in Islam, as the final world religion; the completion of God's favors and blessings on mankind.

Gushing springs of self-assertion and valor, born from the fusion of Arab pride and Islamic commitment burst forth from the arid sands of Arabia, taking the world by storm, as it were. The incredible momentum of the Arab-Islamic revolution of the seventh century, historically speaking, has not yet been surpassed for rapidity of success, in the annals of world history. To my mind, Arab expansion was the result of neither pure racial imperialism, nor of pure Islamic missionary zeal, but rather an inextricable combination of both. To look upon the Arab expansion as nothing but territorial aggrandizement, or as nothing but a spiritual mission, would be to over-simplify a complex historical phenomenon. Arab political expansionism, to begin with, was a violation of the spirit of tolerance. But once the Islamic state was established the Arab Muslims immediately put the Islamic doctrine of tolerance into practice. The people in the conquered territory were invited to accept Islam and become equal partners. Failing this, they could live and carry on their normal activities as protected non-Muslims (*dhimmis*) living in an Islamic state (*darul Islam*). Though the '*dhimmis*' had a slightly lower status, it was, certainly, not a lowly status or a mere euphemism for slavery. There was no recourse to forced conversion of the conquered people.

However, there can be no doubt that Islamic tolerance falls short of the modern idea of tolerance implying complete equality of status, irrespective of religion. Nevertheless, the Arab Muslims were ahead of the times in regard to observing humane rules of war, fair treatment of prisoners and of doing justice to people who had been subjugated but were unwilling to embrace Islam. Historians of repute, including eminent non-Muslim scholars, testify to the above. Short of becoming the head of state, '*dhimmis*' rose to positions of eminence in the service of the state, business, industry, commerce, banking, medicine and the pursuit of learning. In the course of time, the majority of '*dhimmis*' got converted to Islam. But this was certainly not the result of force but of social psychological, political and ideological factors. The great achievement of the early Muslims and Islamic creativity in almost every field of human endeavor genuinely moved millions of Christians, Jews and others to embrace the new faith, as had happened earlier in the case of Christianity and Buddhism.

The process of formal conversion to Islam was a long drawn out affair extending to almost two centuries in Syria, Iraq, Iran, Egypt and other places. Some among the vast Zoroastrian population of Iran migrated to India (where they came to be known as '*Parsis*') on the ground of persecution, but the majority stayed behind, gradually taking to Islam. In a slow and prolonged process of cultural interaction between the ancient and rich culture of the Iranians, and the Quranic and semitic concepts of Islam several Iranian thought forms and cultural patterns became an integral part of the growing Islamic tradition. The same process was repeated later on in India, and subsequently, in Malaysia and Indonesia, with respect to their respective pre-Islamic Sanskrit cultures.

The Prophet himself had set the tradition of tolerance and of interreligious dialogue from the very beginning. The Prophet's agreement with the local residents of Medina stipulated mutual friendship and aid for all citizens, irrespective of their religion. Political expediency and breach of solemn promises by the Jews impaired the inter-religious solidarity and harmony the Prophet had clearly visualized. Indeed, the burden of the Prophet's Islamic message lay in continuity of the great semitic tradition of the Jews as well as the Christians. The friendly relations between the Prophet and the Emperor of Ethiopia are well known. A group of early Muslim converts had found friendly asylum at the court of the Emperor much before the migration to Medina.[23]

Caliph Omar refused to pray inside the Christian Church at Jerusalem (despite requests by the Christians) lest this provide an excuse, later on, for its conversion into a mosque. Omar also had the sagacity and the moral courage to prohibit the Arab invaders of Egypt from displacing the local farmers from their fertile lands in the Nile valley.

Coming to the Umayyad period we come across numerous instances of harmonious relations and friendship between Muslims and non-Muslims. The wife of Caliph Muawiyah (d. 680) was a Christian, as also his secretary of finance. Al-Qasri, governor of Iraq under Caliph Hisham (d. 743) built a church at Kufa to please his mother who was a Christian. Hisham also appointed Zoroastrians to public office. The Abbasid Caliphs appointed Christians as Viziers (Prime Ministers), Ibn Said Yaqut being the most famous. The Caliph Muttaqi (d. 944) had a Christian Vizier. Caliph Mutazid (d. 902) appointed a Christian as the head of the war office, and a Jew, Muhammad bin Ubaidullah, as the Vizier. The Fatimide Caliph, Aziz (d. 996) appointed a Jew, Yaqub bin Killis, as the Vizier. Eventually, Yaqub became a Muslim. Aziz later appointed Isa bin Nestorius, a Christian, as a Vizier. The head of the Babylonian Jews in Baghdad was greatly venerated by the Muslims who viewed him as the direct descendant of David.

Abdur Rahman I (d. 788) of Muslim Spain continued the liberal tradition of the Damascus Caliphate. Hakam I (d. 822), was opposed to the mixing of religion with politics, and stood for restricting the *shariah* to purely religious matters, Abdur Rahman II (d. 852) showed the utmost tolerance to Christians who wielded great power in society. Abdur Rahman III (d. 961) the greatest of all the Caliphs of Muslim Spain and one of the greatest rulers of the world continued the liberal tradition at Cordova. Spain produced a galaxy of poets, thinkers, scientists, historians, artists, architects, manufacturers who came from among the Jews and the Christians, no less than Muslims, and made a permanent contribution to the sum total of human civilization and culture. The Ottoman Caliphs of Turkey also practiced the same liberal tradition, throughout their very extensive multi-racial and multi-religious empire. The Jews and Christians (both Catholics and Protestants) were given the highest posts in the realm and even dominated the industrial and commercial life of the state. Even the personal bodyguard of the Caliphs included Christians.[24]

Coming to the dark side of the picture, several Caliphs (no matter what their other qualities and good points) deviated, in varying degrees, from the Islamic doctrine of tolerance, and discriminated against both Muslims and non-Muslims. Some even persecuted doctrinal dissent within the fold of Islam itself. The most striking case of persecution of doctrinal dissent within Islam is Mamun's prolonged persecution of the great jurist, Imam Hambal, for not accepting the Mutazalite view that the Quran was not eternal but was created in time. Mamun, reputed for his great contribution to culture and learning, sought to impose his own Mutazaiite view on the jurist who held the theological view that the Quran was eternal. Ironically, Muqtadir reversed the position and persecuted the Mutazalites, expelling them from public office.[25] Self-appointed censors invaded homes and burnt objectionable literature. Under Mustanjid, the writings of Ibn Sina were burnt in 1150. In 1192 Abdus Salam, the noted scholar of Baghdad, was accused of atheism and his library was burnt. The persecution of the great mystic, Mansur Hallaj (d. 922) is well known.

Notwithstanding the above, the Muslims in history have shown far greater tolerance than the Christians or Jews in the same period. All impartial historians (including reputed non-Muslim scholars) concede the atrocious behavior of the Christian crusaders towards the Muslims and Jews in the territories the crusaders had temporarily conquered from the Arabs and which remained under Christian rule for an interregnum of approximately eighty years. The defenders of the Cross unleashed a reign of terror and incredible brutality, not only against the non-Christians of Palestine, but against the local fellow Christiana themselves who were far happier under Islamic rule than under the Cross.

## THE PRACTICE OF TOLERANCE IN MEDIEVAL INDIA

Let us now review the practice of tolerance in medieval India. We should avoid drawing hasty and sweeping conclusions from selective views and attitudes and take the totality of facts into account. We would be guilty of 'simplism' if we were to give undue significance to the views of a section of the *ulema* who bemoaned the friendly relations between Muslims and non-Muslims and the power and position of Hindu nobles and top administrators, on the ground that the *shariah* (as interpreted by them) prohibited friendly intercourse between Muslims and the polytheists. Some theologians were not even averse to the permissibility of coercion for saving the souls of heathens, even as a doctor may forcibly administer a bitter medicine for the patient's own good. The expression of such ideas in the writings of some Muslim divines has led some historians and scholars to wrong conclusions regarding the actual state of affairs in medieval India. These scholars tend to ignore the fact that the Sufi, approach to the problem of tolerance was radically otherwise. In fact, a sizeable section of the ultra-orthodox *ulema* held the view that the *Sufis* were pseudo-Muslims. In actual practice, however, the Indian classes no less than masses flocked to the Sufi saints while giving only formal respect to the *ulema*.

*Sufis*, in general, are known for their ethics of tolerance and universal love and the doctrine of the essential unity of all religions and the oneness of the human family, notwithstanding diversity of symbols and forms. Some of the Sufi utterances, really, cut so deeply into the traditional fabric of religious belief as to invite the charge of misunderstanding or blasphemy. Though the great *Sufis* did attract people to Islam through their elevated moral and spiritual status, their emphasis was upon inner purification of the soul rather than upon conversion to Islam. It is highly significant that Muslim sovereigns were attracted more to the *Sufis* than to the theologians.

The point at issue has a great relevance to our own times. It is well known that several Hindu quarters are openly hostile to the non-Hindu segment of the Indian people. Now the spoken and written words emanating from such quarters should not make the impartial observer of the Indian scene today infer that the government of the day actually practice what the Hindu communalists desire or recommend. The declared wishes or inner attitudes of a particular section of the people should not be equated with the actual policy and practice of the government of the day. Unfortunately, this is, precisely, what some scholars, politicians and religious leaders do when they bemoan the plight of Hindu society under Muslim rule in the medieval period. No matter what some custodians of the *shariah* may have thought, the Muslim rulers of medieval India refused to mix religion and politics and followed a policy, which may aptly be called 'functional secularism'. Like rulers, in general, Muslim rulers were more interested in saving their own thrones rather than in saving the souls of others. When things did not go their way, rulers did turn to spiritual help or support from religious sources and symbols. But this was a recipe merely in times of adversity, not the staple food of rulers. As prudent statesmen, the *sultans* and emperors adopted a policy of non-discrimination against their Hindu subjects who constituted the overwhelming majority. This fact rather than sheer force or the supposed degradation of the Hindus helped sustain Muslim rule in medieval India for successive centuries.

The overwhelming majority of the Hindus did not look upon Muslim sovereigns as foreign tyrants, or the Muslim nobility and the military as agents of exploitation of the tyrant concerned. The king or the ruler, no matter what his race or religion, was given all love and loyalty, so long as he was victorious in the battlefield. The Hindu populace, no matter what it might have thought at the time of the very first confrontation with the Turk or the Pathan invaders, soon came to look upon the Muslims as a warrior caste, one among the several castes forming the rich mosaic of Indian society. There is no doubt that when the Muslims settled down in the land of their conquest, they became in their own eyes no less than in that of the Hindus, an integral part of the already much mixed population. True, intermarriage between the Muslims and the Hindus was an unthinkable proposition. But so was intercaste marriage within the Hindu fold as such. The significant point is that the vast majority of the Indian Muslims were ethnically of Hindu stock.

The weaker and socially handicapped segments of an extremely hierarchical Hindu society, bedeviled by caste taboos, had found new hopes of vertical mobility under the umbrella of Islamic social egalitarianism. In addition, Islam being the creed of the ruling class, it offered extra avenues of political power. The sovereigns (with just one or two exceptions) treated Hindus and Muslims with paternalistic impartiality. The Hindu populace enjoyed full freedom of belief and of conscience, and were free to carry on their individual and social life just as they chose. There was absolutely no state interference in matters religious, cultural, and social. Agriculture, industry, the bulk of the trade and administration (at the lower and intermediate levels) remained in the hands of the Hindus. They also had access to assignments at the highest level, but here their proportion was considerably lower because of intense competition from the Muslim side. The upper class families of Turkish, Pathan, Turanian and Iranian descent looked upon themselves and were also looked upon by the rulers as the natural claimants or incumbents at the top levels of power, and even the Muslims of pure Indian origin had to face stiff competition.

The Hindu princes and chieftains who accepted the suzerainty of the central power were accorded high honor, retained their thrones and exercised vast powers, military and civil, in their own extensive territories under the feudal system. There was a common civil levy on the land, apart from personal, laws, which were not interfered with. The law of the land was heavily influenced by the *shariah*, but the sovereigns claimed and exercised discretionary powers in all worldly matters. The sovereigns, firmly and consistently repudiated the claim of the Islamic jurists that the jurisdiction of the *shariah* was all embracing.

The *sultans* and emperors, with the sole exception of Akbar, did not presume to reinterpret Islam, but merely followed the policy of 'functional secularism'. This, in effect, amounted to a pragmatic separation between the jurisdiction of the state and of religion without formally raising technical religious or doctrinal issues, such as the status of India as 'Darul Islam', or the *de jure* authority of the *khalifa* over India, and so on.[25(a)]

Many theologians and jurists disapproved of the above-mentioned pragmatic approach of the *sultans* who, however, persisted in their *de facto* functional secular approach. The rulers got moral support from *Sufi* saints who were, in general, inclined to religious liberalism and humanism and were also more in touch with the populace, Muslim as well as Hindu. Indeed, there was a measure of tension (which persists till today) between the humanism of the *Sufi* and the legalism of the jurist or the theologian. The best Urdu and Persian poets In India and elsewhere express this tension and exalt the spiritual ecstasy of the *Sufi* while decrying the empty legalism of the mullah.[26]

The policy of 'functional secularism' reached its fruition and was sought to be transformed into a basic political principle, as it were, in the time of Akbar. Going beyond mere practical prudence, Akbar sought to bring about complete equality of status and of opportunity between his subjects, and also emotionally integrate Hindus, Muslims and others into one larger Indian family. Akbar's abolition of the '*jizya*' in 1564 (eight years after his accession to the throne) was the most significant reform or innovation, both psychologically and doctrinally, to bring about the desired emotional integration.

However, from the purely fiscal or economic angle, the abolition of this discriminatory tax on non-Muslims did not amount to much. *'Jizya'* was in lieu of the obligatory wealth-tax (*zakaat*) which was a religious duty imposed on all Muslims having surplus wealth at the end of the year. Now whatever the theory of *'jizya'* may have been, in practice, it was an exclusive tax on the non-Muslims, just as *'zakaat'* was an exclusive tax on the Muslims, and the latter tax could far exceed the quantum of *'jizya'* paid by non-Muslims. Moreover, several categories of non-Muslims were exempt from the said tax. The discrimination involved was thus more formal rather than economic. Nevertheless, the discriminative nomenclature must have bred psychological distance between the two categories of tax assesses.

Akbar's administrative intuition and political insight led him to bring all his subjects on par, legally, administratively and fiscally. Unfortunately, Akbar's well-intentioned and far-reaching vision was mis-interpreted by many of his Muslim contemporaries as a repudiation of Islamic *shariah*, or as a sinister move to impose a new religion in place of Islam. The coining of the term, *'Din-e-Ilahi'* and the over-enthusiasm of some of the Emperor's courtiers (for reasons, selfish rather than spiritual) conspired to give a semblance of truth to the misinterpretation of Akbar's religious views as the downright repudiation of Islam or as sheer political opportunism. This misinterpretation still persists, especially among those who glorify the achievements of Aurangzeb, and hold that he saved Islam from being totally destroyed by the follies of Akbar and Dara Shikoh. Numerous non-Muslims, on the other hand, condemn Aurangzeb for his religious fanaticism and persecution of Hindus and Sikhs. Incontrovertible historical evidence is increasingly piling up with the passage of years, thanks to rigorous methods of research by Indian and Western scholars, to expose the fallacy of the above extreme views.

It is clear that Akbar regarded himself as a Muslim, and so did the overwhelming majority of his subjects (both Muslim and non-Muslim). It is also clear that Aurangzeb continued to enjoy the unquestioned loyalty and active support of a sizeable section of the Rajputs till the very end of his long reign. Aurangzeb's declared policy and practice were to employ efficient and honest persons, irrespective of religion or caste. The percentage of non-Muslims among high-ranking *mansabdars*, no less than among lower or middle rank revenue officers, was higher in the time of Aurangzeb as compared to Akbar. Aurangzeb's Deccan and Marhatta policy was not dictated by religious, but rather by economic and political considerations, even as his fight against his father and brothers was a vigorous search for power. His brothers also sought power, but they lost, while Aurangzeb won.

Differences in religious outlook did exist, but the crucial factor in their motivation was the search for power, rather than search for piety. If Dara was poetic and speculative, Aurangzeb was puritanical and legalistic; if Dara came under the spell of the *Upanishads*, Aurangzeb remained in the grip of the *shariah*; if Dara stood for the essential unity of all religions, Aurangzeb stood for the exclusive salvation of Muslims. But the point is that religious bigotry was not the crucial factor in the motivation of Aurangzeb who was far from being an evil tyrant and temple-destroyer. He was rather lacking in political and economic insight.

His failure was due to a relative lack of political insight and a static religious vision, but he was not inimical to others. The re-imposition of the '*jizya*', the excessive territorial expansion of the empire, the concessions to Muslim traders in customs and excise duty, the discouragement of music and other art forms, the long absence from the capital due to his taking over the command of the insurgency operations in the Pune region: all were misconceived and harmful policies, not acts of hostility against non-Muslims. While Aurangzeb did demolish a few temples, he endowed many more in different parts of the country. It is significant that he also demolished a mosque at Golkunda that was being used by Muslim insurgents.[27]

The history of the several independent regional Muslim kingdoms in the medieval period, prior to their incorporation into the Mughal Empire, also points to the tolerant character of the *sultans* and of the functionally secular motivation of their policies and conduct of public affairs. Zaynul Abidin d. 1470) of Kashmir, the most illustrious ruler of the region, was admired and loved by all Kashmiris, irrespective of their religion. He was the patron of Sanskrit no less than of Persian, of the '*sant*' no less than of the *Sufi*. Husayn Shah (d. 1519) of Bengal played a similar role in the eastern region. His example was later on followed by the great Sher Shah Suri (d. 1545) whose enlightened religious liberalism and administrative reforms are still remembered by all Indians, Hindus and Muslims alike.

In the southern region, the Bahmani Sultan, Tajuddin Feroze (d. 1472) gave preference to Dakhnis in state employment, irrespective of religion. His conflict with the neighboring Hindu *Raja* of Vijaynagar was purely political. Mahmud Gawan (d. 1481), the illustrious Prime Minister of the

Bahmani Kingdom followed the same policy. The *Sultans* of Golkunda and Bijapur and the Rajas of Vijaynagar entered into pacts or fought among themselves in their own respective political interests, as they saw them, quite irrespective of their religious affiliations. Ibrahim Qutb Shah (d. 1580) of Golkunda greatly patronized Telugu culture, endowed Hindu temples and even discontinued the '*jizya*'. Vijaynagar thought it fit, in its own political interests, to play one Muslim kingdom against, the other. This game went on until Vijaynagar's eventual defeat in 1565. During this protracted period of shifting alliances, the Muslim ruler of Bijapur sought the help of the Raja of Vijaynagar against the Muslim kingdom of Ahmadnagar. In short, political, rather than religious considerations were the *leitmotif* of the actor's concerned.[28]

Coming to later times, exactly the same remarks apply to the shifting alliances and endemic warfare between the decadent Mughals, rising Marhattas, Rajputs, Pathans, Jats, Sikhs, Rohillas and others, all of whom got sucked into the vortex of the power struggle following the sudden collapse of the great Mughal empire soon after the death of Aurangzeb in 1707.

In the southern region, Tipu Sultan (d. 1799) emerged as the hero, alike of Muslims and Hindus, of *Mysore* (present *Karnataka*). The *Nizam of Hyderabad* emerged as the ruler over a mixed population whose loyalty never wavered till the very end of the British period. However, the Muslim rulers of Mysore and Hyderabad ever remained on opposite sides in the drama of the Indian struggle against British supremacy.

Coming to our own times, the semi-independent princely states, Gwalior, Indore, Baroda, Jaipur, Patiala, Kapurthala, (all ruled by Hindu or Sikh rulers) gave liberal patronage to Muslims of ability and integrity, and they often rose to highest positions of power and trust in the state.[29]

In conclusion, a few comments on the proper interpretation of medieval Indian history would be in order. As is well know, Sultan Mahmud Ghazna (d. 1030) attacked India several times in the 10th century, Muhammad Ghori invaded and conquered North India in the 12th century, Babar in the 16th century, and Nadir Shah and Ahmad Shah Abdali again invaded the country in the 18th century, and all these attackers were Muslim. But it would be a totally perverse view to hold that the above historical processes were instances of Islamic aggression against Hinduism. All the above events flowed, essentially, from the struggle for ascendancy by rising and expanding groups at the expense of older and defensive groups, more or less on the decline, in terms of general human creativity and vigor. This has been the perennial rhythm of world history. In the ancient period, the creative and expanding groups were the Aryans, the Iranians, Greeks, Romans and Chinese, while in the medieval period the Arabs, Turks, and Mongols played the role of the creative expanding group. In the modern era the role was taken over by the Europeans.[30]

It is also worth mentioning that the social paradigm of 'Muslim aggressor' and 'Hindu victim' (even if it were to be accepted, to begin with) breaks down after the first few episodes, since the aggressors and their victims soon became mixed. Here are just a few examples of how the struggle for power and wealth cut across religious or racial distinctions. Babar fought against the combined forces of Ibrahim Lodi and Rana Sanga, Humayun struggled against Sher Shah, and both these contenders for supremacy had allies or supporters from both Hindus and Muslims. The power of the great Mughals flowed from a firm alliance between them and the Rajputs. The victims of Mughal imperialism or expansion were Muslim kingdoms no less than Hindu. The Hindu rulers of South India continually fought against each other even as the *Rajas* in the northern region before the advent of the Muslims. Muslims manned the entire artillery of Shivaji. The victims of Shivaji's lootings of the prosperous port of Surat were Hindus no less than Muslims, even as the victims of the invasions by Nadir Shah and Abdali were Muslims and Hindus alike.[31]

According to the Hindu '*dharmashastras*', every king or ruler was duty-bound to enlarge his dominions and fighting the highest duty of the warrior caste. Territorial expansion was not evil so long as the ruler could win in battle and rule justly over his subjects in accordance with the *shastras*. The *Rajas* fought, won or lost, but the '*praja*', unmindful of the race or religion of the contenders for power, pursued their own peaceful vocations of life, the '*purusharthas*'. This social ethic was also applied to the Muslim rulers when they came on the scene. The Hindu populace, in general, did not grudge Muslim rule, provided the ruler did not interfere in their '*dharma*'. The legitimacy of the ruler was not determined by or dependent upon his religion or race, but flowed from his victory in battle or the struggle for power. Such has been the basic social and political ethic of *Bharat* from times immemorial. Communalism, in the modern Indian sense of the term, was unknown earlier and emerged during British rule.

During the entire medieval period, social gradation cut across the distinction between Hindu and Muslim. Poor Muslims were in the employment of rich or affluent Hindus, and vice versa. Muslim rulers and feudal lords ruled over and commanded the genuine loyalty and admiration of their subjects, Muslim and Hindu alike, and vice versa. Muslim rulers had enemies or rivals among the Hindus, and vice versa. Friends and foes did not belong to any religion or caste, nor did creditors and debtors. There were business and industrial partnerships between Hindus and Muslims who took the same risks and shared the same gains or losses. The common man (Hindu or Muslim) had the same grievances against the *'patwari'*, the *'kotwal'*, the *'sahukar'*, the *'qazi'*, the aristocrat, the burglar, the artisan, and the prostitute, who could be either Hindu or Muslim. And so on. The best commentary on the tolerance and functional secularism of medieval India is provided by the growth of a common or composite culture reflected in the regional languages, architecture, painting, music, dress, entertainments, amusements, proverbs, folklore and folk-religions of India.[32]

# Notes to Essay 5
## Tolerance And Islam

**1.** The word, 'fundamentalism' is a misnomer since its literal sense suggests something totally different from the sense 'fundamentalism' is being used in these days. Understood literally 'fundamentalism' should mean emphasizing the fundamentals of a religion to the exclusion of all secondary or tertiary details. But in actual usage 'fundamentalism' means that the writ of religion runs in each and every sphere of life, every detail of which falls under the discipline of an organized religion. I have termed this basic approach to religion as 'religious totalism', and the opposite of this approach as 'religious liberalism'. The liberal approach to religion demarcates the proper function of religion and lays emphasis upon the fundamental concepts and values of a religion rather than upon cultural, social, economic, political matters which are best left to man's collective wisdom expressed through the democratic process.

**2.** This is precisely what Mawdudi and other critics of secularism do. They first distort the real operative meaning of separating religion from politics and then disapprove of 'politics sans religion' as the naked pursuit of power.

**3.** This simple truth is missed by numerous persons of different religious faiths. In his autobiographical novel, Of Human Bondage, Somerset Maugham refers to how the first realization of this truth freed him from spiritual conceit and contempt for creeds other than his own.

**4.** Existential perplexity is the condition of inner doubt concerning spiritual or moral issues which cannot be settled objectively by observation, experiment or reasoning. In other words, the individual is constrained either to remain in perpetual doubt or to believe on the basis of faith. Existential certainty flows from authentic faith, while objective certainty is the product of systematic perception and inquiry. Not only religious or metaphysical but even ethical and aesthetic truth-claims cannot be established by objective methods of knowing. Empathy is the ability to place oneself in the life- situation of others and to see things from their perspective and in a different light, as it were. Empathy implies the ability to suspend one's own beliefs or views, to become provisionally, as it were, a participant in a different spiritual or ideational world for the purpose of understanding it as an insider rather than as an observer from outside.

**5.** The principle of tolerance is well exemplified in the maxim of the Roman Emperor Tiberius: 'If the gods are insulted, let them see to it themselves'. See, J.B. Bury's classic, A History of Freedom of Thought, London, 1957

**6.** The following extract from the famous Rock Edicts of Ashoka is truly remarkable: 'Whoever honors his own sect and disparages another man's, does his own sect the greatest possible harm...' See, de Bury, W.T, (Ed.) Sources of Indian Tradition, Oxford University/ Press, 1956.

**7.** The early followers of Jesus were humble folk belonging to the weaker sections of the Jewish population of the region.

**8.** The first reported case of death penalty for heresy is that of Priscillian in fourth century Spain, in the reign of Emperor Valens. See Bury, op.cit.

**9.** In the popular perception the Crusades were a bloody confrontation between Christianity and Islam. From a mature sociological and historical approach, however, political and economic factors were silently operative in producing this confrontation, which was far from being a pure and simple religious issue. Indeed, religion provided only a romantic or sentimental coloring to issues, essentially, concerned with the struggle for wealth and power.

**10.** See, Bury, op.cit.

**11.** The tragic story of the Spanish Muslims has been told by reliable historians, Muslim as well as others. See the well known works by Amir Ali, A short History of the Saracens, London, 1955; Hitti, P.K., History of the Arabs, London, 1957.

**12.** The French liberal thinker, Bayle (d. 1706) questioned the validity of St. Augustine's interpretation of the remark 'compel them to come in'. There is a strong similarity between the liberal approaches of Bayle and John Locke of Oxford. Rousseau, Voltaire et al, carried the work of Bayle forward to its consummation.

**13.** The principle of 'Jurisdiction' meant that the jurisdiction of the established religion applies to secular matters no less than to purely spiritual. The principle of 'separation' meant that the affairs of state be kept separate from religion as such, and that the state should function as an autonomous corporation rather than as an agency subordinate to any particular religion. Separation, however, does not mean the absolute or total rejection of religion or of morality.

**14.** This totally absurd war crippled the economy of entire Western Europe. One of the most devastating wars in the annals of human history; it even led to cases of cannibalism for sheer survival.

**15.** Legal disabilities against Unitarians were completely removed in the forties, and against the Jews in the fifties of the 19th century. Signing of the 39 Articles of the official Anglican Church ceased to be a pre-condition of a fellowship at the colleges of Oxford and Cambridge as late as 1871.

**16.** It is both ironic and amusing that Protestants settled in large numbers in Maryland and, on becoming the majority, discontinued the tolerance established by the Catholics, The policy of tolerance was, however, re-established after 1660. See Bury, op. cit.

**17.** It is worth pointing out that the founders of the first secular state in the world were not atheists or materialists, but deeply committed Christians who, however, from the long experience of European religious intolerance and fanaticism had learnt the wisdom of separating religion from politics. The Muslim mind is still struggling with this issue. This principle was incorporated into the letter and spirit of the Indian constitution, thanks to the vision of the leaders of the Indian Renaissance starting in the late 18th century Bengal, and coming to full maturity in the life and work of Gandhiji, Tagore, Nehru et

## The Call Of Modernity And Islam

al. It is true tolerance may also flourish in a state where the principle of jurisdiction holds, for instance, Britain whose monarch continues to be the head of the established Anglican Church. Yet, the American model remains supreme for the rest of the world.

**18.** The Prophet and his companions had to abandon their hearths and homes in Mecca to escape humiliation, ostracism and torture at the hands of their opponents bent upon exterminating the new religion. Even at Medina the refugees were not allowed to live in peace. The overall situation did call for harsh defensive even pre-emptive action by the Muslims. They, however gradually become the dominant political power in the region. See the scholarly and objective exposition (based on original Arabic sources) of this theme in Majid Khadduri's excellent study, 'War and Peace in the Law of Islam', Oxford, 1955.

**19.** Jizya was a graduated tax in three slabs of 12, 24 and 48 dinars per annum. The establishment did not, in general, severely penalize the failure to pay the tax because of financial stringency. See Majid Khadduri, op. cit.

**20.** According to the (spurious) covenant of 'Omar', the 'dhimmis' had to wear a distinctive dress, cut their forelocks, were debarred from using a saddle when riding horses, living in houses taller than those of Muslims, wearing of silken clothes, praying or ringing church bells loudly, and testifying against Muslims. Moreover, they had no legal share in war spoils though they could get an allowance as participants fighting on the side of the Muslims, if a Muslim killed a non-Muslim, the penalty was restricted to fine only. These and similar restrictions or disabilities of the dhimmis were unknown in the earliest normative period of the Islamic commonwealth. Even when they came to be espoused in some Muslim juristic quarters they were not acted upon due to various reasons. However, it is true that evidence of non-Muslims was not admissible against Muslims; non-Muslims could not build places of worship without prior sanction of the state. See, Majid Khadduri, op. cit. Also see Tritton, A.S., The Caliphs and Their Non-Muslim Subjects, London, 1930, and Fischei, W.J., Jews in the Economic and Political Life of Medieval Islam, London, 1937.

**21.** The Zoroastrians were added in the category 'people of the Book' soon after the Arab conquest of Iran during the time of Omar in 642. The Hindus of Sind in India were also included in this category at the instance of Mohammad bin Qasim who conquered the region at the behest of the Umayyad Khalifa, at Damascus in 712. This liberal approach was, however, reversed after Qasim's recall from Sind and his disgrace at the Khalifa's court.

**22.** Muslims are predisposed to see the aspect of missionary zeal alone, while non-Muslim observers that of mere territorial expansionism. Balanced observers and historians such as Gibb, Hitti, Watt et al try to strike the correct note.

**23.** The compact of Medina entered into by the Prophet with the residents of the host city is a document of great significance. (It is worth recalling that an outstanding Indian scholar and public figure, Husain Ahmad Madani (d. 1957) viewed the compact as a sound justification for Muslims and Hindus living together in a united India without any need for creating Pakistan in 1947 as a separate state for Muslims.

Many Arabs wanted to settle down in the fertile lands belonging to the defeated Egyptians. Omar did not permit this, even though Ali reasoned that there should be no objection in view of the fact that the Muslims had earlier displaced the Jewish owners of the fertile farms and lands at Khyber in Arabia. See Shibli's monumental Life of Omar, the Great, Lahore, 1962.

**24.** The instances of tolerance cited have been taken from standard historical works by reliable historians, Muslim as well as non-Muslim, who have laboured hard to go to the original Arabic sources closest to the periods concerned. Amir Ali, op. cit. p. 112-115; 321-322. Hitti, P.K., History of the Arabs, pp.234, 355. The dark side of the picture will be found in the same works: Amir Ali, pp.288-89:301,412. Hitti, pp.353, 359, 360.

**25.** The debate whether the Quran, as the Word of God, is eternal or created in time (just like the rest of God's creation) is one of the most crucial issues in the history of Islamic thought. Under the influence of Greek thought the Mutazilite theologians held that the 'Word' came later in time, since holding otherwise would compromise the essential unity of God's Being. The Asharite theologians held that the Mutazilite view compromised the status and supreme worth of the 'Word of God'. The Asharite held that their view was quite compatible with the unity of Divine Being, while the Mutazalite critics thought otherwise.

**25(a).** It had become a tradition that Muslim sovereigns in different parts of the Islamic world sought legitimacy for their rule by proclaiming, suo-moto, their formal allegiance to the Khalifa, though this was a mere fiction. Indeed, the unity of the Islamic commonwealth had been lost as far back as 750 when the Abbasids displaced the Umayyad dynasty, and the Umayyad prince; Abdur Rahman founded a rival seat of power in Spain. The declaration of allegiance was purely ceremonial. Akbar discontinued this formality. 'Functional secularism' means that secularism in practice went hand in hand with theoretical Islamic rule, even as the secular government in Britain has gone hand in hand with an established Church of England. See, Rizvi, S.A.A. op.cit

**26.** In general, Muslim theologians held that the shariah stipulated the right and obligation of the ulema to overview and regulate the affairs of stale and the acts of the Sovereign. The Sufis, on the other hand, were content with pure spirituality and a rather low profile in the affairs of the state. The Sufis were absorbed in devotional music and meditation and the task of giving solace and comfort to the weaker sections of society instead of asserting their authority in the corridors of power. There were, however, several exceptions to this general rule. Shaikh Ahmad Sarhindi (d. 1624) and Shah Waliullah (d. 1763) are notable instances. Beautiful examples of Sufi poetry abound in the poetry of Attar (d. 1229), Rumi (d. 1273), Sadi (d. 1291), Hafiz (d. 1389), Jami (d. 1492), Urfi (d. 1591), Kabir (d. 1518), Mir (d. 1810), and Ghalib (d. 1869) among others.

**27.** Valuable results have come from the practice of impartial historians to consult deeds of charitable grants by Aurangzeb to several Hindu temples, official lists of Governors, top military commanders, feudal lords, writers etc. and last, but not least, authentic letters or memoranda. See the pioneering study by Athar Ali, The Mughal Nobility under Aurangzeb, Bombay, 1966.

**28.** The details concerning the regional Muslim kingdoms have been taken from Rizvi, op. cit.

**29.** This is not a simplistic indictment of British imperial policy in India. Communalism was also a natural concomitant of the social, economic and political consequences of the process of industrialization and modernization of a given society. The largest single factor which precipitated communalism (in the modern Indian sense) was the introduction by the British of representative secular democracy. This meant that every man was a potential wielder of power no matter what his caste or religion. This inevitably created an almost irresistible temptation to appeal to members of one's own religion, caste, region, or language for winning the battle of the ballot; the passport for political power and wealth.

**30.** In the early medieval period Muslims did destroy some temples and also used their debris for constructing mosques. These actions represented medieval modes of asserting the military might of the victor, though such practices had no Islamic sanction. These acts were, however, not cases of persecution or of forced conversion. While we rightly disapprove of these acts on the basis of our contemporary norms and ideals, this should not make us condemn the medieval period as one of darkness, decay and wholesale tyranny. See Pande, B.N., Islam and Indian Culture, Patna, 1987.

**31.** Shivaji attacked and looted the prosperous port city of Surat first, in 1664, and again in 1670. Nadir Shah attacked and looted north India in 1739, and Ahmad Shah Abdali in 1756. Mahmud's fighting force comprised Hindu mercenaries also. Moreover, Mahmud had Hindu chiefs as allies in the perennial wars for territorial expansion: the declared aim and duty (dharma) of the schattriya caste, according to the dharmashastras. It is significant that when the triumphant Mahmud sent rich presents to a noted scholar-jurist of Ghazna, Qazi Abul Hasan Baulami, the learned divine returned the presents on the ground that Mahmud had not behaved in conformity with Islamic tenets. See, K. A.Nizami's, Religious Leanings of the Sultans of Delhi, 1958. See also, K.S.Murty, The Indian Spirit, 1965.

**32.** Cross-cultural fusion is a universal social phenomenon. The culture or general way of life of the Prophet's time was Arab. The Islamic ethos, as it emerged in the early normative period of the pious Khalifa's and even later, retained much of the pre-Islamic Arab mores. Sociology reveals that the original culture of a society which converts to another religion cannot but subconsciously carry over (to some extent or other) their pre-conversion attitudes and modes of thinking. Thus, while Islam, as an abstract creed, (enshrined in the **kalimah**) is common to all believers, Muslims of Arabia, Iran, Africa, India, and Indonesia etc. greatly differ from each other socially and culturally. See Tarachand's classic, The Influence of Islam on Indian Culture, Allahabad, 1963.

# Essay 6

## Democracy And Islam

### Introduction

The Muslim world is passing through a deep spiritual crisis. The classical interpretation of basic Islamic-concepts and values has more or less ceased to command, the authentic assent of numerous intelligent and informed Muslim believers, and there is a sort of intellectual and spiritual vacuum in The Islamic world. Different ideas and ideologies are competing to fill in the vacuum in the Muslim world, which comprises approximately one-fifth of the human family. Muslim countries have recently won political independence from Western domination, but continue to be dependent on others, technologically or economically. They resist the idea of remaining camp followers and imitators of the Western or Communist establishments. There is an inner demand for re-interpreting basic Islamic concepts, values and institutions to make them viable in the modern age. But an intellectually and spiritually satisfying Islamic vision has not yet crystallized for the vast majority. Expressions such as *'Islamic democracy'*, *'Islamic Socialism'*, *'Islamic Economics'*, *'Quranic constitution'*, *'Sovereignty of Allah'* are tenuous and are often, rather always, used in a manner, both simplistic and misleading.

The word 'democracy' has become a prestigious word (like 'truth', 'justice', or beauty'), and quite diverse political systems claim to be democratic. Many Muslims believe that Islam is the best form of democracy. The purpose of these lectures is:

(a) to make an accurate analysis of the concept of democracy,

(b) critically to assess democracy, and its alternatives,

**(c)** to ascertain how far, or in what sense, Islamic political thought and practice stand for democracy, and finally,

**(d)** briefly to review the acceptability and prospects of democracy in the Islamic world today.

## 1. THE CONCEPT OF DEMOCRACY

The Essence of Democracy: The word 'democracy' is derived from the Greek words '*demos*' (people) and '*kratia*' (rule), and its literal meaning is 'rule by the people at large'. To rule means exercising supreme power in deciding and managing public affairs, maintenance of law and order, security of the realm, fixation of the powers, functions and remuneration of different occupational classes within a hierarchical power structure over-arching plural associations within society as a whole, and finally, the legitimate authority to punish (including capital punishment) offenders of any law, regulation or executive order.

This supreme power is termed 'sovereignty', and the person or persons possessing it the 'sovereign'. The smooth functioning of society, obviously, requires law and order, which in turn, requires an effective power structure. Otherwise, the group identity and unity of the society would disintegrate, and subgroups would emerge, which may further disintegrate for a similar reason, leading more or less to a state of anarchy.

Historically, sovereignty almost always has been exercised over territories of various sizes by single individuals (kings or tribal chiefs), whether or not they had some advisory council of elders or dignitaries. However, every sovereign has always been subject to some form of constraint. The sovereign has always had to contend against those who, while fully accepting his authority as supreme have yet sought to demarcate its proper sphere, not on grounds of rivalry or jealousy, but purely on principle. They are the holy men and the wise and learned men who have ever demanded that the ruler be not merely strong but also good. They have further held that the criterion of good and evil is not the sweet will of the sovereign but some principles, either Divinely revealed to the holy, or discovered by the wise. In other words, while the sovereign wields the power of the sword, the latter wield the power of the spirit. This tension between the two dimensions of power ever irks, and at times, even threatens the sovereign. Indeed, some sovereigns have even aspired to combine the two dimensions of power, but in vain.[1]

The sovereign faces quite a different type of challenge from his rivals, internal and external, who wish to displace him as the sovereign. The constant apprehension of rebellion from some dissatisfied and powerful rival makes the sovereign responsive to the demands of both prudence and morality. This principle also applies when the people become the sovereign in a democratic state, and the government is called upon to resolve peacefully the tensions between different groups and interests.

The Historical Background of Democracy: The first known societies whose sovereign was not an individual but the people, as such, were the Greek city-states in the pre-Christian era. But these city states comprised two categories of people;

(a) the free citizens enjoying equal authority as decision makers in all public affairs, and,

(b) slaves or inferior citizens without any 'say' or authority in public matters.

Since Aristotle accepted the status quo and did not uphold the complete equality of all members of the city sate irrespective of their 'status', he used the word 'democracy" in the pejorative sense of 'rule by the mob'. He equated democracy with 'rule by the mob' and stood for rule, exclusively, by the free citizens. The Romans later on also retained the distinction between the 'patricians' and the 'plebeians', as, indeed, all world religions have rejected the idea of people's power, as such, irrespective of religion, sect, caste, class, or sex. Christianity, for instance, held that power belonged to the Pope, as the *Vicar of Christ*, and to the king, as the *Shadow of God*. Likewise, Islam held that believers should obey God and the Prophet, or his successors. In Hinduism, the *Brahman* lawgivers and *Kshatria* warrior's alone wielded supreme power, while all others were expected merely to perform duties appropriate to their caste.

Earlier still the pagan or tribal ethos had placed supreme authority in the chief who, as the strongest among the strong, could coerce others into submission. However, it was the general belief that his strength and prowess were the gift of the gods who could withdraw their grace if ever the chief did anything to displease the gods. This honest faith restrained the chief from violating the group ethos or abusing his authority. It also implied the concept of magic as a power quite different from normal physical power. And it was the witch doctor who wielded this 'spirit power'.

Judaism, Christianity and Islam believe there is a Divine hand in history, though humans enjoy a limited freedom in the performance of their allotted roles in the great drama of history being shaped by Divine providence. The chief characters, in this drama were, obviously, kings, nobles and priests, while the masses were mere witnesses rather than participants in matters of state. Their participation was confined to simple joys of family life, labor for livelihood, service to their superiors and the worship of God. Obedience to God, for the common man, implied loyalty to the king, the shadow of God. Rebellion against the king who had not broken any Divine law amounted to blasphemy. The common man could not even dream that he had any legitimate share whatsoever in sovereignty.

The modern period, of Western history begins in the 15th century with the Renaissance: an elitist cultural renewal of the spirit of classical Greek Humanism. It was soon followed in the 16th century by the Reformation: a religious challenge to the supremacy of the Roman Catholic Church and the subordination of individual conscience to a supposedly infallible Pope, as the *Vicar of Christ*. Though both these movements had some traces of democracy in their thought and value structures they were not informed by the spirit and temper of social and political egalitarianism and people's power: the essential features of modern democracy. Martin Luther's approach, though anti-authoritarian in relation to the Pope was definitely authoritarian in relation to the populace.

The 17th century, however, saw the first stirring of the republican spirit in Cromwell's England, even the beheading of the king in the name of people's power.[2] The steady progress of natural science and independent philosophical enquiry in Western Europe culminated in the 18th century Enlightenment: the developed and mature version of the Renaissance. The integration of accurate analytical reason and the scientific method led, first to the scientific, and later to the secular revolutions in the second half of the 18th century. Far reaching social and economic changes, brought about by technological innovations in methods of production, combined to bring the capitalist, the merchant, the entrepreneur, the professional manager, the factory worker and the secular intellectual on the centre stage of public activity, thereby relatively side-lining the landed aristocracy, the army and the church. In other words, new power relationships emerged in the British society. The process was weak and slow, to begin with, but gathered ever-increasing momentum in the 19th century. The culmination of this process took place in the early 20th century. *The Parliament Act* of 1911 represents the completion of the process begun in 1832 and signifies the shifting of supreme power from the hitherto dominant sections of British society to the populace in the literal sense.[3]

The idea of democracy is a living and still growing concept. The earliest elitist direct democracy of the Greek city-states, long ago, evolved into the representative (but still elitist) democracy of the Roman Senate. The *Magna Carta* of 1215 and *Bill of Rights* of 1689 were notable landmarks in bringing democracy in England nearer the common man in late medieval and early modern times.[4] The American Revolution of 1776 and the French Revolution of 1789 are significant stages in the growth of democracy. The remarkable social and political reforms in 19th century England, under the inspiration of Bentham's Utilitarianism and liberalism, paved the way for adult franchise for all males. Women acquired the right to vote only after the *First World War* in the 20th century.[5]

The impact of Marx later contributed to the emergence of yet another dimension in the evolving concept of democracy; the state ownership and control of industry. One single word, which best sums up the formative sources and constitutive strands of modern democracy, is 'Humanism'. Humanism implies unconditional respect for the individual and his spiritual autonomy, tolerance of plural viewpoints and of plural results of the human search for truth, goodness and beauty, universal well being, and optimistic life-affirmation despite the trials, travails and tragedies of the human situation. And democracy is the political expression of Humanism.[6]

## 2. SALIENT FEATURES OF DEMOCRATIC GOVERNANCE

(a) People's power and government by consent: People's power and respect for the dignity and freedom of the individual, irrespective of all contingent factors or circumstances, demand that the people be governed with their consent. The freedom of every individual must be subject to the like freedom of every other. This naturally requires the imposition of law and order on the basis of a hierarchical power structure ultimately responsible and accountable to the people at large. Democracy is a system of government whereby people rule themselves through either a sovereign Parliament comprising elected representatives of the people, or through an elected President who, as the Chief Executive, enjoys near supreme power. The elected representatives or the President function as the alter-ago of the people, as it were, and govern in accordance with laws framed after due deliberation in the general interest of society.

Parliament or the President need not consult the people on each and every matter. The people, however, continue to be the sovereign, in the ultimate sense, since Parliament or the President enjoy merely delegated supreme authority for the period for which they have been elected. Thereafter supreme authority reverts, or lapses, to the people who are again called upon to give a fresh mandate to whomsoever they may choose. In any case the individual retains his spiritual autonomy. This, incidentally, is also, the case with voluntary submission to any religious authority and its prescribed discipline. However, if the believer is not free to switch over to some other spiritual or religious authority religious submission ceases to be democratic.

(b) Channelization of the People's will: The Parliament decides policies, frames laws, issues directives, while the council of ministers (which is essentially a committee of Parliament headed by the Prime Minister and fully responsible to Parliament) controls and oversees the functioning of the government. The party system ensures shared views among the members of Parliament and provides a definite thrust and direction to the government. The great powers and prerogatives of the Prime Minister enable him to guide and lead the party. The Presidential system works in a different way, but these differences are immaterial in the present context.

(c) The Right to Govern & the Right to Dissent: The cardinal principle of democracy is that the majority should govern, but the minority has the full and unfettered right of dissent. Each side must respect the right of the other. Dissent must be peaceful and not amount to obstruction, directly or indirectly. The majority should not grudge if the minority actively propagates truth, as it sees it, and aspires to win over the sovereign people by the time the next election falls due.

The right of the majority of the elected representatives to govern for a fixed period is based on the assumption that they represent the general will of the people. In case they flout the general will and cease to translate the general will into effective action they will soon realize their error and rectify it. If they do not do so the people will vote them out of power at the next general election. The right of the minority to propagate their dissent is crucially important because in quite a number of cases voters (as well as the ruling group itself) come to realize the wisdom of the minority opinion.

The concrete method of counting heads rather than weighing them has been adopted because figures or numbers can be accurately counted, while abstract reasons cannot be objectively and accurately evaluated. The verdict of the majority is accepted, provisionally, as the voice of wisdom, but the possibility of error is also conceded and full opportunities are periodically provided for the review and re-evaluation of the issues involved.

(d) Free Enquiry and Freedom of Belief: Knowledge of factual truth is a pre-condition of satisfying human needs and purposes. Now the truths of science are empirically verifiable, while truths of logic and mathematics are self-evident, or can be deduced from self-evident premises. The case is very different in the spheres of morality, religion and economics etc. This is why scientists generally agree, but no agreement exists in religion, politics and economics. Every one strongly feels one's own views and opinions to be right, but no one can conclusively prove his/her truth-claim. Such truth-claims may be called 'cultural' to distinguish them from factual or descriptive truths, on the one hand, and logical or mathematical truths on the other.

All cultural truth-claims, to begin with, are socially conditioned or 'truths of one's milieu', and there is no way to reach objective certainty in the sphere of cultural beliefs. Consequently, plural viewpoints and judgments are bound to remain. The method of following the view of the majority or counting the heads is, indeed, a better way out than the breaking of heads for deciding what should be done. In other words, democracy accepts cultural pluralism, peaceful settlement of differences, and where this does not come about, the agreement to differ without rancor or bitterness. The assumption is that when different observers having different backgrounds, attitudes and interests pursue the path of free enquiry and friendly dialogue there is every chance they would reach some sort of working consensus through mutual give and take. Free enquiry is a continuing self-corrective process without terminating at any point of history.

(e) Freedom of Expression and of Association: The freedom of belief remains meaningless without the freedom of expression. Likewise, the freedom of expression remains incomplete unless it be supplemented by the freedom of association and propagation of truth, as one sees it. These three freedoms go together. Democracy means fully accommodating each and every interest group in the over-arching unity of the sovereign state. Democracy guarantees the inalienable right of all individuals or groups to be respected and heard. It is impossible to improve upon the famous declaration by J.S. Mill, and earlier, by Voltaire in more or less the same words: *'I do not agree with a single word of what you say. But I shall give my life to defend your right to say so'.*

(f) Clash of Interests and their Resolution: The clash of interests is inevitable in the human situation. Whether or not the Marxian theory of class struggle is the whole truth, different interest groups do clash with each other due to limited natural resources and the collective wealth of a societal unit. Different interests get organized sooner or later to promote their respective interests. Proper governance means judicious regulation of group interests for maximizing human welfare. That form of government is the best, which produces maximum human welfare with the minimum conflict and violence. It is not practically possible completely to eliminate violence. But democratic governance is the best possible hope for approximating to the ideal situation. This is so because the democratic permission of free dissent prevents the piling up of destructive passions and their explosion in the form of terrorism or civil strife. The accepted right of the majority to govern and the equally accepted right of dissent cut at the roots of violence. Public ventilation of criticism acts as a safety valve for reducing the pressure of discontent, though the abuse of this freedom often leads to quite contrary results. In general, the good sense of peace-loving citizens results in the virtue of constructive compromise, but, at times, to the vice of appeasement as well.

(g) Consequence of the Exercise of Power: The continuing exercise of power is the source of tremendous satisfaction and the keenest pleasure, but at the same time brings about physical, mental and emotional wear and tear and a corroding effect upon the moral fiber of the rulers. Long years in power result in skill and confidence, but they also make rulers less receptive to new ideas or perspectives. However, very few rulers voluntarily abdicate power, since the lust for power is, perhaps, the most insatiable among human passions.[7] Clinging to power generally leads to attitudes and policies, not best calculated to promote general welfare, but rather the short-term interests of the ruler himself. Now democracy is the only system of government, which makes the public the final judge to decide whether to extend the term of the government or terminate its services. It often happens that despite being unhappy with their rulers the people prefer continuity to change because they are afraid that the alternatives are likely to be even worse.

(h) Independence of the Judiciary: Democracy, as the rule of self-framed law, is opposed to rule by fiat or externally imposed regulations. But the application of laws in concrete situations requires considerable legal reflection and juristic interpretation, specially, when new situations and problems arise in society. The judiciary performs this function independently. If, however, the interpretations placed by the independent judiciary upon the law not be acceptable to the sovereign Parliament, it has the power to change the law. Thus the supremacy or independence of the judiciary and the sovereignty of the people can coexist.

(i) Distinction between Essence and Form of Democracy: The essence of democracy is governance by the consent of the people in the form of periodic free and fair peaceful general elections. Now this essence or nuclear core may be exemplified in different forms or systems of democratic functioning, such as the composition and powers of the chief Executive (President/Prime Minister), the nature and size of the constituencies, the nature and value of the votes cast, the prescribed term of the elected office, the right of recall or other modes of 'citizen vigilance', state/federal legislatures etc. A particular form or system of democracy may be preferred because of practical advantages in a given situation. A different or changed situation may demand modifications for improving the working of the system. A system must be judged as democratic so long as people can really change their supreme managers through free and fair elections, no matter what the system may be. To say this is not to deny the importance of finding out which system best suits the needs and conditions of one's own people.

The question may be asked whether the essence of democracy survives in a situation (which has existed at times in India) where a party comes to power and forms the government on the basis of a numerical majority in the legislature, but does not win the majority of the total votes polled in the country as a whole. The same question may be raised when the largest single legislature party forms a coalition Government. Such situations are obviously not conducive to stability and effective rule. Nevertheless, the spirit of democracy is not negated since the principle of majority rule continues to operate in the legislature, as such, despite its erosion at a different level. If, however, the people do feel strongly on this issue, suitable modifications could be made in the electoral system. Indeed, there is considerable scope for improvement at several points in different democratic systems of the world.

It appears there cannot be any one model of ideal democracy to suit all. Each society will have to think out its own version. But this exercise should not be speculative or limited in scope, but must be done in the light of a critical survey of the experience of the human family.

## 3. Evaluation Of Democracy

Many who strongly criticize democracy hardly seem to realize that the protagonists of democracy are well aware of these defects. In fact, the critical evaluation of democracy by competent Western thinkers is far more penetrating than its facile criticism by the detractors of democracy. But these highly qualified thinkers hold that the alternatives to democracy are even worse, and it is on this ground they prefer democracy. Whatever be the truth of the matter the complexities of the human situation are such that in many cases our choice does not lie between good and evil, but between the greater and the lesser evil.[7(a)]

The main objections are:

(1) Democracy leads to appeasement of voters and corrupt practices.

(2) Elections involve enormous expenditure. Those who get elected are forced to compensate for their heavy investment by resorting to unfair means.

(3) Democracy leads to extremely slow decision-making and divided responsibility.

(4) Democracy results in mediocrity and inefficient administration, and,

(5) Democracy means governance by the unwise majority rather than by the creative and talented few.

I shall now comment on each objection in the above order:

(1) To promote the interests of the society as a whole is the very purpose and function of a democratic government. Should it fail to do so the voters would be perfectly justified in getting it voted out of power. The evil of appeasement sets in only when the government fails to do what is right and reasonable because of the opposition of powerful vested interests who stand to lose or suffer if the right course be adopted. But appeasement is certainly not an inseparable feature of democracy. There are numerous examples of great statesmen who remain responsive to the genuine needs and interests of every group, without fear or favor, but scrupulously avoid appeasing anyone. Likewise, constructive compromise without sacrificing basic principles is a virtue and not a vice.

As regards rewarding of party workers or helpers or shielding them in cases of wrong doings or irregularities etc., public opinion can and should be built against such abuses and other malpractices, say patently false promises at election time, material inducements, harassment of opponents and so on. But to give up democracy merely because it is liable to such misuses would not be the voice of wisdom. The baby should be washed, not thrown away with the bath.

(2) Elections do involve enormous expenditure, and both individual candidates and political parties are forced to seek funds from industrialists and others, which practice, leads to consequences, too well known to be spelt out. Yet, to abandon the theory and practice of democracy on this score, instead of devising ways and means of removing or reducing the evil consequences of huge election expenditure would amount to falling from the frying pan into the fire. Several democratic countries have already taken steps to reduce the costs of democracy. The state funding of political parties and provision of increased facilities to voters and candidates at elections has already commenced and are steps in the right direction. In any case, the expenditure on the elective process should be viewed in the light of the total consequences of abandoning democracy with the resultant evils of authoritarian forms of government.

**(3)** This criticism will not bear scrutiny. Slow decision-making and divided responsibilities are not integral features of democracy, but merely accompaniments due to the operation of checks and balances and committee deliberations. These features have both advantages and disadvantages. In any case, the negative features can be removed through suitable functional innovations and techniques. As for divided responsibility, the concept of constructive responsibility of the minister concerned is increasingly becoming an established convention. Likewise, the progressive increase in the powers of the Prime Minister in several democracies brings about a correlated enhancement in his sense of responsibility and accountability to the country as a whole.

**(4) & (5)** These two objections are, perhaps, the most popular but the least weighty. The criticism that in a democracy the foibles and idols of the market place rather than the wisdom and talents of the elite shape the destiny of the people, or as Iqbal says in his Urdu couplet: '*democracy counts, not weighs heads*' is a highly misleading over-simplification of the matter.

Firstly, there is no agreement among the philosophers and the other wise men who may think that they are born to rule the masses. Secondly, while counting of heads is a clear and understandable procedure, the weighing of heads is not at all a clearly defined procedure for the simple reason that there is no prior agreement as to which weighing machine should be used. Despite the well-known disqualifications of the masses, they do have a store of wisdom and commonsense which redeem all their negative qualities. Moreover, democracy is the only system, which brings out different perceptions and prescriptions into full awareness. The airing of diverse views creates better understanding of the diverse positions thereby promoting the maximum possible reconciliation between them. A really constructive adjustment holds for some time until fresh tensions arise due to the essential fluidity of the human situation. New interests, new avenues of acquiring wealth or power, new rivalries, new power relations, new methods of production, new needs and aspirations, all conspire to create fresh points of social friction and conflict. The previous compromises and democratic solutions demand a fresh look in the light of an ever-developing situation. Thus goes on the democratic human story.[8]

In short, far from being the government of fools pushing the people towards folly or disaster, democracy contains the promise of overcoming the fads and illusions of any one individual or group. The angularities of each get corrected by those of the other in the melting pot of collective decision-making. History shows that the assemblies of the ignorant masses have done less harm to humanity than those great men whose greatness lay in their egos rather than in their vision. This happened because they stood isolated and alienated from the common man, the housewife, the farmer and the worker. The wisdom of the common man is rooted in his experience of sufferings and deprivations, and its value is far greater than the 'sophistry and illusion' of the unverified and unverifiable theories of 'learned fools'.[9]

**Alternatives to Democracy:** If, for argument's sake, we reject democracy, what alternatives remain? It would be futile considering such abstract or Utopian alternatives as 'Islamic democracy', 'party less democracy', '*Ram Raj*', or 'Post-Soviet Communism'. What appears to be an excellent system on paper may function badly, in practice, because of the complexity of human affairs and the unintended consequences of human choices. An ounce of experience of how Western democracy has actually worked has more educative value than tons of arguments in favor of any abstract system.[10] Thus, the only alternatives worth considering are military dictatorship and Soviet Socialism, that is, Communism in current parlance. What has been termed 'Euro-Communism' has recently emerged in some parts of Europe under Russian hegemony. To the extent that plural parties function freely and fair elections are held in these eastern European countries, the new system may well be deemed as democratic. The effective alternatives to democracy are, therefore, Soviet Communism and military dictatorship. For the present we may profitably ignore variations in different models of Communist governments and focus our attention on their common feature; the single party system and the absence of free and unfettered public expression of opinion instead of the present system of internal debate in the top echelons of a monolithic Communist party.

The intra-party freedom of expression permitted in the Soviet Union fails to pre-empt the rise of the attitudes and politics of secrecy, conspiracy and violence in Communist society. It is true that plural democratic parties and the electoral power of the masses tends to breed corruption and appeasement in society. But the single party system breeds the evil of conspiratorial dissent in the body politic, and this, to my mind, is a greater evil. I, for one, hold corruption in a free society to be a lesser evil than conspiratorial politics in an authoritarian regime.

Long experience shows and confirms that authoritarianism (no matter how benign to begin with) inevitably degenerates into tyranny. In the final analysis, our choice is not between benign authoritarianism and corrupt democracy, but the evils generally associated with the two. Now while a corrupt democratically formed government can be democratically changed and reformed, a corrupt or tyrannical authoritarian establishment cannot be de-established without recourse to methods fraught with the evils of conspiracy and violence. In short, the demon inside the ballot is less evil than the demon in the bullet.

## 4. Democracies and Sovereignty of God

Can the foregoing idea of democracy be reconciled with the view that sovereignty belongs to God alone? Is there not a basic contradiction between the idea of democratic freedom and the idea of total surrender to the '*Book and the Example* of the Prophet'? This crucial point merits detailed consideration.

Prima facie, there is a clash between the autonomy of man and the sovereignty of God. But in reality there is no clash, provided believers do two things:

**(a)** make a distinction between the jurisdiction or proper sphere of matters of faith, and the proper sphere of autonomous enquiry through logical reasoning or factual investigation, as the case may be, and,

**(b)** apply the basic principles of semantics to the proper understanding of the Quranic scripture.

In other words, if we make a distinction between objective beliefs concerning empirical and logical matters, and existential convictions concerning transcendental matters, we could well combine autonomy, in the sphere of objective beliefs, with surrender to the Scripture in the sphere of faith in unseen transcendental matters, such as Divine revelation to prophets, life after death, the final reckoning etc.

Questions of fact or of logical implication belong to the sphere of objective belief, and must be dealt with according to the canons of the scientific method or of logic, and not on the basis of any scriptural authority or faith. Truth-claims concerning facts, natural, social, or historical can be conclusively settled, in principle, on the basis of the scientific method of observation, experiment and formulation and testing of hypotheses, but this procedure is ruled out, in the sphere of the 'Unseen'. And here the Muslim believer can very well accept the supreme authority of the Quran. The spheres of objective enquiry and of existential faith should not be confused. If this confusion be avoided, no contradiction remains between spiritual autonomy and the sovereignty of God or faith in the infallibility of the Quran.

It is significant that the Quran does not refer to objective matters (factual or logical) apart, of course, from some biographical matters concerning the Prophet of Islam and earlier messengers etc. and some basic natural phenomena: the succession of the seasons, the night and the day, the cycle of birth, growth and death, and so on. However, such references are not meant to provide factual information or details, but rather to evoke proper attitudes or impart wisdom and moral or spiritual guidance. The tendency to read into the verses of the Quran some theory or other of Physics, Biology, and Geography etc. is a hermeneutic error. It is significant that the Prophet himself never claimed that he had any supernatural access to knowledge concerning objective matters, just as he did not claim any supernatural powers to perform miracles in addition to his gift of prophecy. Here again, the tendency to attribute miraculous powers to the Prophet persists despite numerous Quranic verses declaring that he could not perform miracles and had no knowledge of the Unseen, though the Quran does give him the most exalted status among created beings. There is no reason to doubt that several opinions and beliefs of the Prophet (apart from the contents of the Quran) were derived from his milieu, as in the case of all human beings. Such beliefs cannot be deemed to be sacrosanct. The second *Khalifa* always took this stand.[11]

The crucial question, which we must now answer, is whether social, economic, political, administrative matters belong to the category of objective beliefs or of transcendental convictions. The truth is that they belong neither to the one nor the other, but rather, to the category of cultural beliefs which are based partly on factual premises and partly on value judgments. Now obedience to the clear moral imperatives of the Quran, no less than faith in its transcendental content is binding upon the believer. A clash is, therefore, theoretically possible between the conclusions of an independent or autonomous individual and some Quranic value judgment or imperative.

However, it should not be difficult to resolve any actual conflict between spiritual autonomy and authority of the Quran, if we keep in mind the fact that the Prophet interpreted the Quran flexibly in the light of sturdy commonsense, rather than rigidly or literally.

In fact it was because of his flexible and non-literal approach in the application of Quranic injunctions in actual life situations that led the early Muslim theologians to infer that some revelations were verbal (*wahi-e-jali*) and were included in the corpus of the Quran, while others were silent (*wahi-e-khafi*), though they were equally authoritative or normative for the believers. The above distinction was clearly meant to explain the Prophet's freedom of interpretation with respect to the Quran. The above distinction, however, is not found in the Quran and places believers in a predicament.[12] If they follow the Quran rigidly, in the literal sense, without the Prophet's flexibility of interpretation, they do something the Prophet did not do; if they show any flexibility of their own in interpreting the Quranic texts (*wahi-e-jali*) they risk deviating from both: the text as well as the judgments of the Prophet.

The roots of the above difficulty lie in confused thinking on some basic religious issues. No problem arises, as already mentioned, if we demarcate the proper spheres of faith and of scientific knowledge and also develop a proper methodology of interpreting Quranic texts and of applying the Prophet's example in an ever-changing human situation. Difficulties arise only when we look upon religion or the Islamic faith (in the case of Muslims) as a total guide or map of the good life in all spheres of human activity. When this is done the spiritual or transcendental concerns of religion get mixed up with the concerns of politics, economics and general management of society.

The *Jamat-e-Islami* and other cognate groups shy away from making this basic distinction and persist in their 'totalistic' approach to religion, Islam included. They merely advocate that the *shariah* should be reconstructed or adjusted to suit modern conditions or new factual knowledge. This approach creates deep internal fissures and grave political convulsions in numerous sovereign states that are multi-religious, or multi-ethnic or both. This tends to alienate the Muslim segment from other segments and from the mainstream as such to the detriment of all concerned. Ideally speaking, individuals and subgroups must feel a sense of commonality, not merely with their own religion or nation, but also with the human family as such.

Creative individuals must reach out for all that is best in the human family as a whole.[13]

## 5. SELF-PERCEPTION OF MUSLIMS REGARDING DEMOCRACY

It is quite common to hear among Muslim quarters that Islam is democracy, at its best. Let me examine this line of thinking in some detail. Islam, to begin with, was a set of convictions about transcendental matters. During the entire Meccan period (lasting 13 years) of the Prophet's mission, there were no problems of government before the Prophet. These problems or issues arose in Medina with the rapid accretion of political and economic power to the small but expanding Muslim community. Obviously, the Prophet was not a leader democratically elected by his followers who looked upon the Prophet as chosen and inspired by God. Though the Prophet consulted his followers occasionally and some (specially Omar) gave candid advice on matters, administrative and military, this could hardly be termed as a democratic form of government.

The situation after the passing away of the Prophet shows clearly, that though the *Khalifa* (literally 'successor') was subject to the authority of the *'Book and the Example of the Prophet'* (*kitab Wal Sunnah*) he was not accountable to the community, and there was no definite procedure to review his actions or decisions. The *Khalifa* exercised power on the basis of his Islamic piety and his capacity to convince the people that his policies and orders were in line with the Word of God and the, till then, orally reported doings and sayings of the Prophet. This situation prevailed, to a preeminent degree, during the terms of the first two *Khalifa's*, and, to a lesser degree, during the tenure of the third *Khalifa*. But the term of the fourth *Khalifa* was marked by acrimonious controversies and civil war. The tragedy of the Kerbala, forty-eight years after the death of the Prophet, was the culmination of the civil strife and struggle for power set in motion by the Umayyad clan of the Quraish tribe to which the Prophet belonged.

The crucial points relevant to our central theme are that the *Khalifa* as the chief executive, was not accountable or responsible to the community of believers; there was no definite or fixed term of his high office, there was no clearly laid down procedure for electing or selecting him in the first instance, and for removing him subsequently, there was no standard or authoritative interpretation of the *Book* binding upon the *Khalifa*, apart, of course, from oral reports in circulation about the doings and sayings of the Prophet. In short, there was neither any concept of responsibility to the people (in addition to the *Khalifa's* inner sense of responsibility to God and His Prophet) nor any procedure for unambiguously determining whether the *Khalifa's* actions were in consonance with the *Book and the Example* apart from his own assessment or that of others), nor any procedure for the peaceful transfer of authority from one *Khalifa* to his successor. He could be removed only through assassination or successful armed rebellion. It is significant that the last three of the four pious *Khalifas* were all victims of political assassination.[14]

It is true that the Islamic political doctrine, in the earliest phase of its history, was opposed to hereditary monarchy and stood for a theological form of republicanism, which later on degenerated into hereditary monarchy. Even so, the *Khalifa*, as a monarch, was duty bound to uphold the Islamic canon law (*shariah*). Moreover, his legitimacy or *de jure* authority was conditional upon his upholding the *shariah*. But the theory did not provide any modalities for his 'election' or the peaceful transfer of power from one *Khalifa* to another. In the case of the first four pious *Khalifa's* each became head of the Islamic republic in a different way. The *shariah* did stipulate the theoretical removal of the *Khalifa* in case he failed to uphold the *shariah*. But if he was powerful enough to make his writ run in the realm, there was no modality for removing him apart from armed force.

The *shariah* stipulated consultation as a desirable way of administration or decision-making. But the composition and powers of the consultative body were never spelt out, and in any case, their advice was never held to be binding upon the chief executive. The Quran contains no guidance and gives no clear rules concerning the crucial issue of succession to the Prophet in respect of his political or administrative functions. The Prophet also left no instructions in this regard. The developments, which took place later, are too well known to be recounted, though it must be stated that there is no agreement upon the exact details. Islamic political theory, as it developed in the course of time, became sharply divided into the '*Sunni*' and the '*Shia*' schools of thought. While the *Sunni* view stipulated that the *Khalifa* must be from among the males of the Quraish tribe, the *Shia* view restricted the eligibility of this high office to the house of the Prophet himself.

Thus the concept of equality of status, in the full democratic sense, was at no point of time a feature of the republican temper or constitution of Islam even in the earliest golden period. However, Islam did stand for complete social equality among the believers, in every walk of life: the mosque, the dining table, the battle field and so on. Thus, while Islam clearly upheld egalitarianism and also republicanism, it cannot be said that it stood for democracy, in the full sense of the term.

There are some other serious limitations in the Islamic political and social concepts. For instance, neither the Quran nor the *shariah* ever abolished slavery, as an institution, nor stipulated full gender equality. Again, while Islam stood for a high level of tolerance and equitable treatment of non-Muslims, far in advance of the then prevailing Christian and Jewish norms, the tolerance did not amount to complete equality of all citizens. Thus, **(a)** the notion of the complete equality of the rights, duties and opportunities of the individual and **(b)** the notion of accountability and responsibility of the ruler to the people and a clear modality for the peaceful transfer of *de jure* authority of the head of state, are not present in Islamic political thought and practice.

The Islamic concepts of the fraternity of believers, their social equality, tolerance and justice towards followers of other religions, near-equality of women with men, permission of divorce, permission of inter-religious marriage within certain limits and egalitarian laws of inheritance, certainly represent a creative advance on the then conditions of the human family. A legitimate pride in this fact is natural and also justifiable. But it should not be allowed to stand in the way of an honest and balanced evaluation of its limitations. It is undeniable that the human family has gently outgrown the Islamic level of excellence in all fields of life.

In the sphere of democracy the West has made tremendous advances in building infrastructures and procedures which promote democratic values and human welfare; the separation of the executive and the judiciary, the secrecy of the ballot, the party system, the collective responsibility of the cabinet, the freedom of the press, the system of recall, proportional representation, the permanence of the services, and so on. Avowedly, every institutional mechanism or system has good points as well as bad. Human efforts must ever go on to add fresh dimensions of value in all matters and we must be guided by our own and also the experience of the human family, as a whole. One's own traditions and institutions should not be summarily rejected, merely because of their imperfections or abuses, but we must ever be alive to the need for improvement and innovation. Social space has its own logic, which cannot be ignored. Success in practice is the only test of the value of proposed reforms. No romantic notions or nostalgia for a golden past can be a substitute for the sociological and scientific approach to life.

Obstacles to Democracy in the Islamic Tradition: Some obstacles stand in the way of the Muslims' acceptance of democracy in the modern sense. The first obstacle is caused by the widespread apologetic approach to the tradition. A large number of educated Muslims see only the bright side of Islam and ignore the dark spots on the moon.

The second obstacle is the fear of the social consequences of dissent from the majority position. There is no friendly dialogue between different groups within the Muslims themselves. Keeping one's views to oneself is supposed to be both prudence and courtesy to other Muslims or non-Muslims. One may occasionally open out before very intimate friends, but certainly not express his views in writing. This makes the orthogenetic growth of the tradition either impossible or extremely slow, as happened to Sir Syed's religious reform movement. Even after a lapse of a century his ideas are supposed to be dangerous heresies, which should be politely ignored rather than seriously discussed even at Aligarh itself.

Perhaps, even more serious than the fear of dissent is what the philosophical psychoanalyst, Erich Fromm, calls the 'fear of freedom'. The traditional Muslim develops a fear of independent thinking and suppresses one's genuine attitudes, feelings and intellectual difficulties, as if their mere registration, at the conscious level, would amount to blasphemy or sin. Any spontaneous disagreement from the generally received view is looked upon as spiritual perversion, which needs a spiritual cure. This is why Muslims possessing high technical or professional degrees do not have the moral courage and spiritual creativity to enter into friendly dialogue with the *ulema* and others. Without cultivating and freely expressing an integrated outlook on life religious faith turns into a mere badge lest one be accused of being disloyal to one's group.[15]

Another obstacle to the growth of democratic attitudes is the lack of suitable popular literature on Islamic liberalism, humanism and the social sciences. Islamic literature continues to be almost solely produced by either traditional Muslim writers or by the *Jamat-e-Islami*. The *Jamat* disagrees with the traditional or conservative school of Islam as well as the liberal approach of Sir Syed, Abul Kalam Azad, *et al*. Another obstacle in the way of a wider acceptance of Islamic liberalism is the intellectual isolation of the *ulema* and their almost total neglect of comparative religion, history, social sciences etc. as well as the valuable work of Western scholars on Islam and other religions. They do not realize that contemporary Western scholarship, at its best, is no longer subject to the prejudices and foibles of Christian missionaries, apologists or imperialists, of the previous century, but that they are doing very creative and valuable research on Islamic Studies. Of course there are some rather misinformed and partisan Christian or other apologists, but their activities should not prevent enlightened Muslims from benefiting from the honest scholarly labors of numerous admiring and impartial Western scholars of Islam.[16]

## 6. Concluding Remarks

Islamic resurgence, provided it be on right lines, should be welcomed, not only by the Muslims, but all genuine humanists who look upon humanity as one large family. When, however, the protagonists of Islamic resurgence take to positions, which directly or indirectly, erode the basic values of humanism, spiritual autonomy, free enquiry, equality of the sexes, human rights, tolerance, equality of opportunity etc., Islamic resurgence becomes objectionable not only to non-Muslims but liberal Muslims as well.

Unfortunately, the champions of Islamic resurgence instead of engaging themselves in an impartial and constructive criticism of the human situation and a balanced evaluation of Western thought and institutions, betake themselves to a negative debunking of modernity. This approach may well give them a sense of superiority to the 'decadent West'. But it definitely leads to clouded vision and blurred perceptions of the actual conditions prevailing in Western society. Instead of acquiring an 'insider's insight' into the strength and weakness, the real achievements and limitations of Western modernity, the hostile critics get only distorted pictures, half-truths, over-simplifications, and the like. In other words, they commit the fallacy of 'outsider's negative bias; precisely the same fallacy which they attribute to the Western students of Islam.

In relation to the purely traditionalist Islamic piety the movement of Islamic resurgence of the *Jamat* brand is progressive in many respects. The forward-looking emphasis of the *Jamat* is welcome. But, on a deeper analysis, their language of progress and their pleas for reconstructing and modernizing the *shariah* turns insipid. This happens because they virtually reject the method of free enquiry and the time-tested methodology of the natural and the social sciences, in favor of a newfangled 'Islamic methodology', which is never spelt out, but is merely dangled before charmed Islamic audiences as the panacea for solving all the ills, which beset humanity. They fail to explain how can there be Islamic Physics/Geology/Astronomy/Zoology, or for that matter, Islamic Anthropology/Geography/ Agriculture etc; in contradistinction from these subjects, as they are understood by the world scientific or academic community. The one and only way of the pursuit of truth is the method of free enquiry in a spirit of humility and the readiness to surrender before truth, as ascertained by methods appropriate for the subject matter of the enquiry. The talk of Islamic science or knowledge, or the 'Islamization of knowledge' appears to be a rallying slogan rather than a serious tool of fee enquiry. After all, the power of modern technology flows, ultimately, from the pragmatic truth of the scientific method. Technology will cease to grow the moment the scientific method is discarded. And the womb of the scientific method is free enquiry and the stress on verification. If this spirit weakens or withers away technology will begin to stagnate and eventually collapse.

The *Jamat* forcefully affirms that true religion is not merely praying, fasting and performing other rituals but working to build an equitable social, political and economic order that promotes universal welfare. But the *Jamat* hardly realizes that all good religious people, no matter what their theological creed might be, assert this basic truth. It is, indeed, very true that individual piety is not enough in the absence of a just social order – a surrounding political, economic, and cultural space in which the individual lives and functions. Consequently, if religion aims at true human welfare, it must prescribe not merely individual piety and goodness through spiritual discipline, but also ensure the proper ordering of society as a whole. The mischief, however, begins when the thesis of the social role or relevance of Islam is made into an argument for Islamic separatism or supremacy of the *shariah* in every sphere of life: politics, economics and even knowledge, as such.

The present protagonists of Islamic Resurgence hold that Sir Syed and other Muslim liberal thinkers adopt a 'cosmetic' and soft approach to religion since de-linking it from political activity reduces the power and scope of religion to innocuous rituals. The fact is, precisely, the other way round. Religion loses its power and depth, not through the proper delimitation of its functions, but through an indiscriminate expansion of its jurisdiction. The existential depth and inwardness of religion, thereby, turns into the spatial thinness of fixed rules of conduct at every point of life. Spirituality, the life breath of religion, then gets strangulated either in the weeds of regimentation or the pitfalls of power politics.

The religious liberals who wish to keep religion and politics apart do not ignore the importance of a just, social order. The thesis of the separation of religion and politics does not at all imply the separation of moral considerations and concerns from politics and economics. Since basic moral values are common to all religions the politics of democratic liberal secularism cannot be deemed to be, essentially, 'satanic' or 'Godless'.

Politics, in the sense of seeking and exercising a measure of power, if not supreme power, unavoidably leads to conflict within society. It is primarily the search for supremacy that leads to conflict between individuals, groups or nations, rather than search for truth or God. Ideologies function as instruments of attack and defense in the struggle for power. However, ideas and values also battle against each other. The concept of ideology, in the above sense, antedates the work of Marx. But it was he who brought the above-mentioned role of ideology into sharp focus. Today the above insight has become almost axiomatic for all thoughtful and mature minds, no matter what their religion, race or politics.[17]

The above thesis, however, does not mean that sincerity of faith and honesty of purpose are non-existent in our world and that the talk of religion, values and ideals is pure hypocrisy or, at best, self-deception. Ideals and interests both exist and cooperate with each other, in an extremely complex human situation, which we can never understand with the help of any simple formula. While those who find the doors of opportunity closed, do develop negative feelings of envy and hate against those enjoying power and wealth, genuine impersonal moral indignation at the evils of the human situation also moves the world. Revolutionary fervor directed to rebuilding the world, nearer to our hearts desires and dreams may also be rooted in a deep commitment to moral and spiritual values. Genuine moral indignation and self-interest coalesce, in varying proportions, in different individuals, and even in the same person at different points of time. Their perceptions and levels of aspiration often vary according to their self-assessment of their place on the scale of social recognition and effective participation or of marginalization in society.

The highly complex problems of developing societies cannot be solved by ideology-bound or textbook solutions. In short, the compulsions of development favor (in the long run) the reliance on sociology rather than ideology. In this context, the continuing liberalization process in post-Mao China and the refreshingly new stance of post-Gorbachov in the USSR are of the greatest significance for the entire world. This shows how the compulsions of the developmental process and the logic of sociology score over purely ideological purism and reasoning.

It appears that the Arab oil-wealth explosion and, subsequently, the Islamic Revolution of Iran have jointly imparted a momentum to Islamic resurgence (in its present form), which the movement will not be able to maintain in the decades ahead. The ideological euphoria of Iran will, most probably, wither away in the wake of a revolution that failed. The oil-based Arab euphoria has already given way to economic worries in the wake of the oil recession. The Muslim mind will then awake from both 'dogmatic slumber' and romantic revolutionary dreams. Sociological insights and realistic aspirations would then displace 'ideological mirages. In short, sociology would prevail over ideology, and Islamic humanism and liberalism over pan-Islamism and 'religious totalism.'

This shift of perspective, however, would not be a quick or easy process. Concepts, categories and values evolve like organic species and cannot be created by reformers, philosophers or UNESCO agencies. Western Europe took almost two centuries to complete the process of the scientific and secular revolutions beginning in mid-18th century. However, with the blessings of such tools and instruments of social change, as television and, now, the computer, the journey of the Muslim mind towards Islamic liberalism and democratic humanism, hopefully, may be shortened.

# Notes to Essay 6

## Democracy And Islam

**1.** The Pharaohs of Egypt, Alexander the Great, the pagan Roman Emperors and the Emperors of Japan are some instances. Victory in combat or war has generally been regarded as a sign of Divine favor, though not a certain index. The forces of evil symbolized by the Devil are deemed to be in perpetual conflict with the good and powerful God whose wisdom is inscrutable. Evil sometimes triumphs over good, but these reverses are transient and are meant to test the patience of the faithful. In some cases such reverses are a Divine punishment for the human lapses of the faithful.

**2.** King Charles I was executed in 1659, and Cromwell, later on, became the Protector of the Commonwealth. The restoration of Charles II took place in 1650. His brother, James II, was overthrown in the Glorious Revolution of 1688; a turning point in British and world history.

**3.** Parliamentary and electoral reforms were introduced very gradually in Britain. The Reform Act of 1832 first gave the right of vote to the urban middle class males. The Second Reform Act of 1867 extended the franchise to the lower middle class males in both urban and rural sectors, and also practically the entire urban labor Class, The Third Reform Act of 1884 further extended the franchise to agricultural labor, thus establishing adult male franchise in Britain. The Act of 1911 merely ensured the supremacy of the House of Commons over the House of Lords. Women got the right of vote partially in 1918 and fully in 1928.

**4.** The Magna Carta is the first and fundamental charter of the demand for the rule of law ever made in world history by the subjects of a monarch. The provisions of the charter aimed at controlling the arbitrary powers of the monarch: religious, executive and judicial, and giving to all subjects a sense of freedom and security within the bounds of law.

**5.** Jeremy Bentham (d. 1832) was a distinguished English thinker, reformer and statesman who is regarded as the father of the ethical and political philosophy termed 'Utilitarianism'. John Stuart Mill (d. 1873) made important contributions to this movement of thought and reform. Utilitarianism aimed at emancipating the human mind from the grip of fixed ideas of right and wrong rooted in blind faith or intuition. These two thinkers made the observed consequences of human acts the final test of right and wrong in ethics, politics and religion.

**6.** Karl Marx (d. 1883) also stressed consequences of ideas as the real criterion of their validity or acceptability. Marx also championed people's power, but he thought that it would never accrue to the people in the real sense without violent revolution against the establishment. He further thought that people's welfare was not possible without state ownership and control of the entire means of production. The last two claims are far from being evident.

**7.** History abounds in instance after instance of this crucial truth. Thus the institutionalization of authoritarianism is fatal. No matter how good and sincere a person might be, to begin with, the exercise of power over a long period will have a corrupting influence. Lord Acton's famous dictum, 'Power tends to corrupt, **and** 'absolute power corrupts absolutely', deserves the wide acclaim it has come to enjoy.

**7(a).** This is the near normal position in politics. Very rarely does the choice in politics lie between absolute good or evil.

**8.** Election costs are trivial in relation to the price society pays for violent and bloody struggles for political supremacy. These and some other shortcomings do not invalidate the basic thesis of democracy. Efforts are under way to remove or, at least, minimize these defects. Thus, multiple rounds, of voting could be used to determine which candidate eventually gets an absolute majority. The additional expenses involved in such procedures would be a small price for the immense gains in terms of public welfare.

**9.** Innovations in restructuring democracy have begun and are producing good results. Eternal vigilance is the price of virtue.

**10.** The protagonists of 'Islamic democracy', 'party less democracy' etc. all commit the fallacy of 'abstract Utopianism'. This romantic desire to discover a system of 'perfect democracy' will never help. . 'Islamic democracy' is so far, only a pious ideal or aspiration rather than something real or concrete. Consequently, it is very difficult to be aware of its defects, while those of the Western models have become obvious to all honest students.

**11.** See the following two Quranic verses out of several others in the same vein.

(Al-An'am, 6; 50)
"Say (O Muhammad, to the disbelievers): I say not unto you (that) I possess the treasures of Allah, nor I have knowledge of the unseen, and I say not unto you: Lo! I am an angel. I follow only that which is inspired in me. Say: Are the blind man and the seer equal? Will ye not then take thought"?

(Al-A'raf, 7:188)
"Say: For myself I have no power to benefit, nor power to hurt, save that which Allah willeth. Had I knowledge of the unseen, I should have abundance of wealth, and adversity would not touch me. I am but a warner, and a bearer of good tidings unto folk who believe",

**12.** There was another need for this distinction. It is a fact that the directives or injunctions of the Quran are, so general or non-specific (with a few notable exceptions) that they possibly, could not have been implemented without giving the directives concerned a definite and concrete sense. The Prophet himself naturally and understandably did this. The question was bound to arise whether the interpretations placed by the Prophet upon the revealed verses were also 'revealed' in some way to the Prophet, or were they the products of the thinking and discretion of the Prophet, The concept of 'wahi-e- khafi' was meant to underscore that the said interpretations were the result of hidden or silent non-verbal revelation (as distinct from verbal revelation constituting the Arabic text of the Quran). This way of viewing enhances the status of the interpretations made by the Prophet and renders his directions unquestionable by the faithful. 'The terms 'wahi-e-matlu' (recited revelation) and 'wahi-e-ghair-matlu' (un-recited revelation) refer to the same distinction.

**13.** The only sphere where any modification would amount to violating the sanctity of the Prophet's tradition is the devotional system and its symbolic rites and purely spiritual or liturgical components.

**14.** Each of the four pious Khalifa's was chosen in a different manner. Abu Bakr was elevated by a consensus of sorts, Omar nominated by his predecessor, Usman chosen by a panel appointed by Omar, and Ali was the choice of a faction which was initially dominant but which was soon militarily challenged by dissidents.

**15.** Unfortunately, there is a tremendous dearth of well integrated Muslim scientists and intellectuals. It is quite common to hear of a Professor who teaches the theory of evolution in the lecture room but repudiates it immediately after stepping out from the class on the ground that the said theory is unIslamic. Highly educated persons, when confronted with reasoning or evidence which go against their fixed beliefs, prefer to divide life into separate compartments each sealed from the other. Alternatively, they become inauthentic beings who profess beliefs without inwardly accepting them and without being bothered by an inner schism in the depths of their being.

**16.** See the excellent works of Gibb, Arberry, Montgomery Watt, Annemarie Schimmel, among others, for conceptual analyses of the Islamic belief and value systems. For area studies and objective political, social and cultural information, see (i) Mansfield, P. (Ed), The Middle East, Oxford, 1973, and Piscatori, J. P. (Ed.), Islam in the Political Process, Cambridge, 1984.

**17.** See Isaiah Berlin's excellent work, Vico and Herder: Two Studies in the History of Ideas, London, 1976.

# Essay 7

## The Concept Of An Islamic Economic System

### Introduction

The Islamic Resurgence movement has led to a call for Islamizing society and polity in several Muslim states. The declared rationale for this call is the view set forth by several Islamic intellectuals, theologians and statesmen that Islam is not merely a system of individual devotion and piety calculated to bring about spiritual salvation in life hereafter, but rather a complete way of life, a blue print of the good life in its totality including politics and economics. The concrete contours and details of this map, so they say, ought to be adjusted to the ever-changing human situation with the concurrence of competent *ulema*. Nevertheless the total map must be firmly based upon the Quran and the example of the Prophet.

The advocates of Islamic Resurgence hold that the Muslim liberals of the mid-20th century merely imitated Christian liberalism, which viewed religion merely as a personal relationship between man and God without regulating human political and economic concerns. The advocates of Islamization hold that Liberalism, Socialism and Communism have all failed to cure human ills in the modern age and that the only hope for mankind lies in a return to the Islamic or Quranic system of economics and politics.

In the sphere of economics, the main thrust of the Islamic Resurgence movement is the literal implementation of the Quranic prohibition of usury/interest which is seen to be the root evil. It is claimed that '*zakaat*' (the Islamic wealth tax) and the Quranic law of inheritance would suffice in an interest-free society to cure all economic problems. *Zakaat*, as a 2.5% tax on net wealth at the end of the financial year, was made a statutory tax about five years ago in Pakistan and is being regularly collected by the state directly from banks. In the case of all *Sunni* Muslims (who are the dominant majority in Pakistan) payment of bank interest on deposits and charging of interest on bank loans for industrial commercial purposes have been totally banned since early 1985, though the ban does not yet apply to foreign transactions. A new scheme of Islamic profit/loss sharing by bank depositors has recently been started for promoting investment and economic growth without the lever of interest. It is expected that these innovations would not adversely affect the rate of growth or health of the economy. On the other band, the abolition of interest is expected to promote social justice and general welfare and to remove several social or moral evils inseparable from various non-Islamic politics.

Whatever be the truth of the above claims, the fact is that no attempt has been made, to my knowledge, to present a historical and systematic theoretical analysis of 'interest' or an integrated theory of general economics to show how a totally interest-free world economy would or could work in an admittedly imperfect and 'imperfectible' world.

In what follows I shall analyze the basic concept of an Islamic economic system, as an integral part of the Islamic faith. I shall then examine the basic thesis that the abolition of interest is the root remedy for human socio-economic ills.

## The Concept of an Islamic Economic System

To begin with the Quranic verses dealing with fiscal or economic matters are (with literally two or three exceptions) in the nature of moral exhortations to do the right or the customary and not specific injunctions implying or even pointing to any 'economic system'. Thus, for instance, Quranic verses repeatedly enjoin believers to spend in the way of God, to help the needy, the traveler and the orphan, to avoid extravagance, pomp, avarice and the hoarding of wealth, to be just in weighing and measuring, to fulfill promises and contracts, to avoid bribery and cheating, to be lenient to the debtor, to give honest testimony even when it goes against one's kin, and so on. The only verses which state not mere ethical norms but rather economic rules or regulations are the verses dealing with *zakaat* (tax on surplus wealth) and *riba* (usury/interest).

*(Quran; 2:43)*
*Establish worship, pay the poor-due, and bow your heads with those who bow (in worship).*

*(Quran; 2:275)*
*Those who swallow usury cannot rise up save as he ariseth whom the devil hath prostrated by (his) -touch. That is because they say: Trade is just like usury; whereas Allah permitteth trading and forbiddeth usury. He unto whom an admonition from his Lord cometh and (he) refraineth (in obedience thereto), he shall keep (the profits of) that which is past and his affair (henceforth) is with Allah. As for him who returneth (to usury)--such are rightful owners of the Fire. They will abide therein.*

*(Quran; 3:130)*
*O ye who believe! Devour not usury, doubling and quadrupling (the sum lent). Observe your duty to Allah, that ye may be successful.*

*(Quran; 4:161)*
*And of their taking usury when they were forbidden it, and of their devouring people's wealth by false pretences: We have prepared for those of them who disbelieve a painful doom.*

*(Quran; 30:39)*
*That which ye give in usury in order that it may increase on (other) people's property hath no increase with Allah; but that which ye give in charity, seeking Allah's countenance, hath increase manifold.*

(The above translations are from Pickthall's standard work, *The Meaning of the Glorious Koran*).

The Quran nowhere gives any further details, as it does in the case of some other matters: inheritance, divorce, remarriage, evidence and even the proper procedure of oaths.

It may be thought that since the Quran prohibits usury/interest and implicit obedience to the Quran (the infallible word of God) is obligatory on the believer, the Muslim believer has no option except totally to abjure interest. This line of thinking ignores the methodological principle that prior to drawing any conclusion with regard to 'interest', the exact meaning of the Arabic term '*riba*' used in the Quran should be determined, instead of mechanically equating it with the English word, 'interest'. At times words of a living language undergo great changes in their functional meaning and practical significance due to various factors.

Full investigation into the socio-economic conditions of the then Arab society and the present conditions plus reasoned interpretation of the Quranic text (rather than simplistic literal obedience to the Quran or the Prophet) is the correct approach, not only for the economic historian or social scientist, but also for the committed Muslim drawing inspiration from the Quran and the example of the Prophet.

The advocates of literal obedience to the Quran also ignore (rather much too readily) the historical fact that the Prophet and the pious Caliphs always resorted to juristic reflection on or interpretation of the Quranic text. This naturally led to the admission of qualifications, subtle distinctions in the understanding of the operative or directive meaning of the plain literal texts. For instance, the seemingly categorical Quranic injunction that 'the hands of the thief be cut off' was never applied unconditionally on pain of disobeying the word of God.[1]

The making of relevant distinctions and qualifications is, therefore, also called for in the context of *riba*. This Arabic word literally means increase or growth of any entity: physical, biological or spiritual. Thus the Quran refers to '*riba*' of spiritual merit (*sawaab*) or of punishment (*azaab*). In the economic sphere *riba* means the excess sum demanded by the lender over and above the principal amount lent. Though 'ten thousand' as a lump sum, at anyone point of time, is arithmetically identical with the same amount spread over several years, yet, a consolidated sum has power to purchase an animal, land or tools which augment the wealth of the user, while the same sum spread over a long period of time lacks this purchasing power. *Riba* or usury, thus, has been a universal practice in recorded history. At the same time it has been universally disapproved of since lenders almost always tend to exploit borrowers.[2]

The demand of compound interest makes the situation much worse. Moreover, in ancient times the contract of usury also provided that failure to return the agreed sum in time would entail bonded labor by the borrower from three to seven years. The concept and practice of usury in the ancient and middle ages was, thus, closely tied up with the institution of a form of temporary slavery. This aspect of usury was morally most repugnant in the case of distress loans. The Jewish sense of group solidarity led them strongly to disapprove of usury among themselves, though charging usury from non-Jews was permissible. Subsequently, both Christianity and Islam applied the prohibition to all human beings. This was an advance, upon the Jewish ethos. However, both Christian and Islamic jurists ignored the crucial distinction between usury (in the above mentioned sense) and interest in the modern sense of the term. If we take the expression, 'Islamic economic system' to mean a normative system which is an essential part of the Islamic faith and is permanently binding upon all good Muslims, no such system is found in the Quran or the Sunnah. Nor any such system can be deduced (logically) or inferred (analytically or analogically) from the Quran and the Sunnah. The actual claim by a person, that a particular system is the Islamic norm, is nothing more than a reference to Islamic practice in history, or his opinion how the Islamic system should be. To put it in other words, all such claims are, at bottom, a recommendation that the stated system be accepted as the Islamic system.[3]

What is being called 'the Islamic economic/agrarian system is, indeed, a slow growth which took place in only a marginal sense in the lifetime of the Prophet, and was gradually developed, first by Caliph Omar, and subsequently by other jurists who followed. The process of development spread over two centuries.

The nascent Islamic economic system freely borrowed (quite understandably) from the economic culture of pre-Islamic times. Thus, '*jizya*', (the. tax on protected non-Muslim citizens of the Islamic state) was a medieval Iranian practice going back to the Jews in antiquity. Sovereign Muslim rulers (*Sultans*) in Central Asia, India and elsewhere adjusted and adapted the economic and political ideas and practices of the Umayyad and Abbasid Caliphs to suit local and ever changing conditions. As and when the orthodox *ulema* tried to arrest this practice, tension and conflict developed between the king and the priest, or the state and the church. With a few exceptions, the Indian Muslim rulers or *sultans* (even much before the radical and liberal Akbar) asserted the supremacy of the state in worldly matters and consistently refused to treat the opinions and advice of the *ulema* in such matters as binding upon the state. The so-called Islamic economic/agrarian system, therefore, has never enjoyed the sanctity and binding power as the Islamic precept system relating to prayers, fasting, *zakaat* and the Quranic laws relating to marriage, divorce and inheritance.

## ISLAMIC ECONOMICS

Does the expression 'Islamic Economics' have any significance apart from:

**(a)** economic history or geography of the Muslim world, or,

**(b)** what Muslim social scientists have contributed to Economics?

It might be thought that 'Islamic Economics' is also a theoretical social science that deals with the best method of maximizing material wealth within the parameters of Islam. If so, the scope of 'Islamic Economics' would go beyond the mere economic history or geography of the Muslim believers. According to this concept the social economic polity of a truly Muslim state must reflect and promote the basic Islamic conception of the good life in all its multifarious aspects. However, as soon as we try to spell out the concrete socio-economic features demanded by 'Islamic Economics' we find ourselves faced with conflicting possibilities of choice. And we are thrown back upon our own common sense, economic theory and actual experience in order to clinch various issues.

This difficulty arises because the Islamic values of 'equality', 'fraternity', 'generosity', 'charity', 'sympathy', 'justice', 'compassion' and so on are all abstract concepts. The moment we try to realize them in the framework of laws and a concrete polity, a plurality of social and economic blueprints become candidates for the title 'Islamic' as each claims to be the only true expression of Islam. The same difficulty (to a lesser degree) arises in connection with the two or three specific Quranic economic injunctions mentioned previously.

Thus, 'Islamic Economics', in the sense of prescriptive economic theory, lands Muslims into controversies, which, by their very nature, cannot be solved on the basis of the Quran or the *Sunnah* alone without recourse to independent logical thinking and ethical reflection. In the final analysis, therefore, the term 'Islamic Economics' tends to mislead us into seeking and projecting 'Islamic truths' of economics, or saying that Islam demands the acceptance or rejection of any particular economic system as part of one's faith. However, 'Islamic economics' in the purely descriptive sense as a systematic area study of the economic history of Muslim society or societies

## The Concept Of An Islamic Economic System

or the economic ideas and perspectives of Muslim social thinkers remains a valuable area of study.

Due to semantic confusions several Islamic social scientists, writers and statesmen now find themselves disputing not only with 'secular' economists but among themselves about the identity of the true Islamic system of economics. Paradoxically, prescriptions and injunctions that are taken as Divinely inspired (hence infallible) themselves become injected with ambiguity and liable to be interpreted differently by different believers. One, therefore, cannot help concluding that the directive thrust of the Quran lies in spiritual beliefs and moral exhortation rather than in the sphere of economic legislation. Anyone who claims that the Quran prescribes any particular economic philosophy or system is as off the mark as one who claims that the Quran supports or affirms any particular theory of Astronomy, Physics or Biology. No system could possibly claim a Quranic mandate as in case of laws of inheritance, divorce, prohibited degrees of marriage etc., which are, specifically, contained in the Quran. No positive economic system of Islam could be anything more than a rough logical construction based upon two or three economic injunctions viewed as axioms by the believer.

There can be, I submit, no Islamic truths of economics any more than there could be Islamic laws of Astronomy, Physics, Chemistry, Biology, or Medicine. Economics must be treated as an empirical social science governed by the standard scientific method appropriate to its nature, scope and limits. As a science all its theories, conceptual models, mathematical projections and predictions of mass behavior and social-economic implications of fiscal policies will have to be empirically tested for their validity or truth. All pre-conceived notions, assumptions, untested hypotheses, would hamper the economist's task of analyzing the motives, structure and implications of general economic behavior.

The above task implies a neutral phenomenological analysis of economic concepts, practices and systems (just as a natural scientist analyses natural phenomena) rather than the justification of any pre-rational conviction concerning any particular economic concept or practice including usury/interest. I submit even a committed Muslim economist *qua* social scientist, should do the same instead of assuming that interest is the root of all economic or social evils.

If I, as a Muslim, be inwardly convinced that interest must be evil (since the Quran prohibits it), but do not temporarily suspend this belief while rationally examining the issue, my judgment would not be impartial but rather 'weighted' against interest. Even when I consciously aim to find out the truth rather than to defend any particular view, my perception of the function and utility of interest would be colored by my antecedent beliefs. Likewise, if I have been conditioned by my milieu to hold all religion or pre-modern ideas as infantile myths or as superstitions, I may miss out on some crucially relevant consideration or aspect of the issue. Suspension of belief is, thus, indispensable for a truly detached and balanced approach. To the extent I fail in doing so I shall become selective: noting or emphasizing some features but missing out or ignoring others, thereby confirming my initial slant. However, if I could empty or neutralize my ideological affiliations and predilections or 'ideological vested interests' as it were (as far as humanly possible), I would maximize the clarity of my thoughts and grasp the complex contours of the issues concerned.

I am not suggesting that the social scientist ought to or actually can do away with assumptions about human nature or with moral values. In fact, the committed Muslim ought not, and never can lightly treat the Quranic prohibition against '*riba*'. All I say is that while analyzing and appraising economic concepts and practices, the social scientist must suspend or put in 'brackets' (as the German thinker, Husserl says) all one's preconceived notions and endeavor to discover the structures and interconnections of events or entities and one's own authentic value judgments. If this is not done, one is very likely to be advancing bad reasons for justifying what one takes to be the one and only right interpretation of Scripture. When this happens, all theoretical arguments turn into self-deception.[4]

Suspension of belief for the duration of the enquiry does not imply rejecting the antecedent belief, which might, possibly, even get confirmed as a result of the enquiry. If so, no problem of the conflict between faith and reason would arise. If, however, any conflict does arise the individual remains free to make a well-considered choice. If one chooses the verdict of faith he would not be inclined to 'rationalize' (in the pejorative sense), but merely claim that this course gives him a 'total satisfaction' which he values more highly than mere 'rational satisfaction'. And this would be a very valid stand to take, provided, of course, his sense of 'total satisfaction' is not tainted with fear or doubts. There is nothing objectionable in opting for faith after passing through the discipline of Husserl's 'epoche'. Likewise, there is nothing wrong if the person goes 'where the argument leads him' via the method of Socrates after passing through a struggle between the pull of faith and the pull of reason, provided the final choice is the fruit of authentic freedom rather than of fear, greed, or some hidden motive.

The fear of loss of traditional faith should not stand in the way of the person's quest for authentic being; his inner journey to reach 'the truth of his being' rather than 'the truth of his milieu'. Even if the believer loses his traditional faith or rather its traditional interpretation, this is not necessarily to lose his valuational roots or his spiritual identity, unless, of course, his free enquiry brings about a total rejection of his initial beliefs and values. Should this happen the honest seeker must have passed through a profound inner struggle. And the experience of deep spiritual unrest and honest enquiry yields the pure gold of human authenticity in the crucible of spiritual suffering.

In the final analysis, authenticity or authentic being, irrespective of its contents, is the highest possible mode of human existence. This authentic being is attainable, both by the autonomous philosopher and by the man of faith who has reached the condition of 'blessedness' in the spiritual sense. In practice, however, authentic being appears to be more difficult to achieve at the religious level, when one's religious beliefs or values collide with one's inner rational choices, and thus lead to inner tensions. However, the autonomous philosopher cannot claim any superiority of status over the religious person who freely and authentically submits to an external Authority, provided their degree of authenticity be the same.

The outcome of the above analysis is that Husserl's method of 'epoche' is pre-eminently desirable, even if one loses one's traditional religious beliefs, but attains and retains the condition of authenticity, which is functionally akin to spirituality. It is all to the good if the individual becomes aware of his hidden assumptions and his heightened self knowledge reveals his existential depths and he becomes a more fully integrated person than he was as a 'mass-member' of some 'human herd' or other, no matter what it might be.

## THE CONCEPT OF AN INTEREST FREE ECONOMY

Interest has continued to flourish in the human family though the great historical religions disapprove of it in varying ways. Is this state of affairs merely another instance of the distance between the ideal and the real, or is there some specific social need that interest or usury served and still serves. If so, how will that need be served if an Islamic Society abolishes interest? Again, how or in what precise way is an interest-free society more desirable than an interest-based society? The answer to these important questions should not be given by way of justifying the Quran or the sunnah but must be based on honest and searching reflection in. the light of reliable factual investigation.

The liberal Muslim intellectuals and statesmen of the previous century, among whom S. Khuda Bakhsh occupies an honored place, did indeed, attempt this important task. They made a distinction between:

**(a)** usury and interest, and

**(b)** different types of loans: distress loans, consumption loans and development loans for various purposes.

They came to the conclusion that accepting bank interest on deposits and commercial interest were quite permissible. However, charging interest on distress loans or even on consumption loans was un-Islamic.

Accepting bank interest on deposits is very different from charging interest on loans advanced to others. The depositor places his savings at the disposal of the bank, which invests them, either in the form of loans or purchase of shares in sound industrial concerns etc. Thus, the interest given by banks is, in reality, a slice of the profits, which accrue to them on their investments. Interest-bearing deposits in banks or companies promote investment of idle money for the dual purpose of increasing the owner's wealth without diverting him from his actual vocation as also promoting general material prosperity through increased production and employment of the work force.

The Muslim liberals were correct in their basic approach, but their historical and analytical discussion of the nature and function of interest was too inadequate to convince traditional conservative opinion on such matters. They were unable to provide a rationale satisfactory to both reason and Islamic faith. Perhaps this explains how and why the economic content of the contemporary movement of Islamic Resurgence has gained consider-

## The Concept Of An Islamic Economic System

able vogue in several Muslim countries. To this theme we now turn.

To my mind, most Islamic economists who regard interest as the root of all economic ills start with three unchecked assumptions, which are very far from being self-evident to a dispassionate analyst. The assumptions are:

(a) there is no difference between usury and interest so that the Quranic prohibition of usury implies the prohibition of interest.

(b) the unearned income or gain from a sleeping partnership is morally right, while unearned gain in the form of interest is morally wrong because of risk being present in the first case and absent in the second, and

(c) the abolition of interest would not adversely affect economic activity and growth in general, but rather purge it of social evils.

Let us now examine the above assumptions in some detail.

(a) Usury, in the ancient and medieval periods, was a charge upon all types of loans including distress loans contracted even by the poorest and weakest sections of society. Avaricious moneylenders did not reduce exorbitant usury rates even for distress loans, to say nothing of waiving the interest out of sympathy or compassion. In this regard there is no difference between usury and interest. Yet, it would be quite fallacious to equate the two for the following reason. The rate of usury was fixed on the model of biological reproduction or agricultural growth, which follows geometrical proportions, while interest, in the modern sense, is calculated on the basis of low arithmetical proportion. The difference between the two models of growth is so enormous that to equate usury with interest becomes like equating the domestic cat with the tiger.

The model of biological growth for usury was suggested (quite naturally and understandably) by the average rate of reproductive growth of domesticated animals or familiar agricultural crops, namely, approximately four hundred percent per annum. However, modern interest rates are deliberately kept, relatively speaking, very low in appreciation of the great role of planning and skill of entrepreneur in production and the generation of profit. In other words, in pre-modern times the owner of wealth tended to overvalue his own role at the expense of the merchant or industrialist, and this approach got reflected in the high rates of usury whose model was the rate of biological reproduction or agricultural growth. The biological model was quite understandable in an age when theoretical economics, social science and militant class consciousness were non-existent and the manufacturer or artisan had to borrow money in what may be termed as a 'usurer's market'. No exception was made in the case of distress or consumption loans, whose purpose was obviously quite other than increasing one's wealth. This state of affairs led to the exploitation of the poor or the needy, specially, when non-payment of borrowed amount attracted the penalty of bonded labor.

Interest in the modern sense, however, is computed as a function of the generally viable rate of profit in a given society. This approach has, considerably, pushed down interest rates in the modern age. Furthermore, the law prohibits penal bonded labor if the debtor be genuinely unable to discharge his commitments. Interest in the modern sense is, thus, quite different from usury. The assumption of their structural and functional identity breaks down in the light of historical and analytical scrutiny. The debate among Islamic economists whether insurance involves gambling (which Islam prohibits) is very relevant for correctly interpreting the Quranic prohibition of *riba*.

Insurance finds no mention in Islamic jurisprudence, while gambling and games of chance are prohibited. Since insurance is definitely linked with the workings of chance, the principle of analogical reasoning (*qeyaas*) led most jurists to conclude that Islam also prohibited insurance. However, many modern Islamic jurists now permit insurance. They make (rightly) a distinction between the function of gambling and the function of insurance, and hold that the function of gambling is momentary thrill (without giving anything in return to society) the function of insurance is protection against unhappy contingencies and is, thus, pre-eminently desirable. Now why should not this method of interpretation also be applied to the different types of loans and the issue of interest? While the charging of interest on a distress loan does involve exploiting human misery, does the same apply in the case of a loan for development of industry or commerce? Again, is not ancient and medieval usury involving exorbitantly high rates plus bonded labor functionally very different from interest used as a tool for stimulating the economy and protecting the legitimate interests of the investor, the entrepreneur and society as a whole?

Analytical discrimination and juristic reflection have, indeed always been practiced by Muslim jurists no less than the Prophet and the pious Caliphs. The classical distinction between developed and virgin land, and permitting farming or sharecropping in the former case but prohibiting it in the case of the latter is a good example. The classical Islamic jurists applied the same principle when they waived the Quranic penalty for theft in several cases. Why should not the same approach be followed in the case of interest?

**(b)** We now come to the second assumption. Unearned profit, which is risk bearing, is equitable, but unearned interest, which is devoid of risk, is inequitable. Is there really any moral distinction between the risk-bearing nature of profit and the risk-free nature of interest over and above the purely economic difference that while profit is contingent and flexible, interest is pre-determined and fixed?

It may be thought that since interest is payable to the lender as an absolute claim irrespective of the economic health of the productive enterprise, this causes unmerited hardship to the producer if and when things go badly with his enterprise for no fault of his own. This unmerited suffering does not occur when the lender shares profit or loss in a partnership. There is an element of truth in this contention. But this moral factor becomes relevant only when the producer is close to or actually reaches the state of economic breakdown or the rate of interest be so exorbitantly high as to make the profit almost nominal. Otherwise the factor of risk in a partnership or the absence of risk in the case of interest do not matter except when the rate of interest be so exorbitantly high as to cripple the debtor. In general, when a sleeping partner partakes of profits merely on the strength of supplying capital to the active partner, this appears to me to be as equitable or not as receiving a fixed but small and unconditional return for his monetary contribution to the enterprise.

Social justice is a highly complex goal having several aspects or coordinates. Justice certainly requires that the producer be protected against rough economic weather, but it also requires the reasonable protection of the supplier of capital. It appears that interest (viewed as a fixed charge paid by the producer) tends to motivate him to keep costs down and earn enough to be able to pay the cost of borrowing the capital, while cost-free capital tends to make the economic enterprise much too soft for the entrepreneur and also to slow down the motor of economic growth. On the other hand, when the lender agrees to receiving a low rate of interest he pays a definite price for eliminating the factor of risk in the investment. Choosing a lower share for the sake of security and the elimination of risk does not involve any moral wrong. It is a measure of caution and the creditor's preference for secure returns and paying a price for this advantage. This appears to me as justified caution, and not evil. Charging interest (at high rates) becomes exploitation of the weak only when moneylenders do so in the case of distress loans to the weaker sections of society. However, no inequity is involved when the supplier of capital demands a fixed (relatively low return) for his contribution to the complex productive process and foregoes all profits that accrue to the producer.

(c) Let us now examine the assumption that the charging of interest is an absolute evil and must be abolished in one stroke and that true Muslims must aspire to do so without any 'ifs and buts', and that such abolition and the universal adoption of the 'Islamic model of partnership production' will make the world economy to prosper rather than cause a break-down.

The above assumption is not really warranted by our present state of knowledge and experience. Confirmation of this abstract forecast is a far cry at present. However, to my mind, careful non-ideological analysis does not warrant the optimism of Islamic economists in this regard. The reason is as follows: A sleeping partnership involves full liability without any security for the sleeping partner who supplies capital merely on the trust he places on the bona fides and competence of the managing partner. This, indeed, is the Islamic ideal (as also the ideal situation in general), but the distance between the ideal and the real is obvious. In case the partner be tempted for some reason or other to cheat or indulge in some sharp practices at the expense of the sleeping partner (such instances being too common in the human family to be ignored by any law-giver) the sleeping partner will ever remain at the mercy of the managing partner. It is precisely at this point that the economic function of interest appears in a sharp focus. No other economic mechanism appears to serve the same purpose as effectively as interest.

It is true that if Islamic banks exercise proper vigilance both before and after investment this will act as a strong check upon the misuse of funds by managing partners. In any case human nature being what it is, the degree of security of investment, per force would depend upon the accuracy of the producer's balance sheet. Moreover auditing work would multiply enormously and thereby create scope for concealment and corruption. Now since international trade is unavoidable due to the interdependence of the human family as a whole interest bearing transactions between different counties, would continue. This would create anomalies and complications at different levels. Thus there does not appear to be any justification for permitting unearned profits through Islamic partnerships but prohibiting interest *per se*. In fact, the slogan of profit/loss participation by Islamic banks in place of floating interest-bearing loans to the entrepreneurs is nothing but substituting the theologically acceptable term 'profit' in place of the theologically repugnant term 'interest' without any really meaningful change in economic theory or practice. However, the scheme of advancing interest-free distress or consumption loans at almost zero interest for specified purposes (*qarz-e-hasana*) is a definitely meaningful reform initiated by Islamic economists.

## THE LANGUAGE OF MODERN ECONOMICS

Modern economists have defined interest in various ways putting forward several theories of interest. These theories are, at bottom, attempts to assimilate or reduce interest to some other concept such as profit, rent, price, cost, increment, reward and so on. As a student of philosophy it appears to me, that no theory, which is purely reductive, could ever provide a complete analysis of the nature and function of interest in every possible context. It seems that, in the context of industry, interest approximates 'a factor of the cost of production; in the context of consumption loans, interest approximates 'price or rent of borrowed money'; in the context of state bonds, interest approximates 'reward for deferring enjoyment of one's purchasing power; in the context of distress loans, interest approximates 'callous extortion or exploitation'. No single conception of the 'essence' of interest would thus suffice in all cases. Likewise, no ethical or economic appraisal of interest, in a blanket manner, would be valid. To arrive at a proper evaluation one must take into account the context and the exact function of interest in the type of situation under review. The concept of 'increment' which interest logically implies is, ethically, an indeterminate concept. We shall now briefly review some of the different conceptions of interest without attempting any reductive definition.

One conception of interest is that it is the price a borrower is required to pay for satisfying a need he is unable to satisfy from out of his own available money. The excess payment he makes to the lender, over and above the principal amount, is the price of the borrowed money. Another conception is that the excess is the rent for the use of money belonging to the lender.

Yet a third conception is that interest is the lender's claim to be compensated for depriving himself of the actual or possible enjoyment of his own wealth, which he places at the borrower's disposal. In the context of trade and industry, interest is a relatively small fixed charge upon the theoretically larger profit of enterprise. It may be viewed as guaranteed unearned profit whose justification is that the supplier of capital (one of the necessary conditions of production) is entitled to a small but assured return, for lending capital to the producer who expects to get much larger returns through profits.

The other factors of production (apart from capital) are land, technical skill or know-how, management, labor, and last but not least, leadership and organizational capacity of the entrepreneur. Now each factor of production is severally and jointly essential for the success of the enterprise and thus deserves just consideration. However, entrepreneurial leadership and the supply of capital do occupy a unique position or status in the sense that they jointly create the 'productive space' for the inception and future growth of the enterprise. Without such space having been antecedently provided by the capitalist or the 'captain of industry', the social organism comprising management and labor, would not have come into being at all.

It is, therefore, understandable that the founders and directors of the productive enterprise claim a higher status and a larger share in profits of the enterprise, while the management and labor receive fixed salaries for specified jobs. Between the capitalist and the industrialist, if the former supplies money capital, the latter supplies the 'ideational/volitional capital' – the creative idea, and organizational initiative. The two together create the base for the subsequent productive role of labor and management. Once the organism is born and the infant plant becomes an adult organism, the role of the management and the workers also acquire a key role in raising the productivity and quality of the enterprise. But at the initial stages the capitalist and the entrepreneur do play the crucial role of conceiving and producing a new social organism as such.

If one super-human individual could possibly supply all the different factors of production, he/she could rightly claim to appropriate the entire profit. This is not possible when large investments are made. The need for capital is fulfilled through various mechanisms or modalities: the accumulation of share capital, borrowing on interest (from an individual or a bank or the state or some corporation, or by entering into a partnership). Now is there, really, any conceptual/or ethical difference between the above modalities?

I think they are essentially the same. They are all characterized by a common feature – a claim for monetary return on the strength of some productive contribution towards turning a mere idea or project into a productive concern? And how can this claim be adjudged as morally repugnant in some cases but right in others? It is true that a sleeping partner in an Islamic partnership bears a risk, while the lender of money on interest gets a risk-free and safe return. But how does this economic difference amount to any inherent social injustice. It may be said that the concept of a fixed interest, whether the venture succeeds or fails, is morally evil. But (as stated above) the lender also needs a measure of protection.

In short, we cannot hold that interest is immoral or inherently evil like we judge other wrong actions such as murder, rape, falsely incriminating an innocent person and the like. The abhorrence with which many Muslims look upon interest (which they judge as the root of social or economic ills) arises when they mix different types of financial operations or mechanisms with each other. They firstly confuse the modern idea and function of interest with ancient usury. They also confuse developmental loans with distress loans, insurance with gambling, and risk-free low return schemes for investing one's surplus wealth or hard earned savings with inequitable perpetuation of unearned inherited wealth at the cost of the poor, and so on.

In other words, committed Muslims owe it to themselves to overcome their confusions instead of passing a blanket judgment on the issues of interest and investment returns. There can be no doubt that interest in the modern sense is nothing but a thin slice carved out of much larger expected profits and its function is certainly not to exploit the poor but just to protect the legitimate interests of a large segment of society.

It is true that paying interest to the creditor adds up to the total cost of production and thus certainly adds to the market price of goods and the rigors of the producer. But then it promotes a proper climate for industrial and commercial investments and promotes a ceaseless concern for reducing production costs in a highly competitive market economy. Both its advantages as well as disadvantages must be kept in mind in order to arrive at a balanced perspective.

Indeed, most economists are of the view that interest performs an irreplaceable socio-economic function and that all efforts to eliminate interest from society are futile. It is significant that socialist thinkers and reformers as Robert Owen (d. 1858) of Britain, Rodbertus (d. 1875) of Germany, had condemned interest and advocated its abolition. Marx and Lenin, however, did not hold interest to be the arch evil. Though the Soviet Union had excluded interest, as a cost factor, in the early period just after the *Russian Revolution* of 1917, their ideologues later on gave up this approach. Socialist planners rejected the Capitalist system of production, yet they included interest for computing the total cost of production and for fixing the consumer price.

In short, interest is an economic tool performing several functions only some of which could be taken up by the Islamic partnership model of profit and loss sharing. Social scientists, almost without exception have concluded after prolonged enquiry that there is no effective substitute for interest just as an overwhelming majority of social philosophers and enlightened statesmen affirm that despite the evils of democracy no better substitute is available to the human family.

## Concluding Reflections

Islamic intellectuals and religious leaders must realize the plain truth that the economic directives of the Quran or the classical Islamic polity that gradually developed in early Islam will not suffice in modern times without developing the early economic models and modalities in the light of modern social sciences. The Quranic economic axioms are certainly valid, but they need to be developed in the light of 'economic rationality'. Committed Muslims could, if they so wish, call the developed economic system Islamic or Quranic. Let me explain this crucial point.

The Quranic fixed coordinates of the economic system are only two:

**(a)** the prohibition of usury, and,

**(b)** the wealth tax (*zakaat*).

## The Concept Of An Islamic Economic System

Now all religions prohibit exploitative rates of usury but allow what should be called interest. However, Muslim jurists go by the literal meaning of words and totally disregard the fact that their significance or directive function may clearly change in changing times. They do not see the genuine distinction between the modern concept of 'interest' and the ancient or medieval notion of 'usury' and (innocently) assert that the Quranic term *'riba'* covers both. The same remarks apply to *'zakaat*. In some form or other all religions ordain the rich and affluent among the faithful to care for and generously help the deprived and the weaker sections. The Quranic rate of 2.5% of the net surplus should not be deemed to be a rigid or permanently fixed figure but only a minimum figure as a general guideline for Muslims. To my mind, following an 'open' approach to the Quranic economic axioms would converge with the theories and policies of the school of 'Welfare Economics'.

Islamic economists often criticize that Western economists do not show any concern for values other than maximal growth of material wealth, while Islamic economics is focused on welfare and compassion for all. However, all contemporary social thought interprets the idea of 'economic rationality' as inclusive or fully integrated human welfare that includes material prosperity as an important dimension or ingredient of the *Human Development Index* (HDI). Economists, in their capacity as pure social scientists, may well suggest models of rapid economic growth (in the restricted sense) without moral or humanitarian constraints or considerations. But it is obvious that they are not allowed to cross certain limits that are set by democratic consensus rather than by purely or exclusively economic considerations. Thus, the protagonists of welfare economics adopt the same basic approach, as do Islamic economists.

The basic spiritual and moral values of all universal religions and also secular value systems are essentially similar even though they differ in their theological beliefs and social customs. Such differences, however, do not negate their basic agreements, which suffice for peaceful coexistence and a sense of harmony. In fact whenever a genuine meeting of minds and hearts takes place between diverse groups, a process of mutual learning is set in motion. Does not this go to show the potential unity of basic values underlying the plural metaphysical beliefs, myths, symbols, rites and rituals of the human family?

The fact of the matter is that liberal humanists, utopians, scientific socialists and Gandhian reformers, no less than Islamic economists, stand for the same values in the long run (despite, obviously, differing on details and on the best means for reaching the values concerned). To suppose that the Marxists or the liberals are oblivious to higher values and that creating material plenty is their only objective is to distort the true picture. Thinkers, reformers teachers, poets and artists of the human family as a whole, have the same dreams and aspirations. We register, even magnify, the lapses of others in their pursuit of power; we hardly notice our own lapses. In the final analysis, therefore, the fault lies in the human clay rather than exclusively in any particular system. And, while we can modify or even replace systems, we cannot alter the human clay, much as we may educate or 'condition' it. Wisdom lies in continually improving the system in the light of actual experience rather than of *a priori* formulae (religious or secular) and striving to purify the clay without expecting miracles of success and without losing the heart to march along, despite falls and failures, on the endless road to utopia.[5]

The contemporary movement of Islamic Resurgence aims to overcome the inertia and stagnation of the Islamic world for the past several centuries. This is very welcome, indeed. However, the worldview of their leaders and ideologues suffers from a grave limitation. They have failed to realize the nature and the impact of the scientific revolution of the 18th century upon the religious sensibility of the modern age. In other words, they continue to believe in the medieval view that religion is a total code of conduct applicable to every aspect of human life. This basic approach, inevitably, leads to a rejection of spiritual pluralism and reinforces sectarian communitarianism in some form or other. The earlier 'Islamic liberalism' of the late 19th century, led by Sir Syed of Aligarh and Abduh of Egypt, stood for a spiritualized humanism and a more or less secular approach to politics. Their vision of Islam affirmed that the essential concern of religion is with the transcendental or spiritual dimension of human life, not with political, economic, cultural and administrative concerns. They were quite clear that the essential function of religion in an ever-changing human situation was inspirational rather than legalistic.

The contemporary resurgence movement, on the other hand, for various political reasons, has back-tracked on the earlier liberal humanist approach to Islam and regressed to the medieval view that religion should provide a total code or blue-print of the 'good life' for the true follower. The contemporary champions of Islamic resurgence, for example, the *Jamaat e Islami*, merely seek to 'adjust' the '*shariah*' for meeting contemporary needs, without realizing that there is any need for a deeper questioning of the medieval view of the function and proper jurisdiction of religion in human society and state. In other words, the contemporary movement accepts the medieval theory of religion as a complete and 'totalist' map or code of conduct in every walk of life. This is the essence of what has come to be known as 'religious fundamentalism' or the 'fundamentalist approach to religion', no matter what its creedal content or name. In this sense there is not only 'Islamic' fundamentalism, but 'Hindu' fundamentalism, 'Christian' fundamentalism, 'Sikh' fundamentalism and so on.

The implications of this approach are far reaching, indeed, since this approach implies the definitive rejection of the generic liberal approach in the case of all religions as such, rather than merely of liberalism in the house of Islam. This is why the opponents of liberal Islam also oppose liberal Christianity, liberal Judaism, liberal Hinduism or Buddhism and so on. They (perhaps unconsciously) denigrate the 'liberal attitude' or mind-set as such in the case of all historical religions and judge their emerging liberal versions in the course of history as unwanted aberrations or deviations from their true original. It is common to hear them say that the liberal reformed Protestant Christianity that emerged in the West under the impact of modern science and the industrial revolution is a toothless degenerate version of Church Christianity.

Likewise, the liberal Islam of Muslim reformers or statesmen of the 19th, century in Egypt, India, and Indonesia etc. is only an apology for, rather than true Islam, as such. In short, the ideologues of the contemporary form of Islamic resurgence devalue the contribution of the Islamic liberals of the last two centuries. Rather than take up the torch the liberals had lighted and going forward to complete the unfinished agenda of such noble and enlightened Islamic liberals as Muhammad Abduh of Egypt, Sir Syed, Iqbal and Abul Kalam Azad of the Indian subcontinent, the champions of theocracy and Islamization limit their task to the 'adjustment' of the *'shariah'* (as a total code of conduct) to modern times. They have no inkling of the deeper issue of redefining the proper function and jurisdiction of all religions (including Islam) in the age of modern science and technology and a global society. What is really needed is that the Muslim mind liberates itself from several unquestioned assumptions that are not integral to the essence of the Islamic faith, though they have entered into mainstream Islam due to various factors.

# Notes to Essay 7
## The Concept of an Islamic Economic System

**1.** Though the Quranic command to cut off the hands of the thief is categorical, the shariah admits of several exceptions, namely, when the thief and the victim are close blood relations, or when the stolen amount is below a prescribed minimum. It is also waived in the case of eatables, musical instruments and some other articles.

**2.** Usury on distress loans has been universally disapproved and morally condemned because it implies turning the suffering of a fellow human into an opportunity for material profit. In ancient Babylonia, Hammurabi (app.2000 B.C.) sought to regulate the rate of usury. A new king often declared the cancellation of all debts at the time of his coronation. Judaism prohibited usury in the strongest possible terms making no distinction between distress loans and loans for any other purpose, but permitted Jews to charge usury from Non-Jews. The Christian canon law made the prohibition universal. In the Middle Ages, Thomas Aquinas (d. 1274), the greatest medieval Christian theologian, made a distinction between distress and commercial loans, but the canon law was not altered. In practice, however, the prohibition was conspicuous by its violation due to economic compulsions.

The religious leaders of the mercantile Italian city-states of the early modern era, Florence, Venice and others (which were the pioneers of modern international commerce and banking) were the first to question the ethical and religious validity of the absolute Christian prohibition of interest without distinguishing it from usury when commercial practice had already sharply deviated from canon law. It was, however, John Calvin (d. 1564), the great Swiss Protestant reformer, no less influential than his more internationally famous German contemporary, Martin Luther, (d. 1546) who forcefully pleaded that while usury was morally repugnant, interest on commercial and development loans served social needs. The above approach found ready acceptance in Britain: the first industrialized country in the modern sense and also the country where the seminal work, The Wealth of Nations, published in 1776, by the philosopher, Adam Smith (d. 1790) gave birth to 'Economics' as a social science. Significant contributions by Jeremy Bentham (d. 1832), J.S Mill (d. 1873), Ricardo (d. 1832), Malthus (d. 1834) and others followed to enrich Economics as a pure social science.

The growth of theoretical Economics and the practical constraints of rapid industrialization fostered a new outlook on social and religious problems. The legal prohibition against usury was repealed. Soon afterwards, the statutory ceiling on the rate of interest, and the legal penalty for violating the maximum limit, was removed in the early 19th century in Britain and elsewhere under the influence of the philosophy of laissez faire liberalism, that is, uncontrolled reign of the market place.

The middle of the 19th century, however, saw a reaction against the doctrine of absolutely free and uncontrolled market economy. Several sensitive minds began to think that the much lauded free market economy had bred numerous social and economic evils-uncontrolled urbanization, poorhouse poverty, crime, social uprooting, anonymity, alienation, dehumanization of labor, unemployment, all flourishing in the midst of and despite mass production and affluence. The ideas of co-operative production, state regulation, and finally, of socialism came to the fore in order to remove the grave imbalances created by the free interplay of market forces. There was a spate of social welfare legislation and economic regulations in Western countries to protect the weaker sections. Institutional arrangements were made for the supply of cheap credit to the needy and for protecting insolvents. Thus, while the religious prohibition against usury was done away with, its basic objectives – the protection of the interests of the weak – was sought to be promoted by means of democratic and socialist ideals. Liberal Christian thought contributed to this development but conservative, rather static, quarters within the Church were reduced to the position of perplexed and helpless spectators of the new emerging values.

To complete the picture, a few remarks may be made concerning the ancient Indian approach to usury. The Dharmashastras also strongly disapprove of usury on distress loans. Indeed, one Dharmashastra declares that usury (kuseed) in the case of a distress loan, is a greater evil than even the murder of a Brahman (Brahmhatya). However, commercial interest is permitted. Different lawgivers prescribe different rates of interest bearing in mind different relevant factors and also safeguarding the legitimate interests of the creditor and the debtor and also of the society in general. However, it must be pointed out that there was caste discrimination while fixing the varying rates of interest (the rate being lowest for the Brahman borrower, approx.15% per annum). Moreover, the general rate of interest was much higher than is the case in modern times. Buddhism followed the Hindu practice but without any caste bias.

**3.** Ghulam Ahmad Parvez and some others are inclined to Socialist ideas, Mawdudi, Baqir Al-Sadra and others to free enterprise. See Nijatullah Siddiqi: *Survey of Islamic Economic Thinking*, Leicester, UK, 1980, pp.46-53

**4.** Edmund Husserl (d. 1938) first elaborated the concept of 'epoche'. This means complete suspension of all previous judgments and adopting the posture of 'epistemic openness' without any evasion or unconscious slant and the maximum possible effort to mentally grasp the structure and inter-relations of a specific concept or belief.

**5.** The prohibition of interest, the institution of zakat, the implementation of the Islamic law of inheritance, severally or jointly, would not suffice to solve our complex problems. When there is urgent need of capital for macro development national defense, acute distress or natural calamity etc. borrowing on interest becomes unavoidable. Zakat will not do when savings are almost zero. Islamic inheritance will not do when all there is to inherit is poverty and disease. Moral exhortations will not do when the facts of life have been ignored. The nationalization of means of production will not do when productivity remains low. No economic system will work if we do not give up romantic illusions concerning human nature.

# Essay 8

## Inter-Religious Marriage And Islam

In this article I wish to discuss the objections usually raised against the idea of inter-religious marriage. The prohibition against inter-religious marriage is dinned into our ears from childhood with the result that the idea sounds to most of us as almost unthinkable. When such marriages occasionally do take place they are looked upon as unfortunate social accidents and generate a lot of tension or resentment within the concerned families and also society in general. Such marriages are not tolerated but merely endured by the family. One frequently hears of parents disowning their son or daughter. Both Hindus and Muslims reject the idea of inter-marriage on grounds, which are religious as well as social psychological or cultural. I shall deal with these grounds separately. As far as religious objections go I, as a Muslim, shall confine myself to Islam only.

### (I)

The Islamic canon law (*shariah*) prohibits inter-religious marriage but allows a Muslim male to marry a Jewish or Christian woman. This position is based upon the following two verses of the Quran: (The English version is from Picthall's well known translation of the Quran).

*(Quran, 2:221)*
*"Wed not idolatresses till they believe; for lo! A believing bondwoman is better than an idolatress though she please you; and give not your daughters in marriage to idolaters till they believe, for lo! A believing slave is better than an idolater though he please you. These invite unto the Fire, and Allah inviteth unto the Garden, and unto forgiveness by His grace, and expoundeth thus His revelations to mankind that haply they may remember."*

*(Quran 5:5)*
*"This day are (all) good things made lawful for you. The food of those who have received the Scripture is lawful for you, and your food is lawful for them. And so are the virtuous women of the believers and the virtuous women of those who received the Scripture before you (lawful for you) when ye give them their marriage portions and live with them in honor, not in fornication, nor taking them as secret concubines. Whoso denieth the faith, his work is vain and he will be among the losers in the Hereafter."*

I shall first deal with verse 5:5. This verse provides the textual basis for the Muslim canon law, which allows inter-marriage between Muslim men and Jewish or Christian women, but prohibits Muslim women from marrying Jews or Christians. Two comments are called for. First, the Quranic text does not specify the identity of 'those who have received the Scripture before you' (the Muslims). Second, the basic mood, which pervades the verse, is one of reciprocal symmetrical liberalism with regard to the food and virtuous women of both Muslims, and those who have received the Scripture earlier. The emphasis of the text is upon virtuously living together in proclaimed wedlock rather than in maintaining clandestine relations between the sexes, irrespective of their religion. Now the traditional interpretation of the Quranic verse does two rather unwarranted things, which erode the basic liberal humanistic thrust of the Quranic text. First, it confines the expression 'people of the book' or 'those who have been given the Scripture before you' to Jews and Christians alone. Second, it confines the permissibility of inter-marriage to the marriage of Muslim men with Jewish or Christian women. This interpretation will not stand in the light of careful analysis of the letter and the spirit of the Quran itself.

The Quran expressly declares repeatedly that God's messengers and prophets have been sent in every age and region of the world to guide mankind. If so, the people of, say, India and China, are as much the people of the book as the people of Palestine. Why then should their women be excluded from marrying Muslim men? Second, the one-sided permission of Muslim men to marry Jewish or Christian women does not make sense. Muslim commentators and jurists defend this asymmetrical permission of inter-religious marriage on the ground that the male partner will dominate the upbringing of the children who will automatically become Muslims. But this reasoning assumes that the influence of the father upon the progeny is invariably greater than that of the mother. This assumption is, however, not borne out by actual experience. Quite often the mother plays a more dominant and inspiring role in the education and training of her progeny. It is, therefore, a facile view that the spiritual health of the family will remain satisfactory if a Muslim male is married to a non-Muslim but not if a Muslim women is married to a non-Muslim. In the final analysis, the character and integrity of the spouses and their temperamental compatibility, quite irrespective of their professed religions, will determine the spiritual and material well being of the family.

Let us now turn to the Quranic verse, 2:221. The prohibition of marriage in this verse applies symmetrically to idolaters and idolatresses. According to the traditional Islamic approach the prohibition applies to an entire group labeled as 'idolaters' or 'polytheists' rather than to individuals on the basis of their actual beliefs and practice. This approach, however, ignores the crucial fact that it is always a person or individual who practices idolatry or abstains from it, the group having no existence apart from the individuals composing it. In other words, the proper object of the judgment in question or the proper referent of the Quranic prohibition ought to be individuals rather than an entire group as such.

Moreover, and this consideration is equally crucial, every large religious group always comprises subgroups or sects based upon internal distinctions or differences of various kinds. As a result of these internal distinctions any blanket dichotomous classification of the members of the group becomes extremely misleading. For instance, Hindus who belong to the *Brahmo Samaj* and *Arya Samaj* reject idolatry as much and as categorically as the Muslims themselves. The same applies to the Sikhs. Why, then, should they be subject to the Quranic prohibition on marriage of Muslims and idolaters? Again, numerous individual Hindus repudiate idolatry both in theory and practice, though they do not object if their co-religionists wish to practice it. In other words, it does not stand to reason to hold the entire Hindu community or group to be idolaters.

In the light of the above analysis it appears that the correct or valid interpretation of the Quranic text would be that a Muslim should not marry such Hindus who are idolaters. Now this is a very different proposition from placing a total and unconditional ban upon inter-marriage between members of the different religious groups. To put the matter more directly, the deciding factor for attracting the clear Quranic prohibition should be the actual faith and practice of the parties to the marriage rather than any blanket judgment on the community as a whole. Let me try to explain my point by giving a hypothetical example.

Suppose the Quran had prohibited Muslims from marrying a liar without specifying any other details. It is pre-eminently reasonable to hold that this prohibition would have applied to individual liars rather than to any particular group based on religion, region or race. Moreover, the proper way to act upon the Quranic injunction would have been actually to investigate whether or not a person is a liar rather than declare any particular religious, racial, regional or occupational group as liars who automatically attract the said Quranic prohibition.

There is another very vital consideration, which would confirm the rightness of the view that the Quranic text must be interpreted, as applicable to individuals rather than a group as a whole. The Quranic verse 5:5 allows inter-marriage between Muslims and the 'people of the book', while the verse, 2:221 prohibits Muslims from marrying idolaters and idolatresses. Now, while the Jews are conspicuous for their absolute repudiation of idol worship and their unqualified acceptance of pure monotheism, the same cannot be said of the Christians because of their commitment to the dogma of trinity. Indeed, numerous Islamic theologians honestly believe that the said Christian dogma involves associating others with the one God and that this amounts to polytheism (*shirk*). If so, the marriage of a Muslim male with a Christian woman (deemed permissible by verse 5:5) would attract the prohibition contained in verse 2:221. Now this would land Muslims in a quandary. The only way to resolve this contradiction is to accept the view that the concerned Quranic verses apply to individuals rather than to groups as a whole. On this interpretation the marriage of a Muslim, whether male or female, would be permissible with a non-Muslim provided he or she is not a polytheist and does not practice idolatry.

Marriage is a contractual relationship between two individuals, according to Islam. If the contractual parties do not stand in the list of prohibited degrees of marriage, as given in the Quranic text, as such, (Quran, 4:22-23) differences in race, religion, caste, and economic status should not stand in the way of their marriage, provided the non-Muslim party has clearly repudiated idol-worship in theory and practice. A Muslim marrying a non-Muslim does not violate any basic tenet of Islam so long as the non-Muslim, as an individual, does not commit himself or herself to idolatry.

The Islamic canon law (*shariah*) already allows Muslim males to marry Jewish or Christian women. This amounts to accepting, in principle, the idea of inter-religious marriage. This step was a notable, rather a revolutionary, advance made by Islam in the direction of the humanistic concept of marriage as a loving contract between individuals irrespective of their religion. There is nothing wrong for Muslims to develop the nucleus of the humanistic approach to marriage, already found in the Islamic tradition, to its full and logical conclusion.

The above suggestion will not appeal to conservative Muslim opinion. But new interpretations within a tradition, provided they are essentially productive of human welfare, gradually overcome the natural and quite understandable resistance to change. The following is a random but good sample.

Muslim theologians at one time opposed the printing of the Quran and also books in general. The same applied to translating the Quran in different languages. Many Muslim and Catholic theologians are still opposed to family planning. Several Muslim theologians and jurists oppose music, drama, and painting of animal forms on various grounds. The pursuit of free enquiry, the freedom of conscience, and equal rights to women are deemed to be unIslamic by many learned Muslims. Yet profound changes, slowly but steadily, have taken place in different Muslim societies. It is a different matter that the pace of change has been slow to the point of exasperation, if not despair. However, the pace is likely to increase considerably due to the continuing technological revolution, in general, and the communications revolution in particular.

The thought and value systems of Christianity and Hinduism have responded much more positively and vigorously to the requirements and demands of the modern age. But, unfortunately Islam has been left behind in the quest for a suitable reconstruction of its basic concepts and values to meet new challenges posed by the contemporary human situation. Creative Christian and Hindu scholars and savants have projected their religions in a manner that could claim an almost universal appeal. But most Muslim scholars and divines still equate the medieval Islamic paradigm with the essence of the Islamic faith. To them, any creative response in the sphere of

Quranic interpretation amounts to the stretching and twisting of the Word of God for the sake of worldly gains or making a better 'adjustment' to the anti-Islamic powers of the day. However, I honestly and respectfully submit that the humanistic interpretation of the Quranic texts on the subject of inter-religious marriage is an intrinsically valid insight rather than a mere pragmatic adjustment to the present global society marked by emerging democratic pluralism.

## (II)

Let us now consider the main purely social psychological and cultural objections to inter-marriage.

Perhaps, the most common objection is that children of a mixed marriage are exposed to conflicting religious and moral messages in their formative years due to the opposed beliefs and practices of their parents and wider family members. If both the parents are indifferent to religion than children are spared the evil effects of the divided concerns of their parents, but then they are in the danger of losing all concern for religious and spiritual values altogether. It is further said that religious differences may not prove detrimental in the early years of marriage. But with the passage of time the mischief begins unless one of the spouses subordinates him or herself to the other. The argument goes on to say that while a lot of adjustment is needed in every marriage (even when the couple profess the same religion) the degree and type of adjustment required in an inter-religious marriage become forbidding.

I shall first deal with the social psychological argument and then come to the cultural side of the issue of inter-marriage. It is true that the possession of a common or similar religious background is very helpful in promoting family harmony. But having a common or similar cultural and economic background is no less important. However, the single most important pre-condition of a happy and harmonious family life is temperamental and sexual compatibility of the spouses. In the absence of this compatibility a common religion will be of little avail.

The objection that the clash of religious rituals, ceremonies and festivals prevents the couple from sharing their religious life does not hold good. Sympathetic participation in each other's religious or spiritual world is quite possible even without a common commitment. This type of loving and active sympathy indeed gives immense joy and elevates the human spirit. To give a personal instance, I once happened to travel in the same railway compartment as a distinguished Hindu lawyer of Aligarh. He was known to be an atheist in his circle of friends. As soon as the train reached the Ramganga Bridge, near Bareilly, my friend took out some coins, placed them in the hands of his wife and then threw them into the river below in the orthodox Hindu fashion. Soon afterwards the atheist lawyer gently explained to me that he had done so solely out of respect for his wife and that he himself did not at all approve of this form of venerating river goddesses.

The sympathetic understanding of the faith of another deepens one's own religious faith and promotes the oneness of the human family. True understanding does not necessarily lead to actual commitment. But it enables one to pass from the outer ritual or symbol to the inner core of the faith and to see the world as it appears to the believer. The sympathetic understanding of different faiths does not necessarily waken one's own and does not necessarily make one indifferent to religion. Genuine and sincere communication based on mutual respect actually nourishes one's own faith, to the extent that it is genuine and meets with the inner approval of a mind, which has freed itself from the invisible chains of dogma and the fear of society. The awareness of other religions and communication with their believers dissipates one's own faith only to the extent that it is sheer imitation or cultural conditioning without authentic commitment. That is why it sometimes happens that a superficial verbalization of one's own creed (instilled in early childhood) becomes a deep and living creed, for the first time, only when we come under the influence of a really elevated soul though his formal religion differs from our own.

I shall now examine the view that religious faith cannot flourish in adult life unless parents and teachers inculcate it in the childhood or early youth. Though it is a fact that a religious creed is learnt by the child as he learns the language, manners, morals and music of his group he can grasp the thought and value system concerned, if at all, only when he reaches adulthood. In the final analysis, religion is the depth response of a mature individual to the mystery of man in the universe. Parents can only indoctrinate the child; they cannot lead the child to experience the basic religious feeling of awe and wonder when man contemplates the inscrutable mystery of the universe. Now many psychologists and teachers who are themselves deeply religious souls have come to the conclusion that giving the child objective and sympathetic acquaintance with the major religious traditions of the human family (with special emphasis upon one's own cherished tradition) gives a better religious foundation to the child than sheer indoctrination into a single religious creed. Indeed, some of the most eminent Christian thinkers of our times hold that children should be taught only basic morality, and theology or dogma should wait the advent of maturity. Even more important than the verbal inculcation of moral values is the actual example set by the words and deeds of the role models accepted by the child. Since religions differ primarily in their theology rather than in their ethics parents professing different religions should have no problem in teaching basic moral principles to the children.

The best way of inculcating moral and spiritual values in the children is to relate to them stories or anecdotes that bring out the meaning of the values in a concrete fashion and also motivate or inspire the child to act accordingly. Parents could easily make use of different religious traditions but lay special stress upon their own heroes. As and when the child matures the parents could explain their respective creeds with candor and sympathy, and encourage him to make his own independent choice when he embarks upon adulthood.

Parents and society in general should respect the authentic choice of every adult, even if it be against any particular religious tradition or against religion as such. To the extent that parents encourage the child or the youth to attain to a state of spiritual autonomy and inner honesty they guide the child into the portals of true religion and into the arms of Divinity. No religious creed can, possibly, be proved in the logical or scientific sense. It is, therefore, essential to accept and tolerate the diversity of faiths not as a thorn in the rose but as different flowers in the garden of the human family. Even the total rejection of religion, provided moral values are not abandoned, should be fully tolerated by the parents and by society. Neither the fear of parents, nor the fear of society, nor the lure of worldly gain should constrain the authentic choice of the individual in regard to religion.

The above condition of the soul is beautifully illustrated by an anecdote from the life of Bibi Rabia Basri (d. 801 AD) perhaps, the greatest woman *Sufi* saint in Islamic history. The people of Baghdad once saw her walking on a street while carrying a plate of burning coals in one hand, and a jug of water in the other. When asked for this strange behavior she replied that the coals were meant to burn heaven, and the water was meant to quench the fire of hell, so that humans may neither crave for paradise, nor fear hell, and just act righteously out of love for God.

Belief in God greatly reinforces man's quest for moral and spiritual values. But it is not logically necessary for the good life. Some adults are unable to find God when they try to unravel the mystery of the universe, while some do. One should not try to patronize God by taking upon oneself the duty to establish His existence. God, if He exists, can silence and convince the greatest atheist. True faith is never the product of indoctrination or baptism; it springs froth from man's authentic depths. Not the habitual and conventional verbalization of a creed, but rather a sincere and passionate quest for truth, in the spirit of humility and prayerful receptivity is the way, which brings man to God. Consequently, children who have been brought up in the atmosphere of total truthfulness, respect and tolerance of different points of view, and who have been encouraged to discover their own deepest truth will arrive, in the fullness of time, to a condition of 'peace that passeth understanding'.

Mankind is, potentially, one family, and different religions represent diverse responses to the mystery of the cosmos. Cultural pluralism is not an evil that need to be eliminated. Different religions are different languages of the spirit and can well co-exist just like different natural languages. Those who oppose the idea of inter-religious marriage denude the concept of the oneness of the human family of a vital and crucial dimension. This oneness will remain incomplete if religious plurality is allowed to remain an insuperable barrier against the union of persons who may yearn to share their life in permanent togetherness.

The removal of different prejudices and disabilities on grounds of sex, race, religion, caste, etc. is necessary, but not enough to bring about the full brotherhood of man in all respects. The opposition to inter-marriage is the last and final obstacle in the way of the full unity of the human family based on the principle of cultural pluralism and unqualified tolerance, rather than upon its convergence on any particular religion or ideology.

The belief in the oneness of the human family and the unconditional dignity and quality of all individuals will remain incomplete if inter-religious marriage is not accepted as fully permissible. Marriage is the most intimate form of human association. Only when persons belonging to diverse races, regions, religions or castes readily can strike bonds of friendship and love and feel free to unite themselves in marriage, if they so desire, only then the idea of the oneness of the human family could be said to have turned into a living reality from a mere slogan or empty verbalization. The inner acceptance, rather than the mere grudging toleration of inter-marriage is the acid test of one's belief that all mankind constitutes one family.

# Essay 9

## Sex Morality And Islam

### (I)

In this article I wish to discuss the Western liberal approach to sex morality and to ascertain to what extent it is in harmony with the essential Quranic approach, despite their seeming differences.

Sex morality has always been the central concern of all great religious and moral teachers. As we know, the ideal of chastity and the condemnation of adultery have dominated man's thinking from time immemorial. In fact until very recently the vast majority of the human race thought that an unchaste person could not be morally good or virtuous at all. Though norms of sex morality were frequently broken such violations were shrouded in an atmosphere of fear and secrecy. Moreover, the fear of the social consequences of extra-marital pregnancy was as great, (if not greater) a restraining factor for man and woman than the fear of violating God's commandments.

All this has gradually changed in Western society, which has become extremely permissive in the sphere of sex morality. This does not mean that it has become immoral, but only that it permits the individual to choose his or her own norms of good behavior in a matter deemed to be the private and personal concern of the individual. Barring rape, fraud and bigamy the individual is left free to choose his or her own code of sexual conduct. The case is rather analogous with the permissive approach in the sphere of religious belief and practice. Just as an individual in Western society feels perfectly free to believe or not to believe in God or life after death and has no embarrassment in declaring his authentic beliefs (whatever they might be), so also does he feel free in choosing or not choosing chastity as a major value of life.

The same applies to other personal matters like food and drink, dress, entertainments etc. This freedom to choose one's own values has given rise to such new institutions as life companionship, companionate marriage, single parenthood, homosexuality, apart, of course, from romantic affairs and casual sex.

The above permissive approach to sex morality should not be equated with sexual chaos or amorality, since it merely affirms the value of man's inner freedom to choose rather than any particular choice as such. It is held, that a person who freely chooses chastity and marital fidelity as basic values and a person who chooses otherwise may both be morally excellent persons, worthy of our respect, to the extent that they possess other virtues such as truthfulness, kindness, loyalty, integrity etc. Thus the thrust of a permissive society is not that values don't matter or that one choice is as good as another in all spheres of life, but only that in personal matters like religious faith, artistic taste, sexual conduct, in so far as it is based on mutual consent, the individual should be free to choose his own values. In other words, the permissive society stands for plural value systems rather than the imposition of a single code or the rejection of all values as such.

## (II)

What exactly is the Western liberal sex morality and how did it gradually displace the Victorian mores? The Victorian sex morality was centered on the values of female modesty and chastity with considerable latitude enjoyed by the male sex. This double standard was commonly justified on the ground that un-chastity did not cause any harm to the male, but rather added to his worldly experience and confidence in discharging his duties as the head of the family, while the fair sex, as the weaker vessel, would be utterly ruined by sex outside the sacred bonds of marriage. Monogamy and the indissolubility of the marriage bond (except on grounds of adultery or impotence) were the other two basic ingredients of the Victorian mores or rather of Christian sex morality. The Christian sex morality was an integral part of an inclusive spiritual weltanshauung and value system, which held that man, could not know and pursue the good and the right without God's grace and guidance in the form of a revealed rule-centered morality. This approach gradually developed in Western Europe into the modern scientific humanistic outlook, which stood for a value-centered morality. Humanism or liberalism, in this very broad sense, is just a critical or reflective attitude of mind rather than any specific system of ideas. This attitude which is characterized by a spirit of free enquiry, concern for moral values and tolerance of rival religious creeds was jointly produced by the impact of natural sciences and technology and of social sciences in the 19th century.

The remarkable progress of the social sciences and the global access of Western scholars and thinkers made them familiar with diverse value systems of the entire human family. Abandoning the earlier Christian missionary approach of trying to convert the human family to the one true religion, these scholars and social scientists came to view the different value systems of the human family with sympathetic understanding. They tried to probe into the 'survival-value' of the customs and rites of different wings of the human family, instead of dismissing them as immoral perversions of the barbarian world. Thus polygamy, polyandry, group-marriage, temporary marriage, puberty rites, female circumcision and so on became the objects of objective anthropological studies.

The approach of *'anthropological detachment'* could not but be applied, in the course of time, to Christian sexual mores themselves. Social scientists were soon discussing the survival value of the near universal disapproval of incest, adultery and the prevalence of a double standard of morality for men and women. At about the same time medical and technological progress brought about what may well be called the *'contraceptive revolution'*, that is, man's ability to control conception at will without renouncing sexuality, or man's ability to separate sex from parenthood.

The contraceptive revolution has brought about a qualitative change in the human situation, apart from family planning and control over the growth of the human population. Controlled conception has liberated one half of the human race from the fear and misery of unwanted child bearing and rearing, to the almost total exclusion of other human pursuits. Secondly, it has transformed sexual intercourse, as a mechanism for procreation or, as relief from physical tension, into a language of loving communion between the sexes, independent, of the function of procreation. In other words, man's control over conception has given a new meaning and dimension to sex and marriage. It is indeed significant that the concept of romantic marriage, that is, marriage as a romantic union between equal companions jointly seeking total self-realization was not known in the ancient or medieval world which kept love and marriage as entirely separate and relegated women to a subordinate position. The contemporary idea of romantic marriage, at its best, presupposes the equal dignity of the sexes and capacity and right of woman for a life of intellectual, moral and spiritual creativity apart from the function and duty of motherhood to which traditionally she had been confined. The factors mentioned above combined to usher in what may be called the Western liberal sex morality whose chief features will presently be described.

## (III)

The natural biological consequence of sex union is the creation of new life whose sustenance and maintenance should naturally be the responsibility of the parents. Without accepting this responsibility sexual intercourse becomes mere satisfaction of impulse without acknowledging duties flowing therefrom. The core justification for confining sex activity within the bonds of marriage is precisely the identification of paternity and fixing of responsibility for the maintenance of the family.

Now, adultery violates the fundamental ethical principle that there should be no procreation without acknowledgment of responsibility, since extra-marital intercourse renders the issue of paternity quite uncertain. The moral indignation of the lawful husband and his refusal to be economically burdened by the consequences flowing from the action of another person are thus quite understandable. This is the real psychological and economic basis of the strong and near universal disapproval of adultery and free sex and of the stress upon marital fidelity in different forms of marriage: monogamous, polygamous or polyandrous, as the case may be.

Allowing that the evil of adultery and extra-marital sex is due to the impossibility or difficulty of fixing of the paternity of and financial responsibility for the offspring, the question arises whether or not extra-marital sex is also a moral evil *per se*, that is, evil in the intrinsic and not merely in the instrumental sense? Far from being a purely academic or technical question, this is a very vital practical issue. If one holds that sexual intercourse with consent is not an evil *per se*, then why should adultery or extra-marital sex be deemed to be morally wrong if conception is avoided and if none of the persons concerned has any objection? On the other hand, if one holds that sex, without marriage, is an intrinsic evil it would unconditionally and invariably be evil like, say, rape, murder, fraud, malice and so on, even if there be no procreation of children or any other evil consequences.

This is a basic and crucial issue. Obviously, even the framing of this question was not possible or permissible within the framework of medieval Christian rule-centered morality. And when there was no question, obviously there was no need for any answer one way or the other. But with the advance of independent ethical reflection and value-centered morality associated with the rise of humanism in the late 18th and succeeding centuries some of the most earnest and ablest Western savants gradually converged to the rather revolutionary view that non-procreative sexual intercourse with consent (provided no prevarication or deceit be involved) was not an evil, *per se*, even though it may well be an instrumental evil.

This approach made a clear distinction between sexual intercourse and rape, judging the former to be ethically neutral (in the intrinsic sense) while the latter to be an intrinsic evil, like say, murder, theft or under weighing etc. These actions fill us with feelings of moral revulsion and disapproval quite independently of their being prohibited by most religions. The more we probe our inmost self to determine the depth and persistence of our moral revulsion at the idea of say, murder, ingratitude towards a benefactor, disloyalty or treachery against a friend, business fraud or adulteration, deliberate punishment of an innocent person falsely accused, and so on, the greater becomes our inner certainty of the validity of our moral judgment.

Now the case with adultery is different. To begin with, the unsophisticated Christian or Muslim does feel a deep revulsion against sexual intercourse, outside marriage just as he does in the case of the evils mentioned above. But calm and detached moral reflection often modifies his absolute condemnation of adultery as evil *per se*, even though he may continue to disapprove of sex outside marriage. He may become perplexed whether extra-marital intercourse is an intrinsic evil, like rape or adulteration or whether it is after all only instrumental evil that is, usually productive of bad consequences for the individuals concerned and also society at large. The case is analogous with our reaction to say, polyandry, that is, the legalized marriage of one woman with more than one male. To begin with, the concept of polyandry strikes us as immoral and repulsive or sinful (if we are used to speak the, language of religion). But calm and detached reflection on the socio-economic conditions and legal aspects of polyandry softens our initial revulsion, enabling us to view it as a possibly satisfactory social system in conditions very different from those prevailing in monogamous or polygamous societies. In other words, polyandry ceases to appear to us as an absolute intrinsic evil, even though we may still disapprove of it for ourselves.

Now what are the undesirable consequences flowing from extra-marital sex, according to Western thinkers? Firstly, if the individual does not have the courage to own the truth about himself this erodes his basic integrity of character and leads to a secretive double-faced lifestyle. Secondly, extra-marital sex may lead to procreation without acknowledgment of paternity and responsibility for the offspring. This evil would not result if conception is scrupulously avoided or if the woman has no objection to accepting the responsibility of supporting offspring of the union by herself. Thirdly, extra-marital sex, in the absence of a firm commitment by the partners may lead to an unrequited longing on the part of either for a socially approved permanent union which may not be feasible due to constraints on either side. This leads to a tormenting predicament, which tends to destroy one's peace of mind and capacity for productive work.

The above evils would not result if sex is de-linked with love or a commitment to share each other's lives. But sex without love becomes mere sensation (no matter howsoever enjoyable) and a mere physical transaction or game. Only when sex and love are fused with each other does sexual intercourse become a rite of worshipful union of bodies, a physical symbol of total loyalty and spiritual merger of separate ego hoods, a language of the soul that transports the lovers into the domain of the mystical. And is not mystical ecstasy the deepest bliss humans can taste, if there be any truth in the claims of poets, mystics and saints of all religions? But, then can all persons be expected to have a taste or preference for the mystical, even as can all be expected to have an ear for rhythm or an eye for color harmony? The answer is obvious.

The conclusion of the above analysis is that while rape and deceptive sexual relations are clearly moral evils, there seems to be no clear answer to the question whether extra-marital consensual sex between adults who, otherwise, are absolutely guileless and open to each other and to society is also an intrinsic evil. Under these conditions, liberal thinkers in the West have converged to the view that every individual must probe his or her own authentic conscience, and society must respect that answer.

## (IV)

Let us now analyze the Islamic approach to sex morality. The Islamic ethos gives a high value to sexual fulfillment of man and woman through the institution of marriage, which is not deemed to be an obstacle in the path of spiritual attainments. The Quran also permits much greater freedom and ease of divorce, polygamy, and sexual relations with female slaves with or without marriage, and *Shia* Islam also permits temporary marriage (*muta*), an ancient Arab custom that was given up by *Sunni* Islam. Thus, on the whole, Islamic sexual ethics is 'instinct-affirming' and permissive rather than 'instinct-denying' and repressive. However, it has almost banned the social association of the sexes and it has also gone back to the old Jewish custom of stoning unto death as a penalty for adultery. In some respects, therefore the Islamic approach has been repressive. Perhaps the almost total social segregation of the sexes and the deterrent penalties of flogging and stoning were intended to prevent, as far as humanly possible, the evil of adultery.

Let us now turn to the Quranic concept of marriage. According to the Quran, as also the Pre-Islamic Arab mores, marriage is not a mystical or sacramental indissoluble union (as in the case of Hinduism and Christianity) but essentially a contractual obligation, (intended to be permanent but terminable by the male partner) to 'cohabit', and jointly to maintain the offspring of the union. Further, while the male is permitted to enter into such a contract with more than one female at a time, the woman is permitted only one contractual partner at any point of time. This is the essential core of marriage, according to Islam. The religious ceremony, presence of witnesses, the public declaration and celebration of the contract, though all recommended, are dispensable adjuncts of the essential core of marriage, namely a proposal by one party (whether male or female) and its acceptance by the other based on some 'consideration' or other.

An accurate analysis shows that the thrust of the Quranic text lies in prohibiting secret or casual sexual relationships without any commitment or consequential responsibility flowing there from. Indeed, the permissibility of polygamy, sexual relations with one's female slaves, the simple and easy method of divorce (though only from the vantage point of the male partner), the encouragement of remarriage of widows and divorced women and finally, the permissibility of temporary marriage (though the practice is confined to *Shia* Islam only) all go to show the permissive and liberal approach to sex expression. However, adultery is severely condemned and is punishable by hundred lashes of the whip, provided four witnesses testify to the deed. Again, the Quran lays great emphasis upon the clear identification of paternity by prohibiting women to remarry immediately after divorce or the death of their husbands.

Since the Quranic ethos lays great stress upon paternal identification, prostitution, casual sex, extramarital affairs are all patently un-Islamic. But to the extent that conception is avoided the degree of the evil would be proportionately reduced. Such activities make a Muslim believer untruthful and hypocritical and truth and authenticity are the fundamental values of the Quran.

## (V)

To my mind, the spirit of the Quranic contract for marriage may well be present in a genuine and responsible partnership even without any formal religious or legal ceremony or protocol. However, signing a written protocol or giving solemn oral consent makes it psychologically easier to honor the agreement. In other words, what is called civil marriage (under secular auspices) or even common law marriage is not some act that can be said to be evil in terms of reflective morality. However, extramarital intercourse, especially when one or both partners are already married becomes morally objectionable the moment secrecy or deception enter into the relationship at any level whatsoever. The basic evil of adultery lies in the fact that it seriously endangers the inner integrity and transparency of the character of the persons concerned. Adultery also causes much hurt and pain to innocent victims of secrecy and breach of contract.

The Quran prescribes flogging as a penalty for adultery provided four reliable witnesses testify to the deed. But this condition makes the penalty almost inoperative in practice for quite obvious reasons. The net result of this proviso is to throw men and women back into the realm of pure morality when dealing with such private and intimate actions that never or hardly ever get registered by observes. No law can touch or detect what goes on in the minds of men and their fancies or their private acts away from public perception. By the very nature of the case, only inner constraint, not law can regulate sexual behavior. The inner check may come from fear of God or from authentic commitment to basic values. Both can be present at the same time. But flogging is a poor teacher in a matter that requires spiritual education and nurture rather than fear of the rod. This is the crux of the modern permissive approach to sex morality.

State censorship (as is found in Saudi Arabia), vigilance squads and public punishments produce only terrified puritans or hypocrites, who are held in check by fear, rather than motivated by respect for the moral law. Like the rest of humankind, Muslim society has no workable choice except adopting a permissible approach to sex morality in preference to a harsh legalistic one.

It seems to me that the time has also come for intellectually honest and honest to God Muslims to face squarely the data now available in respect of the considerable incidence of a natural or congenital homosexual orientation among both men and women. The evidence is now too strong to keep matters under the carpet any longer. We all know that until very recently the phenomenon of left handed children was viewed as an unfortunate perversion and parents went out of their way to root out this ugly trait or tendency in some children. Scientific advance has now confirmed that neural circuitry is by no means absolutely uniform in the human species and considerable variations and mutation are found in nature. In all humility and earnestness I submit that harsh condemnations of a congenital homosexual orientation as a heinous vice or abominable evil is no longer justifiable in the light of reliable statistics of inborn homosexual traits from birth.

The modern global industrial society is gradually pushing all religious groups (including Muslims) into accepting the permissive approach to sex morality. The new ethos of human rights and gender equality is turning segregation of women a thing of the past and encouraging the marriage of free choice and family planning. The ethic of marriage as a romantic workable union between more or less economically independent and equal partners is bound to disturb the traditional self-image of the male as the dominant bread-winner and the female as the loyal homemaker and helpmate. The greater the professional attainments and economic independence of the female the more difficult it becomes for her to accept the traditional secondary role as the junior partner in marriage. Nor is it natural and easy for her to accept double standards of marital fidelity after the contraceptive revolution. It is almost inevitable that marriage breakdowns become far more common than they ever were earlier.

The empowerment of women, however, cannot be arrested in the name of domestic harmony and family values by any religious tradition, just as we cannot turn our back to the industrial age in the name of any religious utopia. Humanity can only go ahead with full awareness of the complexities of the human situation and deep spiritual faith in the Unseen Creator and Sustainer of cosmic harmony.

## (VI)

A few observations may be offered at this point on the puritan approach to life in general. Religious puritans arise when any large human group begins to suffer from emotional and economic deprivation, helpless frustration and despair. They begin to devalue or almost reject the softer values of love, compassion, aesthetic delight, and the inner peace and joy of being human. Sheer anger and desperation impels them to overturn the apple cart when they think they have no share in the apples. Sheer anger distorts their judgment and everything becomes rotten for them except their own version of whatever religion they happen to profess. And a negative Puritanism becomes their last refuge from the unbearable pressures, tensions and frustrations of their lot in life. This is how and why the 'Taliban's' among different religious groups reject music, dance, painting, love and romance in literature, innocent gender free social mixing, the pleasures of the palate and contact with nature and several other entertainments and sports. Their moral and spiritual growth, thus, remains ever stunted and fails to reach the higher level of inner-directed discipline that is very different from fear based external control.

Puritanism, as traditionally understood in Islamic circles, is not an integral part of the Quranic ethos. Nowhere does the Quran prohibit the fine arts. Why, then, did the puritanical temper become rather strongly entrenched in orthodox Islam? Well, Muslim theologians and jurists projected personal or regional biases or temporal value patterns on Quranic texts as well as the reported sayings and doings of the Prophet. Pious and sincere as were the learned Islamic divines of the past, their fallibility and limitations should be patently clear to the intellectually honest Muslim believer.

In all humility I would like to recall that the penalty of stoning unto death, banning art forms and music, belief in the exclusive salvation of Muslims, the death penalty for apostasy, opposition to contraception, the total segregation of women, and so on, do not find any clear mention in the Quran and yet they become rather well established components in the thought and value system of medieval Islam.

Rulers and affluent classes all over the world have paid scant attention to puritan protests and warnings, and, most likely, they never will. Perhaps, the show will go on as usual. However, I am quite optimistic that the Muslim world today stands at the threshold of a new paradigm of Quranic Islam minus the gloss of medieval ideas and values, and the most tragic Shia-Sunni schism. This paradigm will certainly not be a patchwork synthesis or an imitation of Western modernity. It will be an organic and orthogenetic understanding of the Quran in the light of timeless Spirit-centered Humanism and the interfaith movement of modern times.

# Essay 10

## Modern Penology* and Islam

### (I)

### Introduction

The political emancipation of Muslim countries from Western domination and their newly acquired democratic freedom has moved Muslim religious leaders and intellectuals to ponder the meaning of the good life according to Islam and how Muslim countries and peoples should shape their political, economic and social institutions in the modern age. The suppressed and deprived sections of Muslims long back had grown demoralized and alienated from the technologically and politically dominant West. It was, therefore, quite natural that after the end of colonial rule their religious leaders and intellectuals should address themselves to questions and issues of Islamic polity in the widest sense rather than to content themselves merely with Islamic piety or theology. This is the essential rationale of the different movements of Islamic reform and resurgence all over the Muslim world in the first quarter of the last century after the sprawling Ottoman empire disintegrated and the charismatic and victorious Mustafa Kamal stamped his own radical ideas upon an unwilling but hypnotized and grateful fellow-Turks. Turkey was the last surviving sovereign Muslim state in the modern age, but Kamal ordered it to embrace a fully secular constitution. And his wish became law. However, as we all know, the Turkish mind is still groping for a fully integrated vision of a good Muslim in a secular state. This is true of Muslims all over the world.

---

\* *The study of the punishment of crime, in both its deterrent and its reformatory aspects.*

Abul Aala Mawdudi (d.1979) is, perhaps, the most illustrious symbol of this very understandable trend in Islamic self-understanding and creative religious thinking. Now there is a lot of talk of Islamic economics, Islamic democracy and the Islamic legal system including Penology. Some Islamic quarters stand for enforcing medieval Islamic sanctions and penalties for theft and adultery in preference to the modern ameliorative and educative approach. These quarters hold that the Western approach has failed to deliver despite the vastly improved material conditions of human life. Such Muslim thinkers and leaders want the prevailing Western system of justice and the laws to be Islamized in the light of the Quran and the shariah. They want the shariah to be dynamic, but they are not prepared to question the diarchy of traditional Islam, which brackets the 'Book and the Example' (Kitaab wal Sunnah) as almost coeval Authorities for the true Muslim. On the other hand, some Islamic quarters honestly feel and believe that modifying the plain and simple directive or imperative verses of the Quran on any ground whatever amounts to saying that human reasoning is superior to that of God; Who has ordained them in the Quran. These quarters, thus, say that if flogging the criminal (avowedly a Quranic penalty) or stoning unto death as a penalty for adultery (not mentioned in the Quran but sanctioned by the traditional shariah) had really violated human dignity or had been really harmful to humankind, God would never have prescribed them in the Quran. In what follows I wish to examine these lines of thinking and present an integrated Islamic approach to Modern Penology.

## (II)

Crime and punishment of crime are timeless and inseparable features of the human situation. Another timeless and universal feature is the belief that crime ought to be punished in the best interests of the victim or victims in question as well as of society in general. The foundational assumption is that the act of punishment gives a measure of psychological relief; sense of satisfaction and security to the victim while the fear of punishment deters others and prevents further crimes.

The primitive form of punishment was to subject the criminal to physical pain of graduated intensity or to deprive the wrongdoer of some limb or part of the body, and in extreme cases, deprive him of his right to live. Thus the hand was cut off as a penalty for theft, the tongue for telling a lie, the feet or leg for trespass, the sex organs for fornication and so on. Eyes were also gouged as an extreme punishment, just short of executing or fatally poisoning the criminal.

The Quran does not contain any penal code as such, nor does it state any theory of punishment explaining the why and what of the proper punishment. The Quran merely prescribes penalties for three or four crimes/sins. It was, therefore, quite natural and inevitable that the Prophet and the earliest Muslims follow the Arab customary laws, unless the Quran prohibited them. The above-mentioned position is beyond contention. What needs pointing out is that the Quran could not, possibly, have prescribed any punishments or penalties that could not have been applied in practice at the then (rather primitive) stage of Arab polity and society. In other words, Quranic penalties had to be simple measures to compensate the victim and deter others. This is the rationale of the few penalties the Quran actually prescribes, such as capital punishment, flogging, amputation of the hand of the thief, house detention for errant females, non-admissibility of evidence offered by malicious accusers. (It is significant that the Quran does not mention stoning unto death as a penalty for adultery). Primitive penalties did not require sophisticated social-economic infrastructures for their implementation, while modern penalties like, secure imprisonment, confiscation of assets, declaration of insolvency, cancellation of voting rights, and so on were inconceivable in earlier times.

# (III)

A little reflection suffices to show that different forms of punishments are, in essence, instrumental rules for promoting social welfare in terms of a set of basic intrinsic values. A deep and unconditional concern to promote basic intrinsic values in the individual and society is the mother of all other virtues and values. It is, therefore, vitally important to ensure that the laws and forms of punishment should actually serve and promote the intrinsic values as such. It is just not enough merely to apply a ready-made set of penalties or instrumental rules, without caring to know whether, at any given point of time and place, they really or effectively do promote the basic values they were meant to promote. Further reflection will also show that instrumental rules whatever their area of concern: administration, economy, law and order, education, individual personal growth, etc. must be treated as subsidiary to the fundamental values they are meant to promote.

Fundamental spiritual and moral values are timeless transcendental truths that cannot be proved and that do not require any proof. Like the axioms of logic or mathematics, they shine by their own light and elicit our inner acceptance or conviction of their validity or truth. Instrumental rules, on the contrary, ever need to be checked or verified for their effectiveness or reliability at any given point of time. In general, any truth-claim that is not self-evident or cannot be logically deduced from some self-evident truth, but spills over into the realm of facts cannot be accepted as unconditionally valid without some evidence or proof.

Modern Penology makes a serious and systematic attempt to study the different types of penalties that can be implemented now but which could not have been carried out in earlier times. These social scientists and reformers first ascertain the causes of crime, its types and categories, make an estimate of the degree of evil or harm of different crimes and the most effective ways of punishment as well as of prevention of crime. They take into account the concepts and insights of Sociology, Psychology and Ethics in the complex task of suggesting a rational and comprehensive penal code based on a careful estimation of the degrees of evil involved in various crimes or wrongs and the most effective ways of preventing or reducing crime as such.

Social philosophers and reformers have come to the conclusion that no single line of attack on the problem of crime leads to optimum results. Thus, giving prime importance to the objective of deterrence without educating and reforming the criminal (on the assumption that the severity of the penalty, by itself, will deter others) does not yield optimum results. Likewise, the implementation of traditionally prescribed punishments without attempting to address the social and economic factors that breed crime leads to poor results. Our approach, therefore, must be multi-dimensional. Western administrators and reformers themselves are not happy at their limited success in controlling the crime rate in different fields. Some time back they were inclined to believe that poverty was the main or prime causal factor of crime. But the high incidence of what has come to be called 'white collar crime' clearly shows that this view is an over-simplification of a complex issue.

Some evidence, therefore, is needed to decide whether flogging or amputation of organs really prevents crimes and improves the total quality of life of individuals and of society as a whole. Such issues can be resolved only when one is willing to think with an open mind and give due importance to reliable empirical data rather than resorting to mere abstract argumentation.

To my mind, the authentic Muslim believer must undertake this task with prayerful humility and the pure search for truth. The Quran itself says that the Creator blessed His apex creation with the capacity for acquiring knowledge and wisdom and with the gift of freedom to choose between good and evil. To my mind, faith in God implies faith in His wisdom when he gave the gift of potential freedom to humankind. Thereby the Creator raised humankind even above His angels. The seeds of both good and evil are present in the human constitution, but the good, by far, predominates over the evil. My faith in God implies that His apex creation will not get lost in the wilderness of evil, if humans use the Divine gift of freedom and creativity in the spirit of humility, compassion and universal tolerance. It is my faith that they will be guided, sooner or later, to the straight path (*siraat ul mustaqim*).

# (IV)

Most Muslim believers, to my mind, have an extremely blurred and unsympathetic image of the worth and wisdom of modern Western culture, though they have no choice but to acknowledge its scientific and technological superiority to all previous civilizations. One must not hesitate to point out the West's feet of clay, but this should not land us into some sort of cultural chauvinism of our own. The West has made a glorious contribution to the sum total of human culture not merely in science and technology, but also in several other fields: philosophy, social sciences, literature, music, art, human relations and the art of governance. Democracy, rule of law, equality of opportunity, gender justice, respect for children, religious tolerance, the welfare state, banking and insurance, the conquest of poverty and disease, planned parenthood, love of adventure, travel and sports, conservation of wildlife and preservation of the grand human cultural heritage, and so on are truly remarkable chapters in the book of human creativity. What the ancient Egyptians, Semites, Greeks, Romans, Iranians, Indians, Chinese and Arabs did in the past to create knowledge and culture the West has been doing in the present era. The story of human culture, therefore, should be viewed as a ceaseless relay race in which every wing of the human family has participated and contributed at some time or the other.

We must not glorify our own race, region or religion and minimize the role of others. Every age excels in some respects and suffers from some limitation in some other respect or respects. We must never hesitate to assimilate the elements of value present in any society or culture into our own distinctive tradition, for in the final analysis, the human family is one. Both the achievements and the limitations belong to the human family, as such, rather than to an in-group or out-group, or to 'we' and 'they'.

The inclusion in the Quran of such primitive and natural penalties, as amputation of hands and flogging, (that alone were available, like air and water, in ancient times), does not imply that believing Muslims are absolutely bound to apply them forever even when other simpler and more effective penalties have come to be known in the light of ever growing human knowledge and experience. This approach to Penology gets support from a report about what the second *Khalifa*, Omar, once did. He thought it quite fit and proper to waive (under famine conditions in a particular region) the Quranic penalty of cutting off of the hand in cases of theft of food.

Muslim jurists, in general, have also traditionally imposed specific qualifications on the Quranic texts dealing with punishments when they pronounced the final judgment. To my mind, therefore, what is needed is an, essentially, reflective, rather than a literal, approach to Quranic texts dealing with punishments. Thus, if there be credible evidence that flogging hardens the criminal rather than reforming him, while some other form or forms of punishment are more effective in the prevention of crime as well as in the inner reformation of the wrong-doer, I submit, Muslim penologists can adopt these forms of punishment without feeling guilty of violating Quranic injunctions.

The Western failure to eliminate crime is not due to the ethic of lenient or mild punishments (as is generally believed in traditional Muslim religious quarters). It is the result of several factors. However, no single factor by itself (severe punishments, speedy justice etc.) will suffice to eliminate crime. Thus, if the intending offender knows that the chances of detection are low, the severest penal code loses on its powers of deterrence. Similarly, if it be known that punishment could be evaded through bribery or political influence, harsh penalties yield low returns.

Western penologists and administrators in developed societies are themselves not very happy at their crime environment. Western penologists earlier expected that universal education, health care and a high standard of material comforts would suffice to eliminate crime just as public hygiene and modern medicine had almost eliminated epidemics and several diseases. However, the extent of 'white collar crime' in many Western democratic democracies has belied this expectation. This shows the great complexity of the causes as well as the remedies of crime.

No single line of attack or treatment of crime would suffice, just as no single objective of punishment can, by itself, suffice to promote human welfare in the best sense of the term. The objective of deterrence is very desirable, but the punishment should not totally exclude the concern for the criminal as such. Likewise, compassion for the criminal is desirable but not at the expense of the larger interests of society as such. The crux of the matter is to determine the optimum balance between different objectives.

The effective prevention of crime is very important indeed. But there is something far more essential to achieve this goal than mere severity of punishment or rough and ready justice. This requires in-depth understanding of human nature and of the laws of social change and growth and the complexity of the human situation. Prevention that flows from the fear of the whip or the rod is fleeting and superficial and does not heal the inner 'sickness of the individual soul' in a state of alienation from its higher self or the divine spark embedded in the depths of the human psyche. This inner healing comes not from the observance of traditional religious rituals or the fear of the rod; it comes through self-understanding that parents and teachers and social institutions bring to bear upon the individual. Most importantly, inner health and healing comes through extremely slow growing self-insight and self-illumination as the soul struggles for and aspires to find the inner peace that 'passeth understanding'. This truth applies to all religions and faiths, and any sense of superiority on the ground of one's theological creed or the language and symbols of one's own tradition of spirituality is as fallacious and conceited as making the color of the skin the criterion or the guarantee of human excellence or one's spiritual status.

The human family as such including the great Islamic segment (for various reasons left behind by other groups) is slowly marching to spiritualistic humanism and interfaith unity. But humankind has miles to go before they can rest. And I hope and pray that they will travel together as fellow pilgrims moving together in a common search for collective human welfare in the spirit of mutual understanding and respect rather than as adversaries in the game of power politics, economic supremacy or the cultural dominance and hegemony of any creed, sect or church.

# Afterword

Several Muslim intellectuals and theologians have referred to 'challenges of modernity' in their books on Islam. I chose the title 'The Call of Modernity and Islam' for my collected essays dealing with the issues of Islam in the modern age. I look upon modernity not as an adversarial challenge to Muslims but rather as a slow flowering of the human spirit in the course of its evolution in history. I do believe technology to be a major causal factor that produces change in the human situation.

The scientific method is the womb from which technology has emerged. The evolution of the scientific method is a fascinating story whose beginnings date back to antiquity but which gathered momentum rather late in human history. Modernity, as we understand the word today, emerged only when the scientific method had reached a high stage of maturity in Western Europe by the beginning of the 18th century.

Modernity is the attitude of accepting and practicing the scientific method in the human attempt to understand the universe, including humankind. The essence of the scientific method is not to accept or reject any truth claim without appropriate evidence. However, the nature of evidence need not be identical or the same for validating every truth claim. If this basic insight is ignored, the scientific method inevitably lapses into a dogmatic fixation upon a particular and rigid procedure, and this leads to the impoverishment rather than the enlargement of knowledge and wisdom. This actually happened soon after the explosion of science and technology in mid 19th century. This led to a theory of knowledge usually called 'Positivism'. Many protagonists of modernity are tempted to reduce modernity or the modern sensibility to Positivism and an aggressive secularism, and tend to devalue the spiritual, ethical and artistic domains of human experience. This is the consequence of their dogma that no truth-claim, which cannot be proved in the scientific sense, could be regarded as either true or false.

This is to say that such truth-claims can be merely opinions rather than knowledge in the proper sense. This outlook or approach has been aptly termed 'scientism'. However, I have no doubt that modernity and scientism cannot be, or rather should not be equated.

The same remarks apply to the relationship between secularism and modernity. Secularism does not reject the truth and proper role of religion, but only liberates the human mind from the illusion that religious faith can be proved, and that only one particular faith is true and therefore worthy of governing every field of human life. Modernity and secularism, thus, liberate people from the chains of ethnocentricity and blind faith in the ideology of exclusive salvation, and superiority to others. Modernity and secularism do not question the crucial importance of ethics for life.

The term 'post-modernity' became current soon after the end of the Second World War under the impact of the one-dimensional mindset of some free thinkers. These minds had become sadly disillusioned due to the sufferings and ravages of the two wars that were fought by the supposedly most advanced and scientifically developed nations of the world. Instead of correcting the one sidedness of aggressive scientism many of these thinkers fell into the trap of cynicism and nihilism as such. However, if the protagonists of modernity had not committed the initial blunder of excluding the truths of spirituality, morality and art from the domain of reliable knowledge, perhaps the term post-modernity would not have been coined at all.

Likewise, no conflict between science and religion would have arisen if their respective protagonists and practitioners had not encroached upon the proper jurisdiction or domain of the two disciplines concerned. Speaking for myself, I have opted, fully and completely to accept the validity of the scientific method in the domain of factual truth and I have opted for the validity of Islam in the domain of spirituality. My chosen paradigm differs from the traditional one in several respects, which must have become clear to the readers of my works. However my paradigm gives me authentic inner peace that passes all understanding while the traditional does not. I entertain the greatest respect for all seekers of truth; no matter where they find inner satisfaction and peace for themselves and whatever religious identity they choose for themselves.

I have the same respect also for those who are unable to resolve their inner perplexities concerning their proper destination. Going still further I find that I cannot avoid respecting those souls who have honestly tried to find God or any other spiritual foothold or anchor, but have failed to find inner peace and rest and have proceeded to identify themselves as atheists. Yet they remain righteous, compassionate, loving and conscientious members of the human family. I find I just cannot bring myself to condemning such souls as wicked wretches who deserve to burn eternally in hell fire.

Here I am reminded of two anecdotes, one of Sufi origin and the other from Judaic mysticism. The famous Sufi saint, Rabia Basri (d. 801), was one day found walking on the streets of Baghdad in a strange manner. In one hand she held a plate of burning coals, and in the other she carried a bowl of water. When asked what she was up to, she replied that she wanted to extinguish the fire of hell with the bowl of water and to burn paradise with the burning coals so that people may do good and avoid evil for the love of God rather than out of love of gain or fear of pain. The Jewish anecdote says that on the Day of Judgment God will not ask humans why they did not follow the Law of Moses, but will only ask why they did not follow the truth of their own inner voice instead of following others.

To conclude, I identify myself as a Muslim and desire that others also identify me as such. I believe in the essential unity of all religions and venerate them. I gravitate to the Islamic tradition (within the parameters of my paradigm) and the Quran as I regard them as my mother tongue in the domain of spirituality. Ontogenetic verses of the Quran, such as the 'verse of the throne' (2:255), and the 'verse of the light' (24:35) and others move, inspire and reinforce my faith that all that exists is somehow the locus of an inscrutable, but sacred, mystery.

At the same time I deeply feel and realize that mere contemplation of and sensitivity to the inscrutable mystery of the universe is not enough. Humans are not angels but thinking, feeling and willing agents who move from situation to situation. They cannot avoid responding in different situations and making active choices in the course of a never ceasing journey. They cannot live without bread, ideas, ideals, and without following instrumental rules and regulations for realizing their ideals. This requires unwavering commitment to ideals, but at the same time, freedom to make fresh rules and regulations in an ever-changing world. The Quranic verse 5:3, '......This day have I perfected your religion for you, completed My favor upon you, and have chosen for you Islam as your religion...' does not imply that on the day the verse was revealed polymorphous perfection had been achieved by Muslim society. After all said and done, perfection is only an ideal and never a fact. All ideas and ideals need perpetual inner growth of the individual as well as in the structure of society and the laws as such.

God alone knows the full truth, and we humans should ever beware of possessing exclusive truth and falling into the pit of spiritual conceit and the delusion of self-sufficiency.

We started this work with invoking the name of Allah and we now conclude it with one Quranic verse that fully illumines the path every truth-seeker has to travel in his journey to salvation, and two Quranic prayers.

*(Surah 3, Verse 7)*
*He it is Who has sent down to thee the Book: In it are verses basic or fundamental (of established meaning); they are the foundation of the Book: others are allegorical. But those in whose hearts is perversity follow the part thereof that is allegorical, seeking discord, and searching for its hidden meanings, but no one knows its hidden meanings except Allah. And those who are firmly grounded in knowledge say: "We believe in the Book; the whole of it is from our Lord:" and none will grasp the Message except men of understanding.*

*(Surah 113)*
*Say: I seek refuge with the Lord of the Dawn*
*From the mischief of created things;*
*From the mischief of Darkness as it overspreads;*
*From the mischief of those who practice secret arts;*
*And from the mischief of the envious one as he practices envy.*

*(Surah 114)*
*Say: I seek refuge with the Lord and Cherisher of Mankind,*
*The King (or Ruler) of Mankind,*
*The Allah (or judge) of Mankind,-*
*From the mischief of the Whisperer (of Evil), who withdraws (after his whisper),-*
*(The same) who whispers into the hearts of Mankind,-*
*Among Jinns and among men.*

Ameen

# APPENDIX 1

## ABOUT THE AUTHOR

Jamal Khwaja was born in Delhi in 1926*. His ancestors had been closely connected with the Islamic reform movement, inaugurated by Sir Syed Ahmad Khan, the founder of the famous *M.A.O. College*, Aligarh in the second half of the 19th century, and the Indian freedom movement under Gandhi's leadership in the first half of the 20th century. After doing his M.A. in Philosophy from the *Aligarh Muslim University*, India, he obtained an Honor's degree from *Christ's College Cambridge*, UK. Later he spent a year studying the German language and European existentialism at *Munster University*, Germany.

At Cambridge he was deeply influenced by the work of C.D. Broad, Wittgenstein and John Wisdom, apart from his college tutor, I.T. Ramsey who later became *Professor of Christian Religion* at Oxford. It was the latter's influence which, taught Khwaja to appreciate the inner beauty and power of pure spirituality. Khwaja was thus led to appreciate the value of linguistic analysis as a tool of philosophical inquiry and to combine the quest for clarity with the insights and depth of the existentialist approach to religion and spirituality.

Khwaja was appointed Lecturer in Philosophy at the *Aligarh Muslim University* in 1953. Before he could begin serious academic work in his chosen field, his family tradition of public work pulled him into a brief spell of active politics under the charismatic Jawahar lal Nehru; the first Prime Minister of India. Nehru was keen to rejuvenate his team of colleagues through inducting fresh blood into the *Indian National Congress*. He included young Khwaja, then freshly returned from Cambridge, along with four or five other young persons. Khwaja thus became one of the youngest entrants into the Indian Parliament as a member of the *Lok Sabha* (Lower House) from 1957 to 1962.

---

* Jamal Khwaja was born in Delhi on August 12, 1926. However, most official records mistakenly show 1928 as the year of birth.

*Appendix 1: About the Author*

While in the corridors of power he learned to distinguish between ideals and illusions, and finally chose to pursue the path of knowledge rather than the path of acquiring authority or power. Returning to his *alma mater* in 1962, he resumed teaching and research in the philosophy of religion. Ever since then Khwaja has lived a quiet life at Aligarh.

He was Dean of the *Faculty of Arts* and was a member of important committees of the *University Grants Commission* and the *Indian Council for Philosophical Research* before retiring as Professor and Chairman of the *Department of Philosophy* in 1988. He was a frequent and active participant in national seminars held at the *Indian Institute of Advanced Study*, Simla.

His works include, *Five Approaches to Philosophy*, *Quest for Islam, Authenticity and Islamic Liberalism*, *Essays on Cultural Pluralism*, and numerous scholarly articles and essays. He was invited to deliver the *Khuda Bakhsh Memorial Lecture* at Patna. He was one of the official Indian delegates at the *World Philosophical Congress Brighton*, UK, in 1988, and also at the *International Islamic Conference Kuala Lumpur*, Malaysia, in 1967, and the *Pakistan International Philosophy Congress*, Peshawar, Pakistan, in 1964.

He has visited the USA and several countries in Western Europe.

He performed *Hajj* in 2005.

## Major Published Works

Jamal Khwaja has written seven major books. Anyone interested in the intersection of Islam and Modernity will find Khwaja to be a reliable guide. His work is magisterial in scope. It is full of passion but remains balanced in perspective. Readers of his work will be in turn, informed, inspired, and intellectually liberated.

As complex issues get illumined and perplexities whither away, Muslim readers in particular, will feel emotionally aligned with the Quran and find themselves empowered to live as authentic Muslims in the heart of the multi-cultural global village.

> 1. Five Approaches To Philosophy: A discerning philosopher philosophizes about the philosophy of philosophy with wisdom and clarity. (2nd Edition). 158 Pages. ISBN: 978-1-935293-51-4

2. Quest For Islam: A philosophers approach to religion in the age of science and cultural pluralism. (Significantly Enlarged 2nd Edition). 364 Pages. ISBN: 978-1-935293-69-9

3. Authenticity And Islamic Liberalism: A mature vision of Islamic Liberalism grounded in the Quran. (Significantly Enlarged 2nd Edition). 244 Pages. ISBN: 978-1-935293-68-2

4. Essays On Cultural Pluralism: A philosophical framework for authentic interfaith dialogue. 268 Pages. ISBN: 978-1-935293-52-1

5. The Call Of Modernity And Islam: A Muslim's journey into the 21st century. 302 Pages. ISBN: 978-1-935293-94-1

6. Living The Quran In Our Times: A vision of how Muslims can revitalize their faith, while being faithful to God and His messenger. 214 Pages. ISBN: 978-81-321-1046-0

7. The Vision Of An Unknown Indian Muslim: My journey to interfaith spirituality. 326 Pages. ISBN: 978-1-935293-96-5

Khwaja's work is the definitive contemporary discussion regarding the collision of Islam and Modernity. Explore it. You will be profoundly rewarded.

For more information, visit www.JamalKhwaja.com

# APPENDIX 2

## THE QUEST FOR THE MEANING OF ISLAM

It is quite common for learned scholars and laymen alike to raise the question 'What is Islam?' and answer it with a sense of assurance and certainty, as if their answer is the only conceivable one. Such persons hardly suspect that this simplicity is superficial. The reason is that Islam is neither a logico-mathematical or scientific concept that could be unambiguously defined, nor a physical object like a chair or table, or a biological organism like, a horse or cow whose properties could be catalogued or described without any room for controversy. The question 'What is Islam?' is very close to the questions 'What is justice?' and 'What is beauty?' and answers to these questions can never be simple, since the nature of justice or beauty is not out there for our perceptual or intuitive inspection, but is chosen by us out of several competing meanings of the words 'beauty' and 'justice'. The individual assimilates the concrete meaning of such abstract words from his milieu, just as he assimilates the language, gestures, or morals of the group. But the individual remains unaware of the fact that his conception of beauty or justice or, for that matter, of Islam is only one particular model among other actual or possible models.

According to the orthodox view, Islam is a set of basic beliefs, values, and practices, which are the defining coordinates of Islam. The core of these beliefs was formulated by the divinely inspired Prophet Muhammad ﷺ. One, who accepts these beliefs, accepts Islam, while one who denies or doubts their validity repudiates Islam. The basic beliefs or pillars of faith are: **(1)** unity of God (*tawhid*), **(2)** revelation (*wahy*), **(3)** life after death (*akhirat*), **(4)** angels (*malaika*); while the five pillars of action are the formula of faith (*kalima*) 'There is no God but Allah, and Muhammad is His messenger', prayers (*salat*), fasting (*soum*), wealth tax (*zakat*), and pilgrimage to Mecca (*Hajj*). But this simplicity is deceptive, for the moment we try to determine what exactly is meant by such words as

'God', 'prophecy', and 'angels', etc., we find ourselves immersed in a sea of difficulties.

The difficulty is due to the fact that one's concrete understanding or interpretation of religious concepts is an integral part of one's basic worldview, which, to begin with, is a product of cultural conditioning. The individual assimilates the interpretation current in his own milieu and accepts it as true. This was as true for the period of the Prophet ﷺ as for any other. Even granting that the Prophet ﷺ was the recipient of Divine revelation, his basic conceptual framework was as much derived from his Semitic milieu as that of his contemporaries. It seems to me that just as the Prophet ﷺ spoke the Meccan style of Arabic, used Arabic syntax and grammar, wore Arab dress, lived in a pre-industrial desert economy, the Prophet ﷺ also shared the generally accepted historical, geographical, cosmological, and medical ideas or beliefs of his times. Most probably the Prophet ﷺ believed that the sun went round the earth which was flat, that mountains and rivers were instantly created by the Creator, that different species of animals were separately created, that plants had no sex, that epidemics and natural calamities were Divine punishment for human wickedness, that women were mentally and morally inferior to men, etc. It seems the Prophet ﷺ must have interpreted the Quranic verses about God saying 'Be', and of the universe coming into being, in the sense of instant creation rather than in the evolutionary sense. Again, if asked to explain the Quranic verse which refers to the motion of the earth, the Prophet ﷺ probably would not have interpreted it to mean that the earth moves round the sun, but in some other sense, which is difficult for us to pinpoint.[1] The implication is that the 'cognitive concretion', that is, the concrete understanding and clarification of generalized concepts such as creation, revelation, and God, etc., is always done within the conceptual framework current in the individual's milieu.

Concrete interpretations need not always be explicitly formulated, but are implicitly present in the general conceptual framework or background of a given period. An implicit interpretation will be formulated or expressed only when there is some stimulus or need to do so. In this process the implicit beliefs become explicit. This is exactly what happened as a result of the impact of Darwin's theory of organic evolution upon Christian beliefs, and the subsequent heated dispute between Christian theology and science. Before Darwin every Muslim and Christian believed that the original ancestors of the various species of plants and animals were first separately created by God, and subsequently they perpetuated themselves through sexual reproduction. This concrete interpretation may or may not have been formulated by any individual. But this was the actual view of almost all Christians and Muslims before Darwin. Similarly, some idea of the total time span was certainly implicit in the awareness of men living before Darwin. We may say that Christians usually believed the world to be about four or five thousand years old. But the geological assessment, as we know, was quite different.

## Religion as an Existential Interpretation of the Universe

Historically every religion has been an organic whole of **(a)** a thought-cum-value system, **(b)** a symbolic precept system, and **(c)** an institutional system. The thought-cum-value system interprets man's cosmic situation and projects intrinsic values and also instrumental rules for realizing them. The precept system comprises the symbolic practices dealing with the transcendental sphere, while the institutional system comprises the approved patterns of behavior in the social sphere.

Thought systems arise because man is never satisfied with bare perceptual experience, but wants to interpret or understand it as part of a wider contextual whole. All human experience stands in need of interpretation in order to become functionally significant for man, since isolated bits of information cannot be used for satisfying human needs. Science is not merely systematic description, but also systematic interpretation of empirical data. The interpretation consists of empirically verifiable and quantitative causal laws connecting different phenomena. Such laws are essential for controlling and manipulating the physical environment. This mode of interpreting physical data is called scientific explanation whose chief feature is its direct or indirect verifiability in terms of human sense-experience. Scientific explanation always has some empirical evidence on the strength of which one explanation is preferred to another.

The above type of explanation, however, does not exhaust the full range of human interpretation, which includes man's ethical, aesthetic, religious, and metaphysical responses, which are not less significant for man's life than scientific explanation. Without the latter man cannot use the environment for satisfying his needs, but without ethical evaluation he loses his sense of direction. Similarly, without the aesthetic response man cannot create or appreciate beauty, and life without beauty lacks a dimension of value. As we know, beauty evokes aesthetic joy, which brings about the spiritual revitalization of man.

The metaphysical or existential response is rooted in man's yearning to decipher the total meaning or significance of the universe as a whole, and to relate himself to it accordingly. Man yearns to grasp the depth-significance of the universe as a complex state of affairs, whose empirical structure is disclosed by science. Biology, for example, tells us about the nature of life and death, but not how to relate oneself, or what attitude to adopt towards life and death. Man could respond to the universe at the empirical, ethical, or other levels without its existential interpretation. But this would amount to ad hoc responses to ad hoc environmental stimuli, and man would not be able to give any inner justification for his different responses. Let us examine this point in some detail.

The universe has some basic features which may be said to be its warp and woof, and which remain the same throughout history, e.g., the features of law and order, harmony and beauty of nature, man's moral sense, as distinct from concrete moral codes, the struggle for survival of the species and of individuals, pain and suffering, hope and joy, birth, growth, decay, and death. Natural science does not concern itself with the significance or meaning of these features of the universe, that is, whether they are just accidental features and could therefore disappear from the cosmic scene, as accidentally as they appeared, or whether they stand rooted in the constitution of the universe arid thus have an ontic status or permanent reality. Now the way in which one interprets these features simultaneously influences the personality orientation of the individual, and is, in turn, influenced by the original bent of the personality itself. In other words, there is a dialectical relationship between the existential interpretation and the personality orientation. The interpretation becomes important, since it influences man's inner responses to the universe in a most subtle manner, though the interpretation has no prima facie bearing upon man's empirical, ethical, or aesthetic response. But the fact is that different existential interpretations constitute different ways of treating the universe or relating oneself to it, and this inevitably influences the individual's life-style and also raises the question as to which particular style is right, and why so.[2] To give an analogy, the practicing scientist does not concern himself with the question whether or why nature behaves uniformly, but takes it for granted, as if it were self-evident or necessarily true, or because it works. But the denial of causal uniformity does not involve any logical contradiction; nor can it be logically proved. We accept it for two reasons: first, our actual experience suggests as if it were true; and, second, if it were not true, no point would be left in our scientific enquiries, which we deem as valuable and worth pursuing. Likewise, there would be no point left or, to be more accurate, the urge to pursue values would be far less intense, if values were chance and ephemeral products of the blind dance of atoms, without the conservation and growth of values being ontologically guaranteed, despite all seeming obstacles. The concept of God is precisely one particular form of this faith. Belief in God implies that values like truth, goodness, and beauty are neither chance products, nor ultimate and un-derived features of the universe, but have their source in the ultimate and Supreme Being with whom man could establish an *'I-Thou'* dialogue. The existential interpretation is neither a hypothesis, nor a partly justifiable postulate; it is a motivational re-enforcer that integrates the individual's thoughts and feelings into a stable inner way of life or mode of treating the universe, as distinct from ad hoc and ever variable responses or attitudes.

An existential interpretation may be compared with dream interpretation or with a poetic metaphor without being reducible to them. The significance of the dream is not a matter of verifiable knowledge but of insight, intuition, or personality projection upon the canvas of the dream. Likewise, the poetic metaphor is not a matter of verifiable description or theory, but of expression of the feelings, emotions, and imagery evoked by some object, situation, or experience. The object of dream interpretation is self-understanding, that of a poetic metaphor self-expression, while that of an existential interpretation, the person's stable attitudinal adjustment or orientation to the universe as a whole, or to some significant aspect of it, e.g., death, conscience, and sexual love, etc. One may, for instance, interpret death as the final release from the tyranny or tragedy of life, or as the blind axe that destroys the tree of life, or as a change of abode or of bodily apparel, or as the destination of life, or as a welcome union with the Infinite. These interpretations have a poetic flavor, no doubt. Their primary aim, however, is not to give pleasure, but to give meaning and direction to life. Likewise, the interpretation that life is a hard and rocky battleground differs from the interpretation that life is a blooming garden, not merely in terms of the imagery, but also in terms of its directive function. The first interpretation suggests the ethic of power and of action; the second the ethic of beauty and of contemplation. Similarly, different interpretations of Eros will imply different codes of sexual conduct, even when there may be agreement on all the relevant facts of life. Similarly, to interpret conscience as the voice of God within man or as the Divine spark makes for a different quality of man's inner life as well as his relationship with society than to interpret conscience as the 'internalized censor'. These existential interpretations enable man to conduct his life in a consistently meaningful manner. In one word, their primary function is orientative rather than aesthetic, although when the proffered orientation really grips the individual, his entire being is suffused with a sense of profound joy, perhaps, more intense than aesthetic pleasure itself.

The existential interpretation is not a substitute for, and hence not a competitor with scientific explanation, just as a poetic metaphor is not a substitute for a scientific description or theory. But an existential interpretation, by virtue of its essential directive function, may well promote or impede scientific enquiry, or in some cases, even of a particular scientific hypothesis. For example, the interpretation that man is the vicegerent of God, Who has granted man power and dominion over the rest of creation, including the sun and the moon, the wind and the ocean, tends to promote scientific enquiry, while the interpretation that man is only an accidental self-glorifying worm, born out of a cosmic accident, tends to inhibit the arduous and sustained labor which science demands. Indeed, as Whitehead points out, the theistic interpretation of the universe facilitated the belief in the ultimate rationality and orderliness of nature as the creation of a perfect Creator.[3] Likewise, the idealistic interpretation of Reality being ultimately mental or ideal might have facilitated the empirical discovery that conation is present in plants and minerals. It also seems to me that Spinoza's concept of *Substance and Psycho-physical Parallelism* was congenial to the growth of an integrated and inter-disciplinary approach to the physical and the biological sciences. Whether or not this likely interaction factually occurred is a matter of research in the field of history of ideas. The crux of the matter is that while an existential interpretation always has an ethical function, in some cases it could also stimulate scientific theories.

An existential interpretation of the universe is by definition not verifiable. However, it must take into account the full range of the different features of the universe without suppressing any feature, which may not harmonize with the favored interpretation. This task presupposes a base of reliable factual knowledge as the data of the interpretation. Thus, one must be aware of the evolutionary feature of life, though knowledge of factual details is not called for. Likewise, one must be aware of the extent of struggle, suffering, and tragedy in the universe (and not merely of its beauty and harmony) to avoid the existential interpretation from being weighted in favor of some selected features of the universe. The interpretation must thus harmonize with the data and reliable conclusions of science. For example, the interpretation that every event serves a cosmic purpose does not appear to harmonize with geo-biological blind alleys and waste. Or the interpretation that God loves and cherishes His meanest creation does not appear to harmonize with the biological struggle for survival. Likewise, the interpretation that the universe was instantly created out of absolute nothingness does not harmonize with the scientific concept of evolution.

If and when the interpretation does not harmonize with the scientific conceptual scheme, a revision of its concrete sense may remove the prima facie discord. We may say, for instance, that God's love for His creation is not the same as mother's love for her child, or that what appears as evil works as an instrumental good in a larger context. This task involves redefining, analyzing, explaining, making distinctions or comparisons either in the spirit of a free exploration of the given data or in the spirit of a defensive reconciliation between theology and science. In the former case, the role of reason is primary, while in the latter it is secondary. The theologian explores new meanings of traditional concepts in a spirit of defensive reverence to the tradition, while the philosopher freely reflects upon the validity of the religious interpretation. He checks whether the actual data of human experience harmonize with the religious interpretation. This activity, however, does not involve deductive or inductive reasoning but existential elucidation, that is, the illumination of one's hidden depth attitudes, choices, interpretative responses, or images. An existential interpretation which is chosen by the philosopher is thus functionally similar to, but genetically or methodologically different from, religious faith.

An existential interpretation of some kind or other is unavoidable. We can only opt for this or that interpretation, but we cannot opt to do away with all interpretation as such. We may claim to avoid all contact with metaphysics or religion, which we may view as the hallmarks of a pre-scientific mentality. Yet the fact is that we cannot live as integrated human beings without some kind of world view or total perspective on the cosmos.[4] And this total perspective, be it religious or philosophical, is at bottom always an existential interpretation of the basic features of human experience cosmic law and order, the mysteries of birth, growth and death, the beauty as well as the fury of nature, good and evil, joy and tragedy.[5] Religious faith is the pre-logical acceptance of an interpretation because of its existential grip over the believer.

Religious faith should not be confused with credulity or trust. A person, for example, may come to have 'faith' in any belief in the sense that he maybe subjectively certain of its truth, and feel no need for testing his belief. Thus, a mother may have such strong faith in the integrity of her daughter or the intelligence of her son, that she may not be bothered by the adverse opinion of neighbors and teachers about her children. Since, however, these beliefs are of a type that can be tested and proved, the refusal to test them cannot be accepted as reasonable. Unshakable faith in beliefs, which could be verified, is not justifiable. But faith in God or life after death is a different matter, since no argument or observation could clinch the issue. It is here that genuine faith touches its proper sphere, and can realize its full possibilities of growth and maturity.

As already mentioned, man passes judgments of fact as well as judgments of value. Those states of affairs which are judged to be good in their own right and, hence, worthy of being established, preserved, or fostered, as the case may be, are intrinsic values, while the means or conditions required for realizing them are instrumental values. For example, punctuality, moderation, courage, industry, endurance, cooperativeness, etc., are all necessary for establishing such states of affairs as universal love, justice, the equality and dignity of man, and his integrated growth. Instrumental values are thus dependent variables, while intrinsic values are independent coordinates of any value system.

The distinction between intrinsic and instrumental values is, however, not rigid. Indeed some values may be both intrinsic and instrumental, while some others may be regarded as intrinsic in one context and instrumental in another. Thus, good health is both an intrinsic and an instrumental value. Similarly, the good will, in Kant's sense, namely man's general desire to do his duty rather than seek pleasure, is both an intrinsic and an instrumental value. Similarly, a clearly instrumental value such as physical cleanliness tends to become an intrinsic good when its cultivation produces aesthetic delight in the individual. Again, an intrinsic value such as social justice or respect for human beings operates as an instrumental value for promoting the self-realization of the members of a group. Nevertheless, the distinction between intrinsic and instrumental values becomes crucial in those cases where adherence to an instrumental value may ultimately obstruct intrinsic values as such.

This tension or clash is not merely a theoretical possibility or a hypothetical situation, but repeatedly occurs in man's history. For example, the early Jewish and Islamic injunction to grow and multiply in order to glorify God was obviously necessary (hence, an instrumental value) for the survival of a nascent group. But under entirely changed demographic conditions, the adherence to this rule obstructs universal self-realization or the integrated growth of human beings. Similarly, many age-old and respected rules, regulations, and social customs such as the position of women and children, rules of marriage, etc., may turn out to be misconceived in the light of factual knowledge, which was not available when the rules were framed. Fidelity to the end is thus more important than obedience to the rules that might stultify the end. This, however, does not imply that means are unimportant and may be ignored without peril. Indeed, the usual formulation of the problem of ends versus means is very misleading, since a complete separation of the means from the actual concrete end is not possible. Nevertheless, intrinsic values or ends desirable for their own sake must be accorded primacy over values that are mere means to their realization.

The emphasis upon intrinsic values encourages the individual to strive for the more important goals of life and not to feel satisfied with mechanical compliance with instrumental rules without bothering to assess their relevance in a changing world. A lop-sided concern with intrinsic values occupying a relatively lower rank in the hierarchy of values must also be avoided. Without the concept of rank of value the individual fails to develop a sense of proportion, which is essential for the good life.[6]

All value systems acquire concrete meaning for a group in its concrete situational context. Without situational concretion abstract values such as justice, charity, chastity, and honesty function as variables whose validity cannot be ascertained. However, no situational concretion can be final. Every age inherits the values of the past but gives them a fresh interpretation. The failure to distinguish between an abstract value system and its situational concretion inclines one to think that any change in the latter destroys the basic value system as such. This makes one cling to the past and stops all ethical growth.

## II

## FIELD TENSIONS AND FIELD INTEGRATION

There is a continuous interaction between the life experience of a religious group and the growth of its religious concepts and values. All cultural systems including the religious are situationally evoked. Many of us are apt to hold that while the beliefs of other religions have been so evoked, our own religion did not grow within an historical situation but was born readymade. But this amounts to the adoption of double standards and is invalid. Even the same individual does not stick to the same meaning at different stages of his life, since experience and reflection continually modify his concrete understanding of general concepts. In the formal sense the nuclear core may remain identical, but, in the concrete functional sense, even the core may change. The concept of God, for example, may evolve over a long period of time, so that the concrete meaning of the word 'God' becomes quite different from its earlier concrete meaning. Yet, the word 'God' may remain intact. Sometimes a new expression, say, 'Being', 'Reality', 'First Cause', may come into use. The choice of words depends upon whether or not one wants to break away from the tradition.

The illusion of changeless fundamental concepts arises through the tendency of words and names to persist in our living vocabulary, in spite of changes in their concrete connotation. Even a radical shift in ideas may take place without a corresponding change in our linguistic habits or vocabulary. This is quite natural though highly misleading, since it tends to conceal the fact of change.

The history of culture shows that all fields of human culture, such as religion, art, philosophy, science, etc., interact and influence each other, so that the total culture of a group is an organic whole. Change in one sphere spills over into all others. There is regional resistance to begin with. But in the course of time significant changes in any one sphere of human culture penetrate the total cultural *gestalt*. To give some illustrations, the invention of photography had its repercussions for painting, the scientific formulation of the theory of evolution profoundly altered philosophy and Christian theology, the industrial revolution led to social, moral, and economic revolutions, and the advent of contraception is gradually influencing

## Appendix 2: The Quest For The Meaning Of Islam

the norms of sexual morality. Religion, as a segment of the cultural *gestalt*, cannot escape transformation in this evolving universe.

Not only the fields of art, literature, and science, but also those of economics, politics, religion, and morality all interact. Religion may claim the right to legislate for all the fields, as if it were the sovereign. Even so, the religious authority is influenced by the inevitable interaction between the different fields of human life. There is a dialectical interaction between a religion or an ideology and the socio-economic field rather than a one-sided dependence of ideology upon the economic structure. In practice this produces field tensions or conflicts between the pull of two or more fields of human experience. Thus the thought-cum-value system of a particular religion may pull us towards a male dominated society, while its techno-centric economy may pull us towards a more or less complete equality between the sexes. Similarly, tensions may develop between the fields of art and science, or art, religion, and morality, etc.

Field tensions may also arise due to conflict between the value system of the religion and the authentic values of the individual, for example, if his religion prescribes human sacrifice, while his conscience rebels against the idea, despite all his sincere efforts to accept it. Likewise, if the Quran were to prescribe stoning as a punishment for adultery (as a matter of fact, this is not the case), and the Muslim's conscience were to revolt against the idea, a field tension would arise and raise the problem of authenticity.[7] The believer could either suppress this tension, or rationalize the command, or, without concealing his disagreement surrender his judgment to the wisdom of the Quran. But if he is not prepared to do so, and wishes to live as an authentic integrated person, he must either attempt the task of field integration or repudiate his religious tradition altogether. In the West, Whitehead and Tillich have followed the first course, while Freud and Russell the latter.[8] It seems the latter course is fraught with the danger of throwing away the baby with the bath. Let us consider in greater detail the various types of response to field tension. They may be called repression/suppression, isolation, rationalization, and, finally, integration.

Field repression/suppression implies that some field or dimension of experience is repressed/suppressed by the individual in order to escape the pain of conflict. One individual may repress the dimension of reason, while another that of spirituality. But neither the intellectual yearning for clear concepts and a unified world view, nor the spiritual yearning to transcend one's private interests and reach out for some higher impersonal values can be destroyed, no matter how much these yearnings may be repressed or suppressed. Even as the sex instinct finds other outlets in the case of repression/suppression, so do the above needs. It appears that class hatred, bigotry, racial prejudice, and chauvinism, etc., are all partly the products of suppression of either the dimension of spirituality or reason or both. Field repression therefore does not produce a lasting inner peace.

Field isolation means that the different fields of human culture are deliberately kept isolated from each other. This approach again proves highly unsatisfactory, since it denies the organic unity of culture. Field isolation cannot withstand the natural impact of the different fields of human culture. The attempt at field isolation leads to a painful sense of fragmentation and the fear of facing life as a whole. Field isolation breeds an inner sense of uneasiness, though it may outwardly help to keep one's faith.

Rationalization is the attempt to overcome tensions by explaining them away with the help of far-fetched alterations in the meaning of words, false generalizations, selective sampling of data, seductive but weak analogies, confusion of meanings, or types of discourse, and, last but not the least, a defensive or justificatory use of reason as distinct from the analytical and exploratory. Field rationalization is a more or less conscious attempt to justify a traditional thought system as a partisan rather than as an autonomous person.

Field integration means a systematic dialogue between the different fields of human experience with a view to overcoming actual or possible tensions between them. The process of integration involves the pruning or revising of definitions or uses of the basic words in question such as God, creation, and justice, etc. A striking need for field integration arose due to the impact of the theory of evolution upon the concrete interpretation of the Bible and the Quran. Intelligent believers felt uneasy at the conflict between the religious concept of Divine creation and the scientific concept of evolution. The concept of 'evolutionary creation', as distinguished from 'instantaneous creation out of nothing' removes the conflict partly, but not completely, between the fields of religion and science. The notion of gradual emergence still conflicts with Divine omnipotence, and the existence of pain and evil conflicts with either God's omnipotence or goodness. These difficulties prompt one to make still further alterations in the concept of God and Divine creation or goodness, etc. The need of field integration cannot be dismissed as the intellectual luxury of philosophical minds. It is rooted in a concern for one's intellectual integrity and disinterested search for truth instead of fragmented loyalties. In the final analysis, field integration is more a search for authenticity than for intellectual curiosity.

The search for authenticity prima facie clashes with an existential surrender to God or Scripture, and appears to be rooted in pride, or a reliance on one's own judgment, and hence the negation of genuine religion, which is supposed to be rooted in surrender to God. But many highly intelligent and deeply religious minds hold self-authentication as an essentially religious surrender to the God within man rather than as a species of pride. This is the existential approach to religion and it enables the individual to retain his spiritual autonomy without the danger of the autarchy of his surface self or the Freudian '*id*'.[9] This approach, however, does contradict the traditional conception of religion, as surrender to an external authority.

The existentialist approach to religion, as I understand it, affirms a three-fold autonomy of science, of individual conscience and of society. This means affirming the autonomy of science in the sphere of empirical truth; the autonomy of individual conscience in the sphere of values; and finally the autonomy of the human community in the sphere of institutional matters. According to my approach, religion belongs primarily to the second category and only marginally to the third. Religion thus becomes an authentic concern with the meaning of the universe rather than an institutional way of life. The meaning is not a propositional truth claim, but an existential interpretation, which quenches the restless longing of man for a stable total perspective or worldview. Spiritual satisfaction can, however, occur only when the perspective is existential and authentic, that is, it wells up from the depths of the person.

A religious response degenerates into a pseudo-religious one, if it fails to grip the individual. A religion should rise from the heart rather than the head, even as maternal love is a demand of her innermost being without the aid of Kant's categorical imperative, or Bentham's (d. 1832) hedonistic calculus. Neither the laws of logic, nor the rules of verification, nor the lure of utility, whether temporal or eschatological, but only the soft whisper of the spirit wields the final authority in the sphere of religion.[10] It may happen that while the basic world view of a particular religion appeals to the believer, he is unable to agree with a particular point or norm of the tradition. Should he then reject the religious tradition, which nurtured him and in which his spiritual roots are embedded? It seems, in such a case self-authentication rather than rejection of the tradition is the proper response. This response presupposes religion in its mature form, that is, religion as surrender to an internal authority rather than to an external.

The inner authority is man's creative conscience or God within man. Submission to an external authority obviously negates freedom, while submission to an internal authority is quite compatible with freedom. Spiritual autonomy is the inner spontaneous demand of man, and submission to an external authority goes against the grain of man, so to speak, even though he may be quite happy and productive, if there be no conflict between the prescriptions of the authority and his own inner demands.

There is another significance of the distinction between an external and an internal authority. If man could submit to an external God without any reservation and with complete authenticity, he would certainly have the inner satisfaction that he would never err to the extent that he obeyed the commands of the infallible God. But the difficulty is that man never encounters God in a direct manner in the same way as he encounters his conscience, or a book, or a person. Submission to God means, in the functional sense at least, submission to God through some mediator or channel. Man's submission to God is thus always indirect and mediated rather than direct and immediate. For example, to a Christian, submission to God amounts to submission to Jesus, the Christ; and to a Muslim, submission to God amounts to submission to the Quran as the revealed Will of God, or, in most cases, to the Quran plus *hadis*. To certain persons, such an indirect submission may not raise any difficulty, and their commitment or faith may be perfect. Indeed, they may be blissfully unaware of the distinction between an immediate submission and a mediated submission to God, just as most non-philosophers are blissfully unaware of the various problems connected with the perception of physical objects, or the mechanism of the perceptual process. They perceive things and are not bothered by the problems or theories of perception. Similarly, many deeply pious believers just believe without being bothered by the intellectual difficulties involved in those beliefs. They honestly feel and believe that the Quran is the Word of God, or Jesus the Son of God, and readily submit themselves before them, as if they had submitted before an unmediated God. But once the reflective impulse or process is set in motion, no matter how or why, man loses the original innocence of faith or commitment. His joy in surrender is corroded by doubts and felt intellectual difficulties. Once the reflective process starts, it cannot arbitrarily be stopped at the portals of sacrosanct beliefs. The reflective process is like an all-consuming fire, which spares nothing. The goal of this process is complete field integration. Should the movement of thought be checked or suspended, man becomes inwardly restless and fragmented. The reflective attitude conflicts with submission to external but not to an internal authority. This makes the distinction between the two crucial.

The difficulties of submission to an external authority have been pointed out. But submission to an internal authority is not free from difficulties of its own. The principal difficulty lies in the fact that man can easily deceive himself into believing that he is submitting himself to the internal authority of his conscience, when, in fact, he may be guilty of rationalization or in-authenticity. Thus, man's spiritual autonomy or freedom is ever perilously near the dark leap into license. 'The fear of freedom', as Erich Fromm calls it, is thus quite natural and understandable.[11] Rationalists are often inclined to dismiss this fear as born of immaturity or distrust in the essential goodness of human nature. But their confidence in human capacities is as one-sided and dangerous as is the fear of freedom, or the evasion of self-responsibility and the resultant surrender to an external authority, whether religious or secular. Consequently, the inwardly free man needs to be extremely cautious that his freedom does not degenerate into license under one garb or the other.[12]

## Field Integration, Science and Religion

Man cannot function in an interpretative vacuum, in the belief that pure morality and science would jointly suffice. To ignore this truth was the crucial mistake committed by many Western science-oriented thinkers in the late 19th and early 20th centuries. The concept of the supposed self-sufficiency of pure morality without some metaphysical foundation or other was generated by the erosion of the traditional Christian theistic interpretation. The case of morality without metaphysics or religion appeared to grow all the more strong with the gradual realization that no metaphysical or religious belief could be proved to be true either deductively or inductively. The Western intellectual's despair pushed him into a positivistic humanism or pure 'ethicism', according to which morality is sufficient for man, and that religion is either a pre-scientific illusion or, at best, a consolation for

William Jame's tender folk.[13] This implied that the progress of science and technology and the eventual eradication of social evils such as poverty and exploitation would ultimately deprive religion of its function as well as its present appeal in the presence of widespread insecurity and injustice. But this belief in the all-sufficiency of science and morality is only a product of man's incurable romanticism.

The history of Western Europe after the First World War shows the inadequacy or falsity of the belief in pure scientific morality without any interpretative support or base. The mono-dimensional fixation upon the peculiar methodology of the natural sciences, or, in other words, viewing scientific explanations as the only model of valid interpretation, generated a new variety of skepticism alter the First World War. This variety embraces not merely particular religious beliefs, but all values as such. This total and all-embracing skepticism or nihilism saps the springs of all human endeavors, generating in man a total despair and a sense of futility or absurdity of life. The logical terminus of this attitude is the quest of death, which is judged as the only means of release from the tyranny of being aware of absurdity, but helpless to overcome it. In some cases this basic despair seeks to disguise itself in a total hedonism. The quest of pleasure and the quest of destruction are desperate attempts to overcome the growing and creeping crisis of the spirit through killing or benumbing the body. The phenomena of drug addiction, alcoholism, 'sexualism', and even such apparently disconnected 'isms' such as extreme nationalism, religionism, scientism, and 'artism', etc., are symptoms of an inner spiritual imbalance or 'ontological deficiency'. They all betray an inauthentic human existence clinging to either escape mechanisms or fragmented loyalties instead of loyalty to an integrated value system. This inauthentic existence turns man into an insecure and anxious being. This breeds suspicion, aggression, and intolerance, etc., and also an inner resistance to the promptings of man's creative conscience. This condition may aptly be termed as a hardening of man's spiritual arteries. Neither the reiteration of traditional creeds nor their intellectual defense cures this malady. Only a dispassionate self-confrontation and more refined methods of philosophical analysis can liberate Western man from his unfortunate nihilism.

The Eastern man, whether Muslim or Hindu, has not yet fallen a victim to this nihilism. He is, however, inwardly uneasy and in need of firm support. Outwardly he may be serene and self-assured, but various field tensions do inwardly disturb him in proportion to his awareness of the contemporary conceptual framework. He is not fully aware of the need of field integration, but inner conceptual fermentation is unmistakably present.

The Muslim having a traditional or conservative approach to Islam would not concede this point. He would assert that the different sciences, both natural and social, do not have any bearing upon or relevance to the proper understanding of Islam. This contention is true in the sense that the detailed theories and hypotheses of science are not relevant to the truth or falsity of fundamental religious beliefs and moral values, which remain unaffected and untouched by the modifications in our scientific theories or advances in factual knowledge. But the scientific perspective or world view comprising such basic concepts as universal causation, uniformity of nature, evolution, relativity, etc., do profoundly affect our concrete understanding of such essentially religious concepts as creation, revelation, miracles, etc. It is true that religious faith is essentially a matter of an existential commitment rather than of a logical or scientific proof; it is also true that the scientific worldview cannot be established through deductive or inductive reasoning alone, but also needs an extra-rational ontological commitment. Nevertheless, the concrete interpretation of every worldview is inevitably molded by the thought system of the person. Since all social and natural sciences are nothing but critically organized thought systems, they are directly relevant to such concrete interpretations. To the extent that an individual refuses to enter into a dialogue with science, he is like a person who refuses to observe or perform a certain experiment, lest this may go against his established beliefs or attitudes.

The reason for this field isolation is perhaps due to a totally false conception about a complete discontinuity between the field of religion and of science. This belief is fairly widespread. It is, however, only due to an oversimplified conception of both science and religion. Science is viewed as purely factual, while religion as purely valuational or spiritual. It is then held that there is no connection whatsoever between facts and values, or between science and religion. Consequently, it is thought, there is no need for a mutual dialogue between these two fields of human experience.

This approach completely ignores the complexity of both religion and science. It is highly misleading to say that religion has nothing to do with facts, which come under the domain of science, or that science has nothing to do with values, which come under the domain of religion. On the one hand, every religion has its distinctive thought system or worldview, apart from a distinctive value system. Every religion thus has a connection with the realm of facts. On the other hand, science generates its own distinctive values, even though it is admittedly not concerned with values, but with the explanation of facts. In other words, science has a 'valuational temper' of its own. For example, the scientific methods of observation and experiment and formulation of verifiable hypotheses lead to a distaste for speculative metaphysics or a hair-splitting theology, both of which fail to possess any operational definitions or concepts. Similarly, a techno-centric society generates the new value of equality of the sexes, or the value of speed, or the ethics of planning, etc. Moreover, science is not only relevant, but also crucial for realizing basic values, and it also has a positive bearing on the concrete interpretation of these basic intrinsic values. The inevitable conclusion, therefore, is that the slogan of a neat demarcation between the domains of science and religion breaks down.

Scientific developments, however, do not prove or disprove religious beliefs such as the existence of God, or life after death. In fact, if religious beliefs could be proved or disproved on the basis of evidence, religious faith would forfeit its distinctive flavor and become just like other beliefs. Religious faith is 'existentially certain', not 'inductively certain' like the factual truths of science, or 'deductively certain' like the truths of mathematics or logic. The developments of science do not, and cannot, prove or disprove our religious beliefs, qua existential interpretations of man-in-the-universe, as distinct from pseudo-scientific or pre-scientific truth claims, involving the subject matter of science itself. But the concrete interpretation of religious beliefs cannot help being influenced by the impact of scientific developments. Science and religion thus interact, and yet they do not interact, in the sense in which interaction takes place between two elements within the same field. The interaction between religion and science is complex, like the relationship between facts and values. Though distinct, facts and values cannot be totally segregated. Concrete value judgments can neither be justified nor realized without adequate factual information supplied by science.

The most significant feature of man's present situation is science or technology. Perhaps the two most vital consequences of this are man's experience of power over nature and progressive inter-cultural communication. The exercise of power over nature tends to corrode those conceptions of religion that discourage man's self-reliance and encourage the ethics of surrender to an all-powerful Divine will.

## Appendix 2: The Quest For The Meaning Of Islam

The ever-growing communication between different cultures progressively transforms more or less stagnant mono-cultural societies into more or less dynamic multi-cultural ones. This renders the traditional commitment to the 'faith of one's forefathers' more difficult. The diversity of thought-cum-value systems generates a healthy doubt as inevitably as prosperity generates parking difficulties in the big cities. The individual is conceptually uprooted from his traditional conceptual soil and pushed into a multi-cultural universe where he has to choose his own conceptual latitude and longitude. Tensions arise between his religious beliefs or thought system and the thought systems of other fields of culture. Tensions may also arise between his expected course of events and the actual course of events or between his aspirations and their fulfillment. This experience of tension, frustration, surprise, and doubt is as essential for man's conceptual growth as is the experience of wonder, uniformity of sequence, success in prediction, and manipulative control over his environment. Tension and frustration induce him to reexamine his beliefs and to remove their inadequacies or mutual contradictions. The leisure generated in affluent societies also tends to promote a growing concern with fundamental human problems, even though this concern is likely to be preceded by a period of an immature hedonism. Affluent societies would eventually be drawn towards a reflective multi-cultural interpretation of religious experience, or a faith that inquires rather than shuns inquiry.

The concrete re-interpretation of basic Islamic concepts thus becomes inevitable due to the growth in our factual knowledge and improved conceptual tools. This reinterpretation involves an ever-growing convergence or integration of the basic concepts of all the different natural, social, and humanistic sciences. This integration does not imply the creation of a super-science or super-philosophy sitting in judgment on the conclusions of the different sciences. All it means is that the basic well-established concepts of the various fields of human knowledge cannot be viewed as irrelevant for the concrete interpretation of the faith. For example, the geological concept of time, that is, an enormous time span with many distinct long periods; or concepts of biology, such as the gradual emergence of life, ceaseless variations, mutations, evolutionary blind alleys; or the conceptions of sociology, such as the impact of patterns of production and distribution on moral and religious ideas; or the concepts of psychoanalysis, such as man's fear of freedom, defense mechanisms; or the concepts of semantics, such as the different functions of language – all these basic concepts are crucially relevant for a more mature understanding of one's religious tradition.

Let us now examine in some detail how some of the above concepts of the natural and social sciences have demanded the reconstruction of basic religious concepts in the case of Christianity.

## DARWIN'S THEORY OF EVOLUTION

The conflict between Newtonian physics and Christian theism was very mild indeed in relation to the conflict between Darwin's theory of organic evolution and theism. Newton's theory had only turned the Creator into a super-mathematician but had not abolished the concept as such. Darwin's theory, on the other hand, abolished the Divine office, since the concept of evolution was supposed to explain and account for all the marvels and complexities of living beings and the universe as a whole.

The entire Christian world was shocked and baffled by this challenge. Initially the Church totally rejected Darwin's theory of organic evolution. But the evidence marshaled by Darwin was too systematic to be ignored. Soon scientists all over the world accepted Darwin's approach. Later on the majority of the Protestant and even Catholic intellectuals assimilated the concept of evolution into their religious framework in varying degrees. This assimilation was done through the belief that evolution was the mode of Divine creation.

This assimilation or integration of biological evolution into the Christian framework satisfied the religiously oriented scientist on the one hand, and the scientifically oriented theologian on the other. But very soon fresh intellectual difficulties were generated. For example, why should an omnipotent God choose such a wasteful and tortuously long road of creation through evolution? The facts of dysteleology and of pain and evil also continued to oppress the religious consciousness. Consequently, the highly sensitive and well-informed intellects of the late 19th century such as Bergson, William James, Paulsen, and Lloyd Morgan, etc., rejected the pre-Darwinian religious conception of creation on the one hand, and Darwin's concept of mechanical natural selection on the other. These thinkers formulated their own conceptions of evolution or evolutionary creation, which are basically similar in spite of differences in terminology.[14]

The Islamic conceptual framework or thought system is, however, still pre-Darwinian. Consequently, a tension exists between science and religion in the deeper recesses of the educated Muslim mind. Integration of scientific concepts with religious concepts is imperative in this crucial matter. To the extent that the official Islamic thought system rejects evolution and its philosophical bearing on traditional theism, it will lack real conviction for the contemporary mind. Only when the followers of the different religions can integrate their respective religious thought systems with well-established contemporary concepts will they become integrated believers who are not pulled in different directions by science and religion.

## KARL MARX'S CONCEPT OF SOCIAL EVOLUTION

The next tension between religion and science was generated by the work of Karl Marx, who may aptly be regarded as the 'Darwin' of Sociology. Marx forcefully and strikingly projected the concepts of social evolution and social causation. What natural selection was in the scheme of Darwinism, technological changes were in the scheme of Marx. Just as the basic concepts of organic evolution and ceaseless variations have been firmly accepted by biologists, the concepts of social evolution and social causation have been firmly established in the conceptual scheme of contemporary man.

A sociological cause is an organic blend of economic, political, cultural, and ideological forces acting upon the human individual or group. Social phenomena are determined by such laws and can be altered or manipulated with their help. Poverty, social inequality, and hereditary class domination, etc. are therefore, in principle, alterable. The prospect of the conquest of poverty was enough to generate a tension between this approach and the traditional view; that the division of people into the rich and the poor is God's own act, just like His creation of mountains, rivers, or deserts, and that man could only shower charity on the poor rather than seek to abolish poverty as such. The actual success of modern Western man in abolishing poverty in the developed nations has prompted creative Western thinkers to redefine the concept of God. This reconstruction has generated a religious ethic of planned action and life-affirmation, as distinguished from the medieval religious ethic of fatalism and other-worldliness.

The traditional Islamic approach, however, continues to be pre-sociological. According to it, social or political changes such as the rise and fall of nations or groups, the fluctuations in wealth, power, or rank, the states of prosperity and adversity, etc., are either due to Divine providence, or at most due to individual human merit. The traditional Muslim is apt to suppose that poverty as well as affluence is the way of God to test the faith and character of human beings, or that the number of children born to a couple is decided by the Will of God, or that poverty can never be abolished. Consequently, the sociological approach that poverty or other social evils are as much eliminable as the physical diseases such as plague, and smallpox, etc. appears to him as being a tall and arrogant claim. He believes that such irreverent interference with a Divinely established social order is inspired by the atheistic materialism of Karl Marx and his tribe.

A corollary of this a sociological orientation is a mistaken reading of history by the average Muslim. History shows many instances of good men or causes losing to bad men or causes supported by brute force. Even where good causes win, careful sociological analysis reveals that mere goodness is not the total cause of victory, but technological superiority always plays a crucial role in such victories. This approach appears to conflict with the traditional Islamic interpretation of history according to which the affairs of the universe including victory or defeat in wars are regulated by Divine providence.

Logically speaking, there should be no difficulty in reconciling the operation of Divine providence with the advantages of technology or the operation of social laws on the analogy of natural laws. But the concept of social law is usually absent from the conceptual framework of the average Muslim. Consequently, he attributes the success or failure of nations in peace and war to purely ethical or moral factors, apart from the Will of God. Thus, sexual laxity, drinking, and gambling, etc., to the neglect of religious obligations and duties, is adjudged the main cause of the defeat and decline of nations. This naive pre-sociological approach is equated with a genuinely religious approach, and contrasted with the atheistic or materialistic interpretation of human history. The average educated Muslim thus misses the complexity of social causation, and mistakes the part for the whole. He misses the relevance of technology and ultimately of the crucial role of the scientific attitude in the rise and fall of nations and the march of history.

The traditionalists as well as many liberal Muslims of the Amir Ali School are also not sufficiently aware of the depth and range of modifications necessary in the traditional understanding of the basic values of Islam, such as brotherhood, equality, and tolerance, etc., for making them relevant to contemporary Muslims who are exposed to the thought of Mill, Marx, and Freud. Unless this is done, many new socio-political and economic patterns are liable to be rejected straight away by Islamic societies, even though those patterns might promote the basic intrinsic values of Islam itself. It is indeed a pity that reputed Muslim writers such as Abul Hasan Ali Nadvi, go on repeating that it is not Islam but the Muslims that need reformation. This is indeed true in the sense that moral and social evils such as dishonesty, selfishness, ignorance, etc., are traits of Muslims rather than of Islam or the Quran. But such a formulation is highly misleading as it obscures the need for the emergence of new dimensions in the Islamic thought-cum-value system.

## Researches in Psychology

Another tension is generated by the concepts of modern psychology and psychoanalysis. Religions affirm that God grants the petitionary prayers of His supplicating creatures. Modern psychology, on the other hand, has empirically proved the crucial role of suggestion and other positive mental attitudes in promoting or maintaining human health, happiness, and success. This approach clashes with the view that health, happiness, and success are the fruits of Divine favors. The psychological approach, on the other hand, implies that human success and happiness are governed by socio-psychological factors.

Freud's psychoanalysis poses a still more powerful challenge to religion, as he provides us with a complete scheme of psychological dynamics governing all mental phenomena without exception. Freud's concept of unconscious motivation is the counterpart of social causation. His concept of sexual or libidinal determinism is the counterpart of the economic determinism of Marx. Again, Freud's concept of repression of the libido is the counterpart of Marx's concept of exploitation of labor. The concepts of '*id*', as a surging sea of irrational drives and repressed impulses, and of the death instinct have debunked man much more seriously than Darwin's theory of man's animal ancestry, or of Copernicus's heliocentric theory. While Darwin's theory had debunked man, it had not destroyed man's confidence in his future. If he had evolved from anthropoid ape to man, he could evolve still further from man to superman. Indeed, this was the actual line of thinking adopted by most of the late 19th century and early 20th century Western thinkers. Freud's debunking of man, on the other hand, left him without hope and faith.

Freud's conception of religion as an illusion is rather dogmatic and one-sided. But the awareness of the numerous elements of value in Freud's depth-approach is essential for acquiring insight into the complexities of human nature. A critical concept of man is the prerequisite of a mature and adequate conception of God. The concepts of suggestion or autosuggestion, father image, fixation, resistance, compensation, wish fulfillment, guilt or inferiority complexes, defense mechanism, neurosis, neurotic fear or anxiety, etc., are highly significant for understanding the dynamics of human behavior and for a genuine and authentic religious commitment, as distinguished from inauthentic faith. But almost no notice has been given to the above concepts by Muslim religious thinkers, apart from literary critics and poets.

## THE PRESENCE OF SUFFERING IN THE WORLD

Another major tension is generated by the extent of suffering in the world. The tension arises due to the conflict between the course of events expected in a world created by an omnipotent and benevolent God and the actual course of events. For example, when a virtuous woman is raped, or a child murdered in front of his parents, or when a life full of promise is cut short by untimely death, while insane or physically crippled patients live on to a ripe old age, or the indiscriminate suffering caused by natural calamities, accidents or infectious diseases; all these facts evoke serious doubts about God's goodness or power. It is the solemn duty of all authentic theists to resolve this tension without intellectual dishonesty.

## TECHNOLOGICAL RESEARCH

In the end, here is an example of a hypothetical tension generated by an ever-advancing technology. Let us suppose man eventually acquires control over the sex of the unborn child. Then there would be a tension between the belief that the determination of sex is an act of God, Who produces the male or the female according to His own sweet will and man's actual control over the sex of the unborn. It should be obvious that if the concept of God has to be retained, it will have to be reconstructed in order to resolve this hypothetical tension and harmonize it with man's actual experience. We could then maintain that natural laws gradually unfold themselves to the inquiring human mind, and that the postulation of natural laws does not contradict the concept of God, viewed as the Primal Source of the law and order in the universe, rather than as an invisible Old Man with a magic wand in His hands.

Tensions arising out of the different fields of human culture must first be acknowledged before they can be removed. The denial of religious difficulties, on the other hand, creates mischief precisely because this merely serves to conceal rather than heal the tensions. The function of field integration is, therefore, strikingly similar to the function of psychoanalysis. Psychoanalysis leads to the integration of the total human personality, while field integration to that of different languages and concepts of the different streams of human culture.

## III

## FIELD INTEGRATION IN EARLY AND MIDDLE ISLAM

Every religion in its early phase is free from interpretative complexities of dogma and doctrine and thus also free from field tensions. This state may well be called the stage of ideological innocence or non-differentiated integration. But with the passage of time field tensions arise and demand resolution.

The germs of inquiry and of field integration in Islam were present in the intellectual approach of the fourth *Khalifa*, Ali (d. 661), and later on of Hasan al-Basri (d. 728) and Jafar Sadiq (d. 765). But the need for field integration came to the fore in a big way with the rise of Mutazilite dialectics (*kalam*) in the 9th century. This movement was followed by the more orthodox Asharite School, which continued to dominate the Islamic world right up to the last century. These movements were considerably influenced by Christian theology and Greek thought and, in all probability; some *Sufi* doctrines and practices of a later period were influenced by Vedantic Monism and Yoga. Let us briefly review these efforts at Islamic self-understanding in the early and middle period.

## THEOLOGY AND PHILOSOPHY

The first source of field tension was the conflict between the belief in free will (which seemed to be a pre-supposition of morality) and the belief that nothing happens without the will of God, and the inequity of Divine punishment if human beings were not free agents. This field tension led to the emergence of the theories of pre-destinarianism and freedom of the will, with their protagonists attempting to justify their views with the help of Quranic verses of their choice.[15] In general the Mutazilites stood for free will, while the Asharites for a qualified pre-destinarianism (*kasb*). This is not the place to go into the details of this controversy. Suffice it to say that it helped in the clarification of the concept of God and His attributes of justice, omnipotence, and omniscience, etc., as well as the nature of man and his capacities and limitations. In other words, the controversy led to field integration between philosophy, psychology, theology, and ethics.

The next source of field tension was the Aristotelian distinction between substance and attributes. God was one, but His attributes were many, like mercy, knowledge, love, power, creation, etc. It was felt that plurality of attributes eroded the unity of the Divine Being. Let us see why this difficulty arose. When, for instance, we say that God is forgiving, we do not mean that He became forgiving at a particular time when He forgave a sinner, but that He is always forgiving or that the attribute of forgiveness is part of His eternal nature or Being. But then, this makes the attribute of forgiveness coeval and co-eternal with God and thus erodes the concept of God's unity. The Mutazilites, therefore, tended to conceive God as pure Being without attributes, which were viewed as anthropomorphic projections upon God's Being, which was essentially unknowable. But this position was difficult to reconcile with the Quranic references to God's attributes and with the orthodox conception of God.

The Asharite theologians held that God's essence is not a bare unity devoid of all qualities. Rather, Divine qualities are the modes of the one Divine Being or Essence, though we are unable to grasp the nature of the Divine attributes, except in metaphorical language, which is only partly applicable to God. It seems to me that the Mutazilite theologians overplayed the distinction between substance and attributes, and rushed to the conclusion that attributes erode Divine unity, and therefore cannot really inhere in God as Substance. The Asharite doctrines of Divine attributes based on the union of metaphor and transcendence (*tashbih wa tanzih*) was far more balanced. In any case, this particular field tension or controversy did a lot to clarify the concept of God.

## Appendix 2: The Quest For The Meaning Of Islam

The most explosive field tension was the controversy about the nature of the Quran. The Mutazilites held that belief in the eternity of the Quran eroded the Islamic doctrine of the unity of God, since; in this case, the Word of God (which is not literally identical with God Himself) becomes co-eternal in time. Moreover, being in the Arabic language, the Quran follows the man-made grammar and syntax of that language, and thus could not possibly be eternal or uncreated. This was not acceptable to many orthodox Muslims for whom the Quran was the pure locus of Divinity without any human elements. The Quranic reference to the preserved tablet (*lawh-e-mahfuz*) also seemed to imply the eternity of the Quran.[16] This position was taken up by the Asharites. They held that the Quran was eternal in the sense that God foreknew the contents of what He would subsequently reveal in time to His chosen Prophet ﷺ. It is true that before the creation of the world there was no language including Arabic. But God's foreknowledge included the Quran in the Arabic language with all its man-made vocabulary, grammar, and syntax, apart from Divine ideas, which, however, our finite minds cannot grasp. However, even if we accept the above Asharite approach, the Quran, in its concrete Arabic form at least, would seem to comprise some human or temporal elements, thereby ceasing to be the pure locus of Divinity. Thus the same difficulty would arise once again. The only way out would be to claim that Arabic has a supernatural origin and a higher status than the other languages of the human family. Perhaps this line of thinking (which was implicitly present) was acceptable to the Asharites, but not to the Mutazilites, who were relatively less susceptible to Arab ethnocentricity and more speculative in their theology.

The above and similar other field tensions were sought to be removed by Mutazilite theologians like Abul Hozail (d. 841), Nazzam (d. 845), Jahiz (d. 868) and Asharite theologians such as Ashari (d. 935), and by philosophers such as Kindi (d. cir. 870), Farabi (d. 950), Ibn Sina (d. 1037), Ibn Rushd (d. 1198) who dealt with a wider range of philosophical problems. In the course of time neo-Platonic theories of emanation and Aristotle's theory of the immanence of form in matter led to the radical redefinition of concepts such as God, creation, revelation, personal immortality, and the eternity of matter, etc. Many theories such as perpetual Divine Creation, the negation of causality in the sense of necessary connection, the growth of lower forms of being into higher, the distinction between metaphorical and literal uses of language, and the essential unity of all religions, etc., were raised and discussed with remarkable thoroughness and perspicacity.

Muslim philosophers had been profoundly influenced by Neo-Platonic thought and held Aristotle and Plato in the highest veneration. Farabi, Ibn Sina, Ibn Rushd, among others, maintained that there was no essential difference between the basic truths of Greek philosophy and the principles of Islam, such as unity of God, revelation, and life after death, etc., apart from the difference in the language of philosophy and of religion. The language of philosophy was abstract and logico-metaphysical, while the language of religion was concrete, anthropomorphic, or metaphorical. But their essential import or significance was the same. Thus, according to them, the Lord of the worlds, as mentioned in the Quran, is the same as Plato's Idea of good or Aristotle's Prime Mover. Similarly, the creation of the universe by the God of Islam is the same as the emanation of different levels of being from the Primal Source, which is pure Spirit. Again the Divine revelation of the Quran to the Prophet ﷺ through the agency of Gabriel (*Jibrael*) is the same as the illumination of the finite mind by the Active Intelligence. Thus the revelatory process is of the nature of melting or fusion of the finite mind into the Infinite or of illumination rather than of the transmission of sounds or signals from an external communicator. It seems this conception of revelation is free from the difficulties in anthropomorphic ideas about God's attributes or acts. But the trouble with Muslim philosophers was that, like all speculative thinkers of the past, they did not bother about agreed criteria of validity of their truth claims.

## Sufism

The other movement, which led to field integration, is *Sufism*, which partly overlaps, but primarily succeeds, the movements of Dialectics and Greek Rationalism. *Sufism* lays primary emphasis upon direct spiritual illumination rather than on reason for removing field tensions and achieving inner peace and serenity (*nafs-e-mutmaiinah*). The seeds of *Sufism* were present in the Quran and the life of the Prophet ﷺ. Instead of giving arguments for God, the Quran repeatedly asks man to reflect on the marvels and mysteries of the outer world and his own self. Many verses of the Quran have a mystical flavor, and the Prophet ﷺ used to meditate throughout his life. Ali was especially interested in esoteric knowledge (*ilm-e-batin*), as distinguished from external knowledge (*ilm-e-zahir*). In the early phase of Islamic political and religious expansion, the influence of Greek thought and Christian theology stimulated the growth of external knowledge, both religious and secular. The spate of philosophical and theological controversies, the barrenness of external morality and legalism as well as later sociopolitical changes led to the growth of Islamic mysticism.

Islamic mysticism or *Sufism* is, however, far from being a way of pure gnosis without any rational or speculative elements, just as Ibn Sina's or Farabi's rationalism is far from being a pure intellectualism without mystical elements. Islamic rationalism is inextricably mixed with mysticism, though in varying proportions in different personalities.

The earlier *Sufi's* were simple pietists who emphasized the inwardness of morality and love of God without neglecting the Islamic religious law and without any metaphysical speculation on the nature of God, soul, and prophecy, etc. But mystics emphasizing the Gnostic dimension gradually emerged and acquired a position of pre-eminence. This in turn was followed by the systematic conceptualization of mystical experience, since no individual can avoid the task of field integration. Even the mystic who stresses direct mystical experience as the true source of knowledge has to live and act at the non-mystical plane for the greater part of his life. Consequently, even he cannot abjure the need of a coherent interpretation of the basic features of the universe, including his mystical experience itself. He cannot avoid reflecting upon the nature and meaning of his mystical experience and its reconciliation with his own normal experiences such as perception, causality, sense of space and time, sense of ego hood, sense of freedom, and a measure of control over the environment. The *Sufi*, no less than the philosopher, is thus drawn into the vortex of interpretative activity, whose range and depth, however, depend upon his intellectual powers over and above his spiritual talents. Some *Sufi's* (like philosophers and theologians) have therefore reinterpreted the basic concepts and values of Islam. But the philosophers were confined to external knowledge alone, while *Sufi* thinkers claimed access to both external and esoteric knowledge. They thus went back to the tradition of Jaffar Sadiq and ultimately of Ali, who was the intellectual and mystic par excellence, while the theologians and philosophers remained at the level of Aristotle and Plato. Perhaps the two most outstanding *Sufi* thinkers are Ghazzali (d. 1111) and Ibn Arabi (d. 1240).

Ghazzali is the greatest mediator between the three main streams of Islamic thought and culture; the legalistic-cum-theological, the rationalistic and the mystical. Up to his time these three streams had developed more or less in relative isolation from each other. The mystical and the metaphysical approaches coalesced in such remarkably gifted figures as Farabi, and Ibn Sina, etc. But the mysticism of such philosophers was speculative rather than pietistic and hence did not attract the notice of the common man who cared for myths and miracles rather than metaphysics and mathematics. Many pietist mystics, on the other hand, were not sufficiently well equipped with philosophy to remove various field tensions. The jurists and theologians, on the other hand, were sharp dialecticians and experts in casuistry, but failed to distinguish religious feeling from religious conformism, and to progress from the realm of law into the realm of the spirit. Thus there was a clear lack of authentic communication between the philosophers, mystics, and jurists of Islam. The genius of Ghazzali led to an integrated multi-dimensional approach which repudiated neither reason, nor intuition, nor law. Unfortunately the cultural stagnation and decay in the Islamic East due to the Mongol violence in the 12th and 13th centuries did not permit further growth or refinement of Ghazzali's irenic approach.

Many Western Orientalists are of the view that the decline of the rationalist temper and of science in the Islamic world was mainly due to the anti-rationalism or mysticism profusely injected by Ghazzali into the arteries of Islamic culture. Ghazzali's masterpiece *'Destruction of the Philosophers'* is regarded as Ghazzali's arrow that pierced into the heart of the philosophical or rationalist movement in Islam and literally destroyed philosophy. This is not the whole truth. What Ghazzali had attacked with great skill and power was not reason or philosophy as such, but rather Greek speculative metaphysics. Indeed Ghazzali's approach in the *'Destruction of the Philosophers'* bears some striking points of similarity with the analytical-cum-positivistic approach of Kant and also of the present. His approach to proofs of God and faith is in tune with contemporary religious existentialism. But Ghazzali, who was so systematic and methodical in his treatment of Greek philosophy, lacked a critical approach in the field of *hadis* literature. Moreover, he could not emancipate himself fully from the pre-scientific thought patterns, prejudices, and limitations of his age, as is indicated by his disapproval of friendly and intimate relations between Muslims and non-Muslims.[17]

Ibn Arabi is, by far, the most daring speculative *Sufi* who has left a permanent mark on the Islamic thought system. He reinterpreted the Islamic formula of faith '*There is no god but Allah*' as '*There is no being but the Being of Allah*'. The monistic interpretation of Divine unity, as the Unity of Existence (*wahdat ul wajud*), in contrast with the traditional interpretation that God had created the universe out of nothing, was a redefinition of the concept of God. Ibn Arabi also redefined other concepts to fit them into his peculiar conceptual framework. His influence upon *Sufi's* with an intellectual bent of mind has been very great, though in his own day the establishment rejected him.

It seems to me that the crucial flaw in Ibn Arabi's approach is the lack of a critical epistemology or methodology, since there is no criterion to test the validity of his mystical-speculative ontology. The traditional Islamic criterion lay in conformity to the Quran, as interpreted by the Prophet ﷺ and his trusted companions. If, however, the mystic feels free to give his own interpretation to Quranic verses in the light of his own mystical experiences, but fails to give any criteria of validity, his interpretation becomes an exercise in uncontrolled speculation. The stand that others could test the truth of the mystic's claims through their direct experience is misleading, since it does not distinguish the conceptual interpretation of the mystical experience with the experience as such. It is quite possible for two mystics to have a similar experience, but they may differ in its conceptual interpretation. Now Ibn Arabi can give us no criterion for the validity of his interpretation of his mystical experience. In this crucial respect Ghazzali scores over Ibn Arabi, since the former is much more cautious in making Gnostic claims. But at times even he floats in the thin air of speculative interpretation of his mystical experience without bothering about the question of validity. The mere fact that the truth claim does not clash with the Quran cannot suffice to make it valid.

After Ghazzali and Ibn Arabi, *Sufism* loses its intellectual vigor and becomes institutionalized. This was perhaps the social consequence of the socio-political upheavals caused by Mongol invasions of the Eastern Islamic world in the late 12th and 13th centuries. *Sufism* in this period ceased to do the job of field integration. But it did promote the personality integration of individual Muslims in troubled times, and also helped in propagating Islam in India and elsewhere through its exalted morality and spirituality. However, spiritual culture without the cultivation of reason is as lame as the latter is blind without the cultivation of spirituality.

## Appendix 2: The Quest For The Meaning Of Islam

The consolidation of Muslim rule in India by the 12th century led to the emergence of a plural society. The vast Hindu population with a rich cultural tradition had accepted the political presence of Islam, but they were in no mood for Islamisation, which had occurred in Iran and Egypt after the Arab conquest. The orthodox theologians stood for the cultural and social isolation of the Muslims, as far as possible, from non-Muslims. But the *Sufis* of the Chishtia order were quick to grasp the social and psychological aspects of the historical situation and stood for a liberal spiritual humanism in place of a theological legalism. This attracted many Hindus to the faith and practice of Islam.[18]

Muslim rulers and administrators in general tended to be guided by reasons of state and preferred the policy of tolerance and non-interference in the religious matters of their subjects. But the orthodox theologians ever demanded the subordination of the state to the Islamic religious law. It appears that but for the pressure of public opinion, under the influence of the orthodox theologians, many more Muslim kings and administrators would have leaned far more to the liberal approach symbolized by Emperor Akbar (d. 1605).

The strongest opposition to the spiritual humanism and liberalism which was gaining ground in the highly sophisticated urban elite during the time of Akbar and his successors in the latter half of the 16th century came from Shaikh Ahmad of Sarhind (d. 1624). The Shaikh, who belonged to the Nakhshbandia *Sufi* order, made it his life mission to rectify the wrongs perpetrated by Akbar and his host, and to restore Islamic *shariah* to its rightful place in India. He was also deeply opposed to the monistic philosophy of Ibn Arabi, which according to him, had corrupted the true Islamic notion of Divine unity. The Shaikh was on strong ground when he said that Ibn Arabi's conception of God was quite different from the orthodox view of God as the Supreme Creator and Lord of the worlds, the beneficent and the merciful, the Hearer of prayers and the Fulfiller of needs, etc. Ibn Arabi, on his part, could justifiably say that no finite mind could claim to understand God's attributes. The only way to understand the nature of God is to suggest a comparison and immediately to transcend it (*tashbih wa tanzih*). So far Ibn Arabi would be in accord with the orthodox position. But when he claims direct knowledge of hidden realities through mystical experience (*kashf*) without giving any criteria of validity of his interpretations his position becomes shaky.

Shaikh Ahmad's critique of Ibn Arabi's position was thus quite powerful and made considerable impact on *Sufi* circles. But the unfortunate thing was the Shaikh's rejection of the spiritual humanism and liberalism of the Persian mystical tradition represented by the classical Persian poetry of Attar (d. 1229), Rumi (d. 1273), Sadi (d. 1291), and Jami (d. 1492), which was flourishing at court circles ever since Akbar. The Shaikh on the other hand stood for a rigid adherence to the *shariah* as a complete and closed code of conduct rather than for a creative fidelity to the Quran. The Shaikh had no understanding of the requirements of a plural society and the point of view of his non-Muslim Indian brethren whose ideals and interests pulled them towards a secular polity rather than the rule of Islamic law. He was also not sympathetic to the *Shia* Muslims. He, thus, put back the clock of the Indian secular movement, as it were.[19]

In the 18th century Waliullah (d. 1763), the greatest Muslim philosophical theologian of the age, brought some fresh air and light into the portals of the Muslim mind through his concept of a common '*deen*' underlying the revealed Semitic religions, his permissive approach to denominational conformism within the four orthodox *Sunni* sects, his rationalistic approach to Quranic hermeneutic, and his irenic approach to the controversy between Ibn Arabi and Shaikh Ahmad. But he accepted the Islamic *shariah* as an organic totality, and his approach to the putative sayings of the Prophet ﷺ was not sufficiently critical. Moreover, his approach to socio-political issues was rooted in concepts and values common to both medieval Islam and Christianity.[19A] These ideas, which had started changing in Western Europe during the Renaissance, underwent a perceptible difference by the middle of the 18th century. This is the century, which witnessed the American and French revolutions, and also the industrial, the secular, and the sociological revolutions, which were rooted, in the earlier scientific revolution of the previous two centuries. The 18th century enlightenment blossomed into the knowledge explosion of the 19th and 20th centuries. This has now compelled the Islamic thought-cum-value system to come to terms with modernity.

# IV

## Field Integration in Recent Islam

The 19th century is of crucial significance for not only Islam but all other religions, since it was in this period that Darwin's theory of evolution brought the conflict between modern science and religion to its sharpest point. For Islam it is significant for the additional reason that the process of slow cultural and political decay going on in the entire Islamic world for several centuries reached its point of culmination. The entire Islamic world became a virtual dependency of some European power or other, and all hopes of success in the future appeared illusory. This total political and economic defeat of the bearers of the Quran and of God's best community (*Khairul Umam*) inevitably evoked fresh questionings in the minds of the thinking Muslims the world over from Egypt to Indonesia. Thus the nadir of defeat and despair proved to be a stimulus for a constructive probe into fundamental problems of religion and human destiny.

Of all those who reflected on these problems in the 19th century three persons stand out as outstanding: Jamaluddin Afghani (d. 1897), Muhammad Abduh of Egypt (d. 1905), and Syed Ahmad of India (d. 1898).

## Jamaluddin Afghani

He vigorously pleaded for a united pan-Islamic state as a precondition of the political and cultural re-emergence of Islam in the modern world. Gifted and dynamic as he was, Afghani had a merely pan-Islamic rather than an international perspective. He was certainly right in criticizing the evils of theological hair-splitting and a static religious piety totally divorced from a living concern with socio-political problems and concerns. But he was unable to register the full meaning and implications of the scientific attitude, which is the differentia of the modern age. Grievances against the excessive conservatism of the Mullas does not constitute the full meaning of a truly liberal and rationalist approach to religion and life. Afghani was thus more of a dashing publicist for a pan-Islamic renaissance rather than a creative scholar who could integrate contemporary concepts and values into the traditional Islamic thought-cum-value system.[20]

## MUHAMMAD ABDUH

He took inspiration from Afghani but did not entangle himself in politics. He devoted himself to reforming both the administration and the teaching of al-Azhar, the oldest living university in the world. Abduh played a crucial role in weakening the hold of a static tradition upon the Arabic speaking Muslims. He never abandoned the traditional interpretation of fundamental Islamic concepts and values, but only stood for a limited adaptation of the institutional system of Islam to contemporary needs and the aspirations of a liberal mind. His reconstruction of basic Islamic concepts and values was marginal. Perhaps this cautious and moderate approach, together with the great prestige of al-Azhar, as a symbol of traditional Islamic learning, greatly facilitated the propagation of his ideas in the Egyptian milieu. His ideas were different from those of the conservative and stagnant minds of his associates, but not too different to isolate him from the broad thought patterns of his associates. He was a modernist in relation to the outlook of his milieu. But in comparison with Syed Ahmad or Iqbal he was rather conservative.

## SYED AHMAD

He was the principal architect of the Aligarh Movement, the father of Islamic Modernism, and the first to be aware of the need of field integration between religion and modern science. His sharp mind pierced through the armor of the medieval pre-scientific understanding of basic Islamic concepts. He realized that Islamic thought had not even caught up with the Copernican revolution, to say nothing of the Darwinian. One cannot help admiring his efforts, even though one may be unable to agree with some features of his approach.

Syed Ahmad was a great admirer of Waliullah, but knew that the latter's basic conceptual framework was essentially medieval. Waliullah, for instance, retained the medieval polarity between the Islamic religio-political community and the non-Islamic world. Syed Ahmad, on the other hand, had outgrown this Islamic communitarianism.[21] He had genuinely accepted secular democracy and liberal nationalism with the implication that religion was a personal relationship between man and God rather than a total way of life in the medieval sense. In other words, the cast of mind of Syed Ahmad was almost (though not completely) modern. He went further than any previous Islamic thinker in viewing Islam as a simple Quranic theism without an all-embracing institutional system. He separated the proper spheres of religion and the state within the organic unity of a spiritual perspective, which was rooted in religious tolerance. This approach led to a pluralist fellowship of faiths in the place of the traditional concept of a religious brotherhood or community, be it Islamic, Christian, or Hindu.

Syed Ahmad was, however, primarily a philosophical theologian and apologist for Islam who used all the resources of his fertile mind to reconcile science with the Quran, accepted as the infallible and literally revealed word of God. His basic thesis was that science accurately and objectively describes the physical world, which is the Work of God. Now there cannot be any contradiction between 'the Word of God' and 'the Work of God'. The seeming contradiction was due to the mistaken interpretation of Quranic texts on the basis of pre-scientific ideas. In the light of this basic assumption Syed Ahmad proceeded to reinterpret those Quranic passages which seemingly violated the postulate of the causal uniformity of nature and also other well-established scientific theories of the time. This led Syed Ahmad to deny the actual occurrence of miracles, though he conceded their logical possibility, or God's power to perform them. Since, however, God had Himself willed the laws of nature and expressly said in the Quran that there is no change in Divine ways, nature always behaved uniformly.

The other basic thesis of Syed Ahmad was the essential harmony between reason and revelation, both of which were Divine gifts for man's guidance. Reason was given to all, but revelation was confined to the prophets alone. Their source was one and the same, though their spheres of operation might be different. Syed Ahmad thus stood for a scientific empiricism and speculative rationalism without, however, having a clear and critical methodology of science and philosophy. He accepted the findings of science as well as the findings of reason no less than the Quran, which is infallible, and then, proceeded to reconcile any apparent discrepancy between them with the help of a speculative hermeneutic. The attempted reconciliation involves rejecting the ordinary meanings of Arabic words or expressions. Syed Ahmad thus rejects the separate existence of Satan (*Shaitan*), of angels, of heaven and hell as locales, arid of the literal truth of verses about the creation and fall of Adam, the ascension of the Prophet ﷺ, and the virgin birth of Jesus, etc.

## Appendix 2: The Quest For The Meaning Of Islam

Syed Ahmad's metaphorical or philosophical reinterpretation of the Quranic texts in question was bound to disturb, nay alarm, the religious establishment. The orthodox and conservative sections naturally dubbed him as a naturalist or as a champion of reason rather than of revelation. But the truth of the matter is that Syed Ahmad was not a pure rationalist philosopher, but a scholastic with a pre-rational faith in the Quran, as the revealed word of God, as well as a pre-critical faith in the harmony between revelation and reason. This concept of a pre-established harmony between revelation and reason was his heritage from classical Islamic philosophers: Kindi, Farabi, Ibn Sina, and Ibn Rushd, etc.

Let us now briefly examine the validity of Syed Ahmad's position. It seems to me that Syed Ahmad commits what may be called the rationalistic fallacy; a fallacy which is committed by all those philosophers or theologians who claim to prove the truth or validity of their faith, which (according to them) was initially accepted because of the accident of their birth, but which is retained by them because of its coercive rationality or objective truth. This approach was the common feature of medieval Islamic and Christian thought, and continued right up to the time of Kant. Descartes, Leibniz, Locke, Paley and many others always stressed the reasonableness of the Christian faith, and advanced putative conclusive proofs of God. It was Kant who denied the coercive power of such proofs and examined the proper scope and limits of reason. Barring a brief interlude of Hegelian rationalism, almost all post-Kantian philosophers and theologians such as Schleiermacher, Kierkegaard, William James, Bergson, Otto, and many others have abandoned the rationalistic approach to religion in favor of a broad voluntaristic or existentialist approach. According to this viewpoint, religious faith is qualitatively different from logical or objective certainty, and is essentially incapable of any coercive proof. Thus there can be no proof of the existence of God, Divine incarnation, prophecy, and life after death, or of the truth of a particular religion. Indeed, if a coercive proof were possible, either in the logico-mathematical or scientific sense, no occasion or room for faith will be left at all, just as there is no room for faith in the spheres of logic and mathematics, etc. (Though there is a sort of 'faith' in the truth of the postulates of science or even of a scientific theory). Religious faith presupposes that the beliefs in question are not logically provable. In other words, faith is not like objective knowledge, but like the subjective truth of ethics and aesthetics. It is this essential non-provability, which gives religious faith its inwardness, tension, depth, and poignancy as distinct from the external or objective tension-free certainty of science or logic. Syed Ahmad's rationalistic approach to Islam thus can be said to be valid only in the sense that it does not shun rational or scientific enquiry but affirms its need. But his approach is invalid when it claims that the truth of religion in general and Islam in particular could be rationally proved.

Syed Ahmad's approach to Quranic miracles and his Quranic hermeneutic are also invalid. The Quran contains several references to miracles performed by God or His prophets, even though Prophet Muhammad ﷺ had no power to perform miracles (according to the Quran). Now Syed Ahmad explains away the prima facie Quranic references to miracles by interpreting them as reports of natural events, which were misconstrued as supernatural due to the general human craving for the supernatural. Perhaps the most striking instance of this type of Quranic hermeneutic is Syed Ahmad's interpretation of the Quranic verse that no man had touched Mary who was with child. Syed Ahmad interprets this verse to mean that no man, other than her husband, had touched Mary who had conceived a child. Another instance is the Quranic verse that God punished sinners through natural calamities. Syed Ahmad says that natural phenomena are governed by natural laws, but men view them as a punishment for their sins.[22] Similarly, he gives a naturalistic interpretation of verses describing angels, demons and the people of the cave (*ashab al kahaf*), etc. Syed Ahmad shows great linguistic skill in reinterpreting Arabic expressions, even though his command over the language may not be perfect.

Syed Ahmad had a twofold orthogenetic justification for this type of hermeneutic. The first was the clear statement of the Quran that the Prophet ﷺ had no miraculous powers and was an ordinary mortal like other human beings, the only difference being that he was the recipient of Divine revelations. (The implication was that if the greatest of all prophets could not perform miracles, other prophets too must have been without any supernatural powers.) The second justification was the Quranic statement that it contained two types of verses; the clear and categorical commands (*muhkamat*), and the metaphorical or ambiguous verses (*mutashabihat*). Armed with this twofold principle of interpretation, Syed Ahmad perhaps felt no qualms in explaining away all Quranic references to the supernatural. This approach is quite valid and fruitful up to a point, but Syed Ahmad did not realize its limitations and went to the extremes of semantic speculation just to prove his point.

Forced interpretations of a text involve the fallacy of projection of one's own ideas upon the revealed text. It may be said that, by the very nature of the case, there can be no standard meaning of Scripture, and that all meanings are inevitably cases of projecting our own ideas upon the propositional canvas of the Quran. But it seems to me that the interpretations made by the Prophet ﷺ and his trusted companions, who were directly inspired and instructed by the Prophet ﷺ himself, must be treated as normative interpretations, at least in spiritual and moral matters. Now if the Prophet ﷺ believed in miracles, but miracles do not really occur, the Prophet ﷺ was mistaken in his interpretation of the Quran. This would imply that though he was the messenger of God, he was not the infallible interpreter of the Word of God. Syed Ahmad did not actually draw this inference but, it seems, this approach was latent in his thinking.

Syed Ahmad's attempted field integration led to his denial of miracles, including the Prophet's ﷺ bodily ascension to the highest heaven (*meraj*), his affirmation of revelation as the highest form of Divine illumination of the human consciousness without any intermediary role of angels, in the literal sense, his denial of the virgin birth of Jesus; in brief, a thorough 'de-mythologisation', of the Islamic thought system. This was no mean achievement, and one cannot but admire Syed Ahmad's imagination, clarity, candor, and courage.

But in his quest for integrating religion with science and philosophy, Syed Ahmad deprived Islam of its mystique or spiritually romantic elements, without, however, providing a critical and mature philosophy of religion, which could appeal to the modern Muslim mind. His approach lacked the organic unity and inner consistency of an authentic existential interpretation of man in the universe. This is why neither his closest friends and admirers nor the orthodox could agree with his peculiar blend of faith and reason. However, as the principal architect and inspirer of the Aligarh Movement, which produced or influenced a whole galaxy of liberal Muslims such as Chiragh Ali, Mehdi Ali, Imtiaz Ali, Hali, Shibli, Amir Ali, and Ghulamus Saqlain, among several others, Syed Ahmad acted as the master trend-setter. The work initiated by him in the 19th century was carried forward in the present century by Muhammad Iqbal (d. 1938) and Abul Kalam Azad (d. 1958), both of whom were men of genius.

# IQBAL

Through his book, *'Reconstruction of Religious Thought in Islam'* as well as his moving philosophical poetry, Iqbal has reinterpreted Islamic concepts and values in the light of contemporary thought. Iqbal realized that one's concrete understanding of religious concepts is organically related with one's basic conceptual framework, which grows with the growth in man's factual knowledge. But he also held that scientific knowledge based on sense perception could not disclose the nature and destiny of the human ego and of ultimate reality, as distinct from its appearance to our sense organs, or its conceptual reconstruction in scientific theories. The ultimate nature and destiny of the human ego, its relationship with God; the ultimate Ego, the attributes of God, the nature of prophecy or revelation, etc., are beyond the ken of human reason and can be known only through revelation or spiritual intuition which is a Divine gift to a chosen few. Iqbal, therefore, makes no attempt to prove God's existence, and immortality, etc., but follows Kant in rejecting the putative coercive power of the classical proofs for God. He emphasizes love and intuition rather than reason as the path, which leads to God, so that his approach to religion is existentialist. At the same time Iqbal reconstructs the concrete meaning of basic religious concepts to integrate them with the conceptual framework of contemporary science. He was an erudite scholar, though not an analytical thinker of genius like Kant, Jaspers, or Wittgenstein.

Iqbal rejects the anthropomorphic concept of God's attributes and actions such as creation, guidance, and punishment, etc. Though the nature of God can never be grasped by man, He may best be viewed as the Infinite Ego Who is the Source of all finite egos or monads which are centers of energy or the will to affirm one's existence. The ultimate reality for Iqbal is thus not matter, or even matter in motion, but the Divine Ego Who creates finite egos or centers of will as a manifestation of His creative powers and glory. Man is the highest created being. But his latent powers have not yet been realized with the exception of the Prophet ﷺ who was the perfect man and exemplar for all mankind.

Man, as the vicegerent of God on earth, can subjugate and direct all creation through the application of natural laws, which have been willed by God. God does not change them to perform miracles though He may do so. Scientific laws are not logically necessary but are empirical generalizations.

## Appendix 2: The Quest For The Meaning Of Islam

In Iqbal's view, the proper way of self-realization or the growth of the ego is neither metaphysical speculation, nor mystical absorption into the Infinite Ego, but the conquest of nature through science and the conquest or disciplining of the human ego through obedience to the Quran and the *sunnat*. The conquest of the ego does not mean the suppression of its individuality but rather its growth through the full cultivation of the Divine attributes of power, wisdom, love, mercy, etc. The developed ego can then control and discipline its lower urges, not at the behest of external commands of God, but as the inward demands of his own developed nature due to the assimilation of the Divine attributes. The developed ego, however, remains the servant (*abd*) of God and at the same time experiences itself as free or autonomous.

The commands of God are to be found in the Quran, which is the revealed Word of God. We cannot understand the mechanics of revelation, but the conviction of its Divine Source may arise in us if we approach the Quran and the Prophet ﷺ with receptivity and humility in an earnest search for truth. Iqbal rejects all anthropomorphic models for understanding the mechanics of Divine revelation, that is, the model that Gabriel first gets the message from God and then communicates it to the Prophet ﷺ, or that Gabriel appears in the human garb before the Prophet ﷺ, or the model of an angel on the sky, or of mysterious sounds reaching the Prophet ﷺ, as if from nowhere. The Quran does refer to these modes of revelation, but they fall in the category of metaphorical verses whose mystery cannot be deciphered. However, poetic and artistic inspiration as well as psychical phenomena such as telepathy and veridical dreams do confirm the existence of modes of human experience over and above normal perception and reasoning. Just as the gift of poetic or musical genius is not universal, the gift of prophecy is confined to a few Divinely chosen persons. Iqbal's concept of prophecy is thus basically the same as that of Syed Ahmad, who in turn followed Waliullah and the tradition of classical Muslim philosophers.

Iqbal rejects the literal interpretation of the Quranic verses dealing with the creation of Adam and his expulsion from the garden, universal resurrection of the human body, heaven and hell as external locales. Iqbal accepts the evolutionary hypothesis. But he qualifies the mechanistic conception of Darwin since he holds that the evolutionary force is rooted in the individual will to live and to assert its power, corresponding to its endowment (*taqdir*).[23] Evolutionary change, therefore, is not the mechanical result of the combination of chance variations and natural selection (in Darwin's sense) of the better adjusted species, but rather the result of a striving for self-perfection and a more intensive and permanent ego hood. The peak of evolutionary growth is man who is next only to God. Iqbal agrees with the famous lines of Rumi describing the different stages of growth; minerals, plants, animals, man, and higher still.[24] The urge to grow and develop comes from God Who is the ultimate Source of all being and value, and without Whom the evolutionary process would not have begun at all.

Iqbal's conception of evolution is very similar to Bergson's Creative evolution. But while Bergson posits an '*Elan Vital*', which is the vital ground or immanent principle of movement.

Iqbal holds the vital ground to be not merely an impersonal immanent *Elan* but a supra Personality or Super Ego, Whose mode of existence is, however, beyond human comprehension. The Divine Ego responds to human prayer, though not in the sense of a Heavenly Father wiping the tears of His children and giving them sweets. Iqbal's concept of evolution adumbrates Aristotle's view that every member of a species strives to reach the perfection appropriate to its form.

Iqbal holds that Islam is not merely a set of metaphysical beliefs and rituals but also a complete code of conduct. It thus differs from Christianity, which makes a clear distinction between the church and the state and enjoins on the Christians to render unto Caesar and Christ what respectively belongs to them. Iqbal holds that from its very inception Islam has been an organic whole demanding a total loyalty from the Muslim. Thus the Prophet ﷺ and the pious *Khalifa's* were the spiritual and temporal heads of the Islamic community, and there was no distinction between the sacred and the profane or the spiritual and the secular. However, the law and polity of Islam are not intended to be static. Indeed they must ever be renewed within the framework of the Quran and the *sunnat* to keep pace with the ceaseless creativity of human values. The Quran only gives basic guidance to the Muslim and exhorts him to exercise his reason within those limits. The *sunnat* too must be given the utmost importance but it can never equal the status of the Quran. This is because human reports about the Prophet ﷺ may be mistaken, unlike the complete authenticity of the Quran.

The principle of movement or independent reasoning, however, applies only to the institutional system (*muamilat*) and not the prescriptive system (*ibadat*) as fixed by the Prophet ﷺ. Independent reasoning may be exercised not only through the consensus of the jurists (*ijma ul ulama*) but also through the consensus of the Islamic community (*ijma ul ummat*). Iqbal, however, does not give any further constitutional details in this context.

Let us now attempt a critical estimate of Iqbal. His existentialist approach to religion, his vitalistic and voluntaristic ontology and evolutionary cosmology, his rejection of life-negating mysticism, his ethic of self-realization through the conquest of nature and a dynamic religious morality and law, his awareness of the limitations of scientific knowledge, his emphasis on creativity of values, his concern for social justice, and his rejection of narrow nationalism are all very valuable. But Iqbal's concept of Islam as an organic total code of conduct (even though possessed of an in-built mechanism for inner growth); as well as his theory of Islamic communitarianism, is not valid for our times. Let us examine in some detail why this is the case.

Iqbal does not seem to realize that right up to the 17th century not merely Islam but all religions had been total guides to life rather than merely a set of rituals. It is true that the church and the state were never one in Christianity, though the two were united in Islam. Thus in Christendom the Pope and Emperor symbolized the domains of Christ and of Caesar, while in Islam the Caliph (*Khalifa*) was at once the spiritual and the temporal head of the Islamic community. This difference was, however, due to the historical situation of Christianity and Islam in their early history.[25] When Christianity became the state religion of the Roman Empire in the fourth century the Christian Church too claimed spiritual jurisdiction over the state, and the Church held Christianity to be a complete code of conduct for the believers. When Martin Luther (d. 1546) repudiated the authority of the Pope in the 16th century, this repudiation was made in the name of true Christianity represented by his own Church, rather than in the name of secularism. The break from the Church of Rome did not imply any change in the conception of Christianity as a total conduct of life. Likewise, Calvin (d. 1564), who also founded his own church soon after Luther, claimed to provide complete guidance to his followers, including the spheres of trade, industry, education, law, and government, etc.

The effective breakthrough in the conception of Christianity however came in the 18th century as the cumulative result of the gradual scientific revolution in Western Europe between 1500 and 1700, and its impact upon the social and industrial life in the 18th century. The scientific revolution was nurtured by the works of Copernicus (d. 1543), Kepler (d. 1630), Galileo (d. 1642), Newton (d. 1727), Descartes (d. 1650), while the revolution in social and religious ideas by the impact of Locke (d. 1704), Voltaire, (d. 1778), Rousseau (d. 1778), Adam Smith (d. 1790), Kant (d. 1804) *et al.*

Let us now consider the exact way in which scientific developments led to the gradual transformation of traditional Christianity as a complete way of life. Traditional Christian theism implied that every event, whether social, natural, or Divine, was purposive. The category of purpose or final end was the supreme explanatory principle of the cosmic process, though finite mind could not grasp the purpose of many events, which prima facie went against reason or justice. Human reason had, therefore, to be subordinated to faith. However, the rise of Mechanics and Dynamics culminating in the grand Newtonian cosmology showed that natural events could be accurately described and predicted in terms of pure mechanical causes without any reference to any purpose or end, whether human or divine. Reason was still necessary for formulating hypotheses and developing their implications, which were empirically tested. But reason was no longer the supreme and sufficient oracle, which decided what was the case.

The steady growth of natural science inevitably led to technological innovations for the satisfaction of man's practical needs. Technological innovations in turn led to social and economic innovations, like mass production factories, banks, joint-stock companies, insurance firms, managing agencies, auditing firms, etc. In the course of time these social forms or phenomena became objects of systematic theoretical study like natural phenomena in the earlier period. In other words, social phenomena also came under the jurisdiction of the scientific method, first, the economic behavior of man, and later his social, moral, and religious behavior. All this naturally led to a shift of intellectual influence and power from the church leaders to the university intellectuals and the business and industrial community whose interests lay in adopting a secular and scientific approach to problems of social organization in place of the closed ecclesiastical approach of the medieval period. This may be called the secular revolution of Western Europe, partly overlapping and partly succeeding the Industrial Revolution of England. The secular revolution was nurtured by Locke, Hume, and Adam Smith in England, Voltaire, Rousseau, and Montesque in France, Kant and Lessing in Germany, and Benjamin Franklin and Jefferson in

America. The secular revolution did not dislodge religion but transformed Christianity as a complete code of conduct into the modern conception of religion, as primarily a spiritual perspective upon the universe. In other words, religion came to be viewed as a personal relationship between man and his Creator rather than as total guidance or a mandate for every sphere of human life.[26]

It seems Iqbal was unable to look upon the secular revolution as a factor in the evolution of a mature religion. This was because Iqbal remained under the spell of the medieval conception of religion as a complete code of conduct, or what may be called religious institutionalism or 'religionism', in short. Iqbal does not realize that 'religionism', be it Islamic, Christian, or Hindu, raises quite unnecessary social, psychological, and administrative difficulties which make it unfit for plural societies, even though it may work relatively better in the case of the homogeneous. Iqbal's approach is utterly unsuitable for plural societies where it is absolutely essential to separate macro-social matters involving the entire nation, from micro-social or transcendental matters touching sub-groups or individuals. Muslims living in plural societies cannot accept Iqbal's understanding of Islam, which is rooted in medieval 'religionism' rather than in modern secularism.

The rejection of 'religionism' is not dictated by prudence or the situational compulsions of a plural society, but is the result of mature insight into the essential and non-essential functions of religion and the role of reason in human affairs. To hold that Iqbal's conception is true, but not prudent for Muslims of mixed societies would imply that such Muslims are second class Muslims who are compelled by their historical situation to acquiesce in the rupture of the organic unity of their religion. Nothing could be more misleading than this conclusion, which seems to be logically implied by Iqbal's conception of Islam. Just as Iqbal holds that a dynamic approach to the *shariah* is intrinsicly desirable and valid rather than merely prudent, similarly, many contemporary religious minds, be they Muslim, Christian, or Hindu, genuinely accept the religion of the spirit rather than medieval 'religionism'. This implies that secularism is right and valid not only for plural societies like, say, India or Nigeria, but also for predominantly Muslim countries, say, Pakistan or Turkey, or a Hindu country like Nepal. Indeed secularism becomes a principle of the good life, like democracy or socialism, rather than a matter of policy or prudence.

It may be that Iqbal was prejudiced against the 18th century concept of secularism because it eventually led to agnosticism and atheistic materialism in the succeeding centuries, though the founding fathers of the secular revolution (like the earlier creators of the scientific revolution) were all sincere Christian deists. But secularism as such is pre-eminently neutral towards the truth of religion or the truth of a particular religion, though it does clearly and emphatically reject religionism.

It is noteworthy that while many brilliant Western minds of the later 19th century rejected not only religionism but also the religion of the spirit, the best Western minds of the present century are much more cautious in this respect. Indeed they have become deeply aware of the dangers and limitations of a new brand of dogmatism, termed scientism; the belief that scientific knowledge exhausts the full description and meaning of the universe. Contemporary thought has realized that reality is far more complex than the scientific picture paints it to be.[27] Many eminent thinkers now seem to be willing to concede that mere morality without an existential interpretation of the universe fails to sustain man's quest for value and plunges him into a destructive nihilism. In other words, though morality without God or Spirit may and does flourish, the cultivation of the spiritual dimension of man reinforces morality and creativity in general, thus enhancing the inner quality of life. Iqbal's fear of secularism, as it were, is thus not justified, in view of the perfect compatibility between secularism and the religion of the spirit.

Let us now examine Iqbal's theory of Islamic communitarian ism and the implied critique of nationalism. According to this theory, the primary determinant of group identity and loyalty is the religious community rather than the nation, race, etc. He repeatedly criticizes nationalism as a narrow and restrictive focus of loyalty, as compared to a religious community rooted in shared ideas and values transcending all barriers of race, region, and language, etc. Iqbal was even critical of the League of Nations since its basis of membership was the nation-state, thus perpetuating the very evil it sought to cure.

Consistency demands that Iqbal concede that all religious communities are justified in making their religion the primary determinant of group identity and focus of loyalty. Iqbal cannot deny them this right on the ground that religions other than Islam are false. Now the moment this is done, humanity again becomes divided into rival religious groups, if not warring nation-states. Is not strife between partisan ideological groups as bad as strife between partisan nation-states? The answer is quite plain. Moreover, if relations can be friendly between different religious groups they could also be friendly between different national groups. What makes nationalism harmful is thus not territorialism as such but rather chauvinism and aggressive intolerance. And these can also vitiate the virtues of communitarianism. It seems Iqbal equated nationalism with chauvinism just as some tend to equate faith with fanaticism. But one equation is as wrong as the other.

It is true that nationalism or rather nationalistic chauvinism has played havoc in modern Western history and Iqbal's fear of nationalism is, therefore, not groundless. But it is equally true that communitarianism or rather ideological fanaticism had played havoc in the medieval period producing endless strife between Catholics and Protestants or between Christians and Muslims, etc. Indeed reliable historians have claimed that casualties in the religious wars or persecutions of the medieval period far exceed the losses inflicted by nationalist wars in the modern period. Thus, in view of the smaller world population in the medieval period, religious communitarianism caused greater friction than has nationalism in the modern.

Let us now see how far communitarianism is feasible in the present world situation. We find that human societies have gradually become mixed or plural due to migrations, wars, and political integration, etc. Communitarianism with its stress on religious differences creates problems of emotional integration for the different religious groups, while territorial nationalism makes for a smooth and harmonious relationship between the different sub-groups composing the nation. Again, the world is today organized on the basis of nation-states, while communitarianism demands an entirely different focus of primary loyalty. Communitarianism thus leads to emotional stress for minority groups in mixed societies, as it tends to displace the state as the primary basis of macro-social identity and the focus of loyalty.

Take for example an American Jew, who is a member of two classes; the class 'American' and the class 'Jew', and by implication, of a third class, 'American Jew'. Now no conflict would arise as long as the class 'American' is deemed to be the primary group which includes Jew, and Christian, etc., as secondary classes or, in other words, when the dominant principle of functional classification is membership of a common state rather than a common church. When, however, religion seeks to become the dominant basis of functional classification in a mixed society a tension is inevitable between the two rival bases of classification, each of which seeks for the pride of place.

Even if human society becomes religiously homogeneous, it is condemned to be spatially, racially, and occupationally plural and sexually dual, and all these differences will inevitably generate special affinities over and above the bond of religion. Under these conditions the administratively most convenient basis of macro-social unity is the nation-state comprising all the different religious, racial, linguistic, regional, occupational groups as parts of an harmonious and integrated nation.

Nationalism is not opposed to internationalism or humanism since both complement each other. Nationalism is also not opposed to religion but only to religionism. Again, nationalism does not imply the rejection of local or professional loyalties and interests since there is no mutual conflict, provided we accept a scale of values. Suppose several candidates apply for a job, or several sites clamor for a steel plant, or two nations dispute over some matter. Now nationalism, properly understood, does not mean siding with my country, right or wrong. Likewise, professional or local loyalty does not mean siding with my club, my profession, my city, my team, right or wrong. We must always back the right principle and not any religion, nation, or region. However, a conflict may arise between patriotism and justice in the case of a war. But this conflict is also possible when the belligerents are divided into religious communities rather than nation-states. This problem is thus not peculiar to nationalism.

The nation-state, as it now exists, cannot however be deemed to be an immutable and sacrosanct institution. The concept of sovereignty in the classical sense is in the process of being transformed into the concept of national autonomy within a supra-national confederation based upon cultural and economic interests. In the past smaller principalities combined, whether by force or by free will, to form the nation-state. In the future the present sovereign nation-states may evolve further into supranational confederations, like multi-national common markets and corporations within the present framework. Religious ties will facilitate economic and cultural cooperation since a common religion does constitute a powerful bond between individuals or nations. But a common religion is not the only bond, and by itself alone it can never suffice for inter-regional collaboration unless the people share common politico-economic ideals and interests. Consequently, if the emphasis on religious brotherhood does not lead to religious parochialism or communitarian discrimination in international relations, the forging of special relations between sovereign states with a common religion is quite justifiable. This is the only valid sense of the traditional notion of Islamic brotherhood.

The history of the pan-Islamic movement also points to the same conclusion. Jamaluddin Afghani stood for the political union of all Muslim countries and Iqbal shared this ideal. But gradually Iqbal veered to the idea of a confederation of Muslim states functioning in close harmony but retaining their separate identity. But even this would not work in the absence of shared politico-economic ideals and international cooperation on secular lines. Pan-Islamism, therefore, must be secularized and not merely regionalized in Iqbal's sense.

There is nothing wrong with Iqbal's deep concern for the welfare of the Islamic community and the touching lamentations in his poetry over the decline and fall of the political and cultural glory of Islam in the past. But what strikes me as odd in a philosophical poet of Iqbal's stature is that he never sheds tears at the decline of other great cultures. Again, he is severely critical of the evils of Western diplomacy, but is apt to overlook the core of genuine idealism in the life and work of Western savants such as Mill, Matthew Arnold, Tolstoy, Max Mueller, Blunt, etc. Iqbal gives the impression of being a devoted partisan of the Islamic community rather than a universal savant who can look upon the fads and foibles of the human family with a sense of detachment rather than of resentment or bitterness.

To turn to another aspect of his social philosophy, Iqbal seems to waver in his evaluation of democracy and socialism. He believes in Islamic democracy and socialism but does not spell it out anywhere. He is apt to confuse the question of the structure of Islamic polity with Islamic piety. Thus he dwells on the need to avoid pomp and show, to be charitable and kind to the needy, to be prompt in paying wages to the worker, etc., but he does not spell out the ideal Islamic polity.

Iqbal's approach to the status of women is also unsatisfactory. Iqbal does not permit his ideal woman to be man's equal partner in life but regards woman as a perpetual ward and man as her natural guardian. Iqbal's ideal woman at best can only aspire to be the mother of the male super-man but not super-man herself."[28]

In conclusion, it may be pointed out that Iqbal omits to deal with the crucial problems of pain and evil and of authenticity. But his greatest shortcoming is his rejection of secularism and inter-religious fellowship or universalism. It is important to point out these limitations of Iqbal since his medium is poetry, which, as sheer poetry, is one of the treasures of world literature. Indeed, as a poetic genius, Iqbal has the power to cast a spell on his readers through his word-magic even when one may totally disagree with his social philosophy.

## Maulana Abul Kalam Azad

In his early *al-Hilal* phase, Azad stood for a romantic pan-Islamism and a more or less traditional interpretation of Islamic concepts and values. But in his second phase, represented by his monumental commentary on the Quran, Azad formulates his mature conception of Islam.[29] His existentialist approach to proofs of God is much more in harmony with contemporary thinking than the pre-Kantian rationalism of Syed Ahmad. Azad outgrows the Muslim scholastic or rationalistic approach to the proofs of God and confines himself to the Quran, which does not give any arguments for God's existence, but only invites the reader to ponder over the mystery of the various aspects of nature and of man's inner self, and then listen to the inner response of his total being. The implication is that if man looks at the order, harmony, and beauty of the macrocosm and the microcosm, in the spirit of pure receptivity without any preconceptions or theories, the inner conviction will well up from the depths of his being that the universe is not a chance or accidental event or a brute fact, but a purposeful cosmos.[30] This cosmos cannot be the result of the blind dance of atoms without serving some end or purposes, even though the purpose may not be primarily anthropocentric, that is, centered on human welfare. This inner existential conviction can of course never be proved in the logical sense. But then logical proof is needed only when one is in doubt and not when one is existentially certain. When the lover's eyes meet those of the beloved in wordless communion, is there any need left to prove that one loves the other?

The intuitive conviction of the existence of God does not imply that we have intuitive knowledge of His attributes as well. In fact the finite mind can never grasp the Infinite. But the attributes of God, as mentioned in the Quran, do give us analogical or metaphorical knowledge of the Divine

Being. Azad thus steers the middle way between theological gnosticism and philosophical transcendentalism or 'negationism'. He is at once aware of the limitations of the popular anthropomorphic conception of God and also of the extreme agnostic negation of Divine attributes. The view that no attribute like love, wisdom, mercy, power, and creativity, etc., could be predicted of God, and that all we can properly do is to affirm His existence but negate every quality (in order to avoid inner contradictions) virtually amounts to the negation or denial of God. The qualified analogical affirmation of Divine attributes, on the other hand, leads to the spiritual growth of the believer through the partial assimilation of the Divine attributes. Azad thus believes in a personal God in the non-anthropomorphic sense.

Likewise, Azad accepts that God reveals His will to His chosen prophets through revelation (*wahy*), but Azad's conception of Divine guidance is rooted in his philosophical conception of fourfold Divine guidance through instinct, perception, reason, and revelation. Let us examine his conception in some detail.

Azad points out that the Quran uses the word '*wahy*' in the wide and narrow senses. In the wide sense '*wahy*' refers not only to suggesting or making signs by one man to another but also to God's guiding the bee to collect honey.[31] Azad holds that the instinctive behavior of animals is not the product of blind impulse, but of God's guidance to animals to perform those actions which are essential for their preservation and the realization of their potential excellence, in the Aristotelian sense. Thus Azad regards unlearned drives which have survival value for a species as a Divine gift to animals. In a similar vein, the capacity for sense perception through different sense organs is another form of God's guidance to His creatures. Sense perception enables the individual to perform instinctive actions more accurately and effectively. In many cases perception triggers the instinctive response and gives it concrete content and direction, as in the case of the searching for food or a mate. Thus instinct and perception fuse into each other in the economy of life.

The capacity to reason is the next mode of Divine guidance to His creatures, but this form of guidance is restricted to man alone, animals possessing it only in its rudimentary form. When the conditions of perception, whether internal or external, are not standard, that is, not in accordance with the Divinely intended structure and functioning of the sense organs, reports given by the senses are not reliable, for example, the sun appears to be a disc when it is, in fact, much bigger than the earth itself, or the stick appears to be bent in water, when it is, in fact, straight. In such cases reason corrects or amends perception. Moreover, reason also enables man to intuit logical truths or the connections between concepts and propositions through direct inner vision, as if reason were a spiritual lamp, which illumined man's consciousness. Thus reason and perception mutually complement each other at the human level, just as perception and instinct do at the animal level.

The last form of Divine guidance is revelation. But even in this case there are two levels – the lower level of the intuitive flash of the poet, artist, and scientist, etc., and the higher level of prophecy (*wahy*). We can never understand the nature and dynamics of '*wahy*', which is restricted to the prophets alone. But it is clear that revelation is the highest level of the fourfold Divine guidance, since it complements and completes God's guidance to His creatures. There is no clash between revelation and reason if their proper spheres are not confused. Revelation guides man in the sphere of spiritual and moral truths, while reason, in the sphere of logico-mathematical and perceptual truths. However, reason does help us to discover instrumental rules for realizing basic ethical truths disclosed by revelation. Man's conscience, as a form of reason, also gives ethical guidance up to a point, but such reasoning in the sphere of morality and spirituality, without the confirmation of '*wahy*', ever remains subject to doubt and disagreement between men.

The net result of Azad's concept of Divine guidance is to demarcate the proper spheres of the operation of instinct, perception, reason, and revelation and to put forward the ideal of a balanced and integrated conception of Islamic piety and of obedience to the Quran and the *sunnat*. Neither the Quran nor the *sunnat* is treated by Azad as a textbook of law, politics, economics, physics, or astronomy, but as the fount of spiritual and moral truths. The Muslim must use his powers of perception and reason, which are as much Divine gifts as revelation, for acquiring knowledge of nature and also for the detailed ordering of society.

Azad makes a clear distinction between Islam as '*deen*' and as '*shariah*'. '*Deen*' may be defined as authentic faith in God and an authentic concern for right action for its own sake. *Shariah* is the law rooted in the Quran and the traditions of the Prophet ﷺ. Now Azad holds that all prophets have preached the same '*deen*', though legal codes have differed from prophet to prophet. But these differences do not negate the essential oneness of all religions. Doctrinal differences arose because of misunderstanding the original '*deen*'. The removal of these misunderstandings plus righteous action rather than a formal acceptance of the Islamic '*shariah*', suffice for inter-religious understanding and salvation. Just as the biological structure of man is the same despite differences in complexion or facial features, similarly, the basic oneness of the '*deen*' is the same despite differences in the religious law. This leads Azad to the concept of a federal religious unity of mankind rather than a conception of unity, which deems conversion to Islam as the condition of brotherhood in this world and of salvation in the next.

Azad's stress on religious tolerance and pluralism, however, does not imply that he gives up his belief in the uniqueness of the Quran and of the Prophet ﷺ as the last of the long line of prophets. What Azad rejects is the view that a Muslim, as a member of Muhammad's ﷺ community (*ummate-Muhammadi*), has a higher spiritual status than non-Muslims without any consideration of his ethical or spiritual condition. Spiritual merit and status depend upon spiritual attainments rather than upon membership of a particular race, family, religion, etc. It is sheer conceit to hold that an immoral Muslim ranks spiritually higher than a highly moral non-Muslim simply because of the formers faith in the Quran and the Prophet ﷺ.

Azad rejects Iqbals conception of Islam as a total guide to the good life without any distinction between the spiritual and the secular, and also Iqbal's conception of the Islamic community (*ummat*) as the primary and supreme determinant of group identity and loyalty. In these two respects, Azad accepts the essentially secular and nationalist or rather humanist outlook of Syed Ahmad. Both Syed Ahmad and Azad stand for Islamic universalism as distinct from the Islamic communitarianism of Iqbal. They also have the same concept of '*deen*' as the basic unity behind the variety of religious laws. Their common emphasis on '*deen*' as the essence of religion enables them both to accept the special status of the Quran and the Prophet ﷺ, without the implication that non-Muslims will not be saved, or that a formal Muslim is *ipso facto* superior to the non-Muslim, or that human brotherhood is not possible without a world Islamic umbrella.

Azad's Islamic universalism made him full of sympathy and concern for the welfare of the human family rather than the Muslims alone. It seems to me that Azad's spiritual humanism was unfortunately misconstrued by his political opponents as an ideological concession to his political ambitions in a country where the majority consisted of non-Muslims. Many alleged that Azad had compromised his authentic faith of the *al-Hilal* period at the altar of political ambition. This most unfair interpretation of Azad's genuine spiritual evolution must have weakened the potential appeal of his line of thought to his fellow Indian Muslims.

The crucial issues not raised by Azad are the problems of pain and evil, the problem of authenticity, the problem of moral and legal growth, and the concept of social justice. Let us now briefly deal with the above matters.

The problem of pain and evil arises when we encounter unmerited suffering and evil in a universe created by an all-loving and all-powerful God. Azad emphasizes the beauty, harmony, and goodness of the universe and dwells at great length upon the wonderful ecological balance and teleology of nature. But Azad almost completely ignores the suffering caused by different species and members of the same species struggling for existence, and also ignores the presence of evil. Azad follows the traditional approach that evil is merely a means for promoting a greater good. But this leaves unanswered the crucial enigma why an all-powerful Creator should resort to evil for promoting good.

The problem of authenticity arises when the individual experiences an existential conflict between his conscience and some scriptural injunction. One's conscience, for example, might demand complete equality between men and women, while the Quran definitely gives a higher status to man. Or, one may have a conscientious objection against the penalty of severing the hands of the thief, or against whipping. Azad's distinction between '*deen*' and '*shariah*' is very pertinent, and it may be said that the above matters are not part of '*deen*' but of the '*shariah*', and that Muslims are free to modify the law. But any amendment of any clear Quranic injunction implies that the Quran is not perfect.

Azad stands for secularism but he nowhere spells out the details of the politico-economic and social institutions, which he approves. One would like to know, for instance, what Azad thought about inter-religious marriages. We know that many individuals, both Hindu and Muslim, who loudly proclaim the virtues of secularism, view inter-religious marriages as an obnoxious evil, without realizing that this violates the meaning of secularism.

Similarly, Azad did not spell out his concept of social justice and socialism, which he professed. Azad did not concern himself with the crucial question as to what were the features of the ethically good society over and above the virtues of the good individual.

## Mawdudi

According to Mawdudi, Islam is the acceptance of unqualified and exclusive sovereignty of God in every sphere of human activity. In practice this boils down to implicit obedience to the Prophet ﷺ. Islam's ethic of submission is totally opposed to the humanist ethic of inner freedom, which is the common denominator of all man-made 'isms' like Democracy, Rationalism, Communism, etc. The individual Muslim, however, retains ample scope for exercising his freedom within the bounds of the sacred law. Similarly, the Islamic community also retains ample scope for the joint exercise of its discretion (*ijtehad*) to meet new problems in accord with the spirit of the Quran and the *sunnat*. This reform must conform to the spirit of the *shariah*, and only the Islamic scholar-jurists are qualified to decide what the spirit is. Hence, for all practical purposes, Mawdudi makes the consensus of the scholar-jurists (*ijma til ulama*) the supreme arbiter of the destiny of the Islamic state. Perhaps his followers do not adequately realize this crucial implication of Mawdudi's interpretation of God's sovereignty.

Mawdudi, indeed, speaks of the need of a new Islamic reconstruction of the basic concepts of all the natural and social sciences. Yet he rather dogmatically rejects the evolutionary hypothesis about the origin of the human species. Although he criticizes traditional Muslims for their conservatism and mechanical conformity to the letter of the *shariah*, in practice, Mawdudi himself remains as much tied down to the letter of the *shariah* as any other theologian, except in rather minor and marginal issues. He thinks that his significant message to contemporary Muslims is that they should reconstruct the traditional Islamic institutional system. But Mawdudi's concrete views on social or politico-economic matters, such as the position and status of women, polygamy, socialism, and equality of opportunity, etc., reflect an essentially justificatory approach to tradition rather than its sympathetic but critical appraisal.

The burden of Mawdudi's thought is **(a)** the sovereignty of God, **(b)** the organic totality of Islam as a complete code of conduct, and **(c)** Islamic communitarianism. The implication of the first is the rejection of the Western concept of the autonomy of the individual and the sovereignty of the state; the implication of the second is the rejection of secularism; the implication of the third is the rejection of nationalism and secular internationalism. It will be seen that all these are already found in Iqbal, so that there is nothing new in Mawdudi. What is new is his political activism and dedication to the party, which he founded and still continues to lead. The secret of his appeal, in my opinion, is his simple but polished and powerful Urdu prose, the sheer volume of his writings on themes, which really touch the interests and imagination of his audience, his valuable translation and commentary on the Quran, together with a remarkably detailed and systematic index and, last but not least, the fact that much more than Iqbal, Mawdudi's understanding of Islam remains closer to the traditional thought-cum-value system. Iqbal had rejected many traditional concepts, such as, the view that the sayings of the Prophet ﷺ were implicit revelation (*wahy-e-khafi*) as distinct from explicit revelation (*wahy-e-jali*) or the Quran. It is Mawdudi's great contribution to the full understanding of Islam that he makes explicit what was implicit in the traditional concepts. Mawdudi thus cannot be ignored. The contemporary Muslim must either accept Mawdudi or the secular revolution.

## Parvez

The voluminous writings of Ghulam Ahmad Parvez (containing Quranic quotations in almost every paragraph) attempt a systematic reconstruction of the basic concepts of Islam in the light of modern ideas. He takes from Azad the concept of Divine Providence (*nizam-e-rububiyat*), but in all other matters he relies upon Iqbal without, however, being a mere imitator.[32]

Parvez' uniqueness lies in his Islamic or Quranic socialism. Iqbal had also criticized capitalism because of its exploitation of the poor, but he had never claimed that the Quran prescribed socialism. Similarly, Ubaiduallah Sindhi and Hifzur Rahman had also stood for socialist ideas on secular grounds.[33] But Parvez actually deduces a socialist polity from the Quranic text by giving novel interpretations to Arabic words such as '*salat*', '*zakat*', and '*akhirat*', etc. Thus Parvez holds that '*salat*' or establishing of prayer does not mean merely the ritual of prayer but the establishing of a just social order. Likewise, '*zakat*' does not mean merely a tax on savings, but the appropriation by a welfare state of all the surplus wealth of individuals for running a planned economy. Similarly, Parvez interprets the term '*akhirat*' as worldly welfare in addition to its usual eschatological sense.

## Appendix 2: The Quest For The Meaning Of Islam

To the objection that, if the Quran stood for socialism, why does it give such detailed attention to the laws of inheritance, Parvez replies that socialism could not come about at a stroke; detailed laws were, therefore, given for the transitional period. The advent of socialism will make these laws in fructuous rather than invalid, even as improvements in hygiene eliminate the need for curative medicines. To the further objection that if this were the real intention of the Quran why was this not accepted by the earlier Muslims, Parvez holds that the vested interests of the establishment and the essentially non-Arabic (*ajami*) ideas of the previous ages distorted the proper interpretation of the Quran and *hadis*.

Let us examine the above claims. Parvez commits the fallacy of projectionism by reading his own thoughts and values into the propositional canvas of the Quran. While it is quite permissible to interpret the Quranic reference to instantaneous creation as an evolutionary beginning, or the Quranic reference to six days as six geological periods, or the Quranic reference to the motions of the sun and the moon as motion in the Copernican framework, the situation becomes quite different if one interprets '*salat*' as an injunction to establish socialism. This amounts to a far-fetched stretching of the plain meaning of terms to make them conform to one's own ideas. One may well accept socialism on rational or ethical grounds and hold that, since the Quran does not oppose socialism, Muslim society ought to go socialist. In other words, matters of polity should not be mixed up with transcendental matters.

It seems Parvez attempts to seek Quranic support for a socialist polity for two reasons; firstly, because he thinks this would strengthen his case, and, secondly, because Parvez (under the influence of Iqbal) accepts Islam as a complete code of conduct meant for every walk of life. But his purpose is totally defeated, as is evident from the situation in Pakistan where the opposition to politico-economic leftism has not been softened or overcome merely by finding Quranic sanctions or support for socialist ideas. In fact, as sociology tells us, the roots of the opposition lie in the vested interests of the privileged classes who will quite understandably continue to support the status quo, justifying it in the name of orthodoxy. Thus Parvez' socialistic interpretation of the Quran will not work even in a Muslim society. But even if it did to some extent, it would not work at all in plural societies especially where Muslims are in the minority. Parvez' approach will give a religious turn to an issue which cuts across religious groupings and which, as an essentially politico-economic matter, requires a national rather than a group consensus in a democratic state. In the final analysis, therefore, secularism provides the only route to socialism for Muslims, whether in homogeneous or in plural societies.

The difficulties of Parvez arise because he is unable to accept secularism, which implies delinking the politico-economic system from the purview of religion. It is significant that out of the about 6,200 verses of the Quran only about 250 are prescriptive in character, and out of these only about 10 deal with politico-economic issues.[34] Thus, for all practical purposes the Quran does not prescribe any polity. This was worked out by the early Muslim jurists and administrators starting from Umar, and will have to be modified by each generation to suit its own situational needs. If so, there is no point left in Iqbal's theory (faithfully reiterated by both Mawdudi and Parvez) of the organic unity of Islam and the implied rejection of secularism.

Secularism does not erode the Muslim's freedom in the transcendental *'I-Thou'* sphere. However, every society, whether homogeneous or plural, and every state, be it secular or religious, must inevitably constrain the freedom of the individual in social relationships. Consequently, the sense of external restraint is inseparable from the individual consciousness as such. The only difference is that in a plural society, which is predominantly non-Muslim, the sense of restraint will appear to flow primarily from an out-group, while in a homogeneous Muslim society, from an in-group. But it is pertinent to note that since the in-group itself can never be absolutely homogeneous, social-psychological tensions will again tend to arise between the constituent sub-groups. This is happening in Pakistan, which was established as a pure ideological state. Consequently, mutual understanding between different religious, linguistic, regional, and occupational groups becomes equally essential in both homogeneous and plural societies. Secularism is, thus, more relevant to the human situation in general than Iqbal's communitarianism with its restricted appeal to Muslims in a homogeneous or predominantly Muslim society.

V

# A New Look

Arab, Turkish, and Iranian Islamic modernists such as Ali Adbul Raziq

(d. 1965), Taha Husayn (b. 1891), Ziya Gokulp (d. 1924) *et al.* also accept secularism, but they take another stand. They want the 'essence' of Islam to be maintained, while all accretions and details to be thrown away unceremoniously without any qualms of disloyalty to a long tradition. They are quite right up to a point, but unfortunately they oversimplify the issues involved and miss the essentially organic character of religious faith.

Ziya Gokalp and Raziq identify the essence of Islam with a simple monotheism minus the traditional conception of revelation, according to which the Quran is the infallible revealed Word of God. The conception of Islam, as entertained by Gokalp thus reduces Islam to a sort of 18th century British or French Deism, and to the view that religion is a matter of a personal relationship between the individual and God, without any beating upon the collective life of mankind. In other words, man is left free to order the social web of human life in accordance with his collective wisdom. The assumption is that men are quite capable of regulating their affairs satisfactorily in a democratic manner without any religious authority. This is a rejection of the traditional conception, according to which Islam offers complete and perfect guidance in every walk of life.

Ali Raziq's radical conception of Islam is marked by the incongruity and inadequacy of retaining the traditional Islamic conception of God without the corresponding traditional conception of revelation. If the traditional Islamic conception of God is retained, but the traditional conception of revelation is repudiated, mere belief in a God Who creates but does not guide His creatures, either through incarnation, in the traditional Christian sense, or through revelation, in the Islamic sense, satisfies neither the heart nor the head. A lacuna is left in this approach to Islam. Turkish and Arab Islamic modernists do not seem to be aware of the intellectual and spiritual difficulties inherent in combining an unqualified secularism with traditional Islamic monotheism. What Muslims all over the world require is the reconstruction of the traditional Islamic concepts of God and revelation so that they no longer conflict with science and secular humanism. In the absence of such a reconstruction the combination of secularism with Islamic monotheism strikes a jarring note of discord between two incongruous concepts. Such a combination is an artificial or mechanical juxtaposition without inner organic harmony, and is liable to disintegrate. Such a patchwork synthesis leaves men as divided selves and split personalities, even though they may not be fully aware of their subtle spiritual predicament.

The same remarks apply to all those persons who are inclined to think that all will be well with Muslims, if their economic problems are solved, and that the reformation of Islamic concepts does more harm than good as it generates religious controversy. This line of thinking completely ignores the vital relationship between theory and practice in human life. Just as man finds it very difficult, if not impossible, to pursue morality without some sort of a theoretical basis or set of reasons for being moral (whether this base be supplied by theism, pantheism, or humanism, etc.), similarly it is very difficult, if not impossible, to pursue socio-economic objectives without a suitable theoretical rationale. Thus, if the members of a society consciously or unconsciously believe that poverty and riches are created by God rather than the results of human actions, their motivation will never be as powerful as of those who regard poverty a man-made evil. Similarly, the ideal of human brotherhood will never inspire a group, if it believes those who are outside the group will not find a place in heaven, no matter how morally good they might happen to be. Modernism as a mere socio-political expression will never suffice unless it touches those depths of the human personality where religion resides and operates.

We are thus justified in concluding that reconstructing the basic concepts and values of Islam is an unavoidable responsibility of Muslim intellectuals. Mere changes in sociopolitical infrastructure or, in other words, the schemes of modernization, as advocated by some Islamic liberals in India, Pakistan, and West Asia, will never prove effective unless they are rooted in a systematic and consistent thought system. Similarly, Mawdudi's program of the marginal reconstruction of Islamic polity will also not prove satisfactory. Neither Mawdudi nor the Turkish and Arab modernists attempt to reconstruct the basic Islamic thought system in the light of the ever-expanding frontiers of human knowledge. All said and done, only Indo-Pakistan thinkers like Iqbal (d. 1938), Azad (d. 1958), Fyzee, and Fazlur Rahman (d. 1988), etc. are sufficiently aware of this vital need.[35]

## FIELD INTEGRATION, CONTINUITY, AND CHANGE: THEIR PSYCHOLOGY AND ETHIC

A fresh look at Islam by Muslim intellectuals is essential for giving enlightenment and guidance to the common Muslim, who stands totally perplexed by the antagonistic pulls of theocracy and democracy, clericalism and secularism, traditionalism and modernity. The average Muslim is more or less a split personality and must be helped to integrate himself.[36] The traditional conception of a monolithic religion poses a serious problem to him. As long as the inner logic of traditional Islam leads the Muslim in the direction of monolithic theocracy, and at the same time the logic of his historical situation pulls him in the direction of secular democracy, he can have no inner peace. To the extent that he refuses to come to grips with this basic conflict, he will continue to remain a split personality. The split is due to the basic conflict between the contemporary concept of secularism underlying the present Indian polity and the traditional concept of Islam, as a revealed code of conduct for every facet of human life.

The traditional conception further implies not only the Muslim's duty to submit himself to the discipline of the *shariah*, but also to try to convert non-Islamic states into Islamic ones. This approach makes non-Muslims suspect that all Muslims perpetually attempt to convert, if not subvert, their ways of life. The Muslim resents the suspicion of his loyalty, and feels that his loyalty to the Sovereign Lord of the universe is immensely more important than his image in the eyes of others. He believes that in trying to establish a Quranic world state he is really serving his fellow men better than they know how to serve themselves, rather than imposing an alien way of life.

Any alteration in one's religious convictions on grounds of political expediency or improving the community's image in the eyes of others is definitely wrong in principle. What is really needed is a genuine field integration and the realization that all cultural traditions, including Islam, need ceaseless self authentication, if they are not merely to endure but also prevail. This approach stands in quite a different category from opportunism and signifies inner growth rather than the loss of one's soul for the sake of worldly gain. It leads to an integrated human vision rather than to an eclectic compromise or patchwork synthesis dictated by situational needs or demands.

A mere pragmatic adjustment can never convince the person at the existential level, that is, in the depths of his being, even though it may appear to possess the virtue of situational expediency. No matter how well such a position may have served in the past and may promise to serve in the future, it will lack that power of existential conviction that prompts a Socrates to drink the hemlock with a smile, or a Husayn to embrace death as his highest destiny, or a Vietnamese woman to accept destruction in a foxhole, without the consolation of heaven, just for making the socialist dream come true for posterity. Now, whether we like it or not, some of the Western secular thought-cum-value systems such as Democracy, Socialism, and Communism, etc., do possess this inner structural harmony and existential appeal to their respective followers. This fire of conviction, needless to say, had once burnt in the hearts of the early Muslims also. But the fire gradually cooled down leaving behind only the ashes of a once living conviction. Religious faith is indeed like passionate love, which cannot be produced or extinguished at will. If love be present, the lover is carried on the wings of a sacred passion which makes the sacrifice of his comforts, nay life itself, a ready giving to the beloved rather than a painful duty. But if love be absent, neither logic, nor allurement, nor force suffices to impel such sacrifice, though prudence or sense of duty might prompt the service of others.

A basic difficulty that besets the traditional Indian Muslim is that he honestly believes in the superiority of his religion to all other religions, especially to polytheistic Hinduism, as he understands it. At the same time he finds himself in a hopeless minority as a result of the new democratic set-up in the country. Right up to 1750 A.D. the Indian Muslims had been the politically dominant minority in the country. Later the advent of British rule had deprived them of their dominant position, but they had never become dependent upon the Hindus. At present, however, the Indian Muslim is at a loss to know how to relate himself to Hinduism about which his information is very meager, in spite of the long contact between Islam and Hinduism. All that he does know about Hinduism is derived from a period in which Hinduism was decadent in many respects. The vital and creative period of Hinduism had ended with Harsha (d. 647 AD) almost four centuries before the effective political penetration into north India by the Ghorid Pathans in the late 12th century. Indian Muslims, therefore, never had any opportunity of seeing or studying Hinduism in its earlier period of creative glory. The early Arab scholars of the Abbasid period, who avidly translated Sanskrit classics into Arabic and learnt Indian numerals, astronomy, arithmetic, and chess, etc., must have entertained an image of Hinduism considerably different from that of the Ghorid soldiers and administrators who established themselves in Hindustan without much opposition. Perhaps something of the unconscious group pride still clings to the Indian Muslim mind. This was precisely the situation, which prevailed during the latter half of the 19th century after the establishment of British rule in 1857. But then the problem was posed by Christianity and the Englishman, with the result that Syed

Ahmad was perpetually on the defensive against charges of appeasing the English and of watering down Islam to suit the then existing conditions.

It is thus necessary to correct and supplement the rather distorted and one-sided image of Hinduism in the minds of many Muslims. The grave evils that unfortunately crept into Hindu society long ago need not be glossed over by Muslims. Nor should the rather chauvinistic approach of some Hindu sections be silently accepted. At the same time the numerous elements of value in the long and rich Hindu tradition should be appreciated by the Muslim. In doing so the Muslim would find himself in a very distinguished company, indeed the company of some of the finest intellects of the world: from al-Bairuni to Max Mueller. It goes without saying that the Indian Hindus too must acquire an authentic and well-informed understanding of Islam, as distinguished from the rather superficial social contacts or mere political cooperation for short-term objectives.

Man is born egocentric, bred ethnocentric, but he is potentially 'value centric', that is, inwardly free to assimilate new values or to cultivate new dimensions in the traditional values. The inwardly free man is engaged in an eternal pilgrimage with no sectarian barriers in his way. His heroes are not Muslim, Hindu, or Christian, but just beacons of light that guide his own authentic quest for value. He is neither an imitator nor an originator, but only a truth-seeker gathering the pearls of truth wherever he finds them.

The study of the history of other religions will prove useful for acquiring a deeper insight into our own. Just as it is easier to detect the psychological defense mechanisms or motives of self-interest of others than one's own, so is it with groups. The limitations of other religions are much more easily grasped than those of one's own. Consequently, a critical sociological survey of other religions helps us to understand better the stages and laws of growth of our own culture or religion, its strength and its limitations. This comparative sociology of religions tends to dissolve our natural ethnocentricity and group self-conceit. Self-conceit prompts us to treat our own religion as a class by itself, and hence exempt from sociological laws that apply only to religions other than our own. Once we put aside natural ethnocentricity or 'group snobbery', if I may call it so, we are in a much better position to appreciate the points of excellence of our own religion and its unique contribution to the human family at large.

History avers that no group or tradition can grow and prosper without intelligent self-interpretation. Modern Western culture has been particularly receptive to self-criticism and it is precisely due to this that it continues to grow and flourish. Protestant Christian thinkers such as Matthew Arnold, Tolstoy, Schweitzer, Bultmann, Tillich, Niebuhr, Ramsey, Robinson and others have revised traditional Christian concepts and values without breaking away from the tradition. The Catholic Church has not approved of these essays in conceptual reconstruction, and remains conservative in its approach. But now it is also displaying a new dynamism. Hinduism has been reinterpreted by Rammohun Roy, Vivekananda, Tagore, Aurobindo, and Radhakrishnan, etc. But it appears to me that the systematic reconstruction of Islamic concepts and values has relatively trailed behind in the modern era, though Muslim thinkers were in the vanguard of field integration in the medieval age.

The spiritual and religious history of the West is deeply relevant to Muslims. The achievements of Christian thought must be sympathetically studied for the light it could throw on our own problems and prospects. The counsel of some to accept Western science and technology, but not bother about its spiritual and religious history is both superficial and barren. Conceit is as irrational as blind imitation.

It seems to me that Muslims are relatively more sensitive than non-Muslims to criticism, no matter how objective and academic, on religious issues. It is a common grouse of even highly educated Muslims that Western non-Muslim scholars knowingly or unknowingly distort the truth about Islam due to religious prejudice or political hostility, etc. This makes Western scholarship suspect in the eyes of traditional Muslims. This is indeed most unfortunate. While most Christian writers were manifestly prejudiced against Islam right till the closing years of the last century, the approach of contemporary Western scholars of non-Christian cultures has undergone a qualitative change due to a number of reasons. It would be sheer folly and misfortune for the Muslims to ignore the sympathetic yet critical and balanced evaluations and findings of a Gibb or an Arberry merely because their agreement with traditional Islamic views may not be complete. A dogmatic or defensive rejection of the fruits of free enquiry is no less undesirable than mere fashionable imitation of things Western.

No cultural system, whether religious or secular, can be completely free from spatiotemporal traces. The sincere effort to transcend the limitations of the tradition while remaining loyal to its basic values constitutes creative fidelity to the tradition. The jurists of Islam have in theory evolved a very rational procedure for bringing about orderly changes in the situational concretion of the Islamic value system. But changes based on individual reflection (*ijtihad*) have been very slow and halting, utterly failing to keep pace with a rapidly changing and fast moving world. Even when changes have been accepted by some liberal Muslims, others have continued to question their bona fides. The true conservative seldom gives up the pious hope that the erring members of the group will recant one day. Consequently, he is averse to the 'legitimization' of even the *de facto* changes wrought by time into the religious tradition. However, if the changes take deep roots, showing no sign of dislodgement from the liberal sections of the group, the conservative in time becomes partly reconciled to them.

The creation of new values and the conservation of the old ones that have stood the test of time are both equally necessary. In fact they depend upon each other. The creation of new values presupposes a valuational base or support. Similarly, the effective maintenance of this base demands awareness of the subtle changes in the nuances of human experience. Eternal and intelligent vigilance is the price of keeping old values alive in the condition of dynamic interaction with the environment, rather than as showpieces in the museum of man's heritage.

Creativity ever spurs men to go ahead in the realm of values and to yearn for the better rather than be content with the good. The function of tradition, on the other hand, is to strike a note of caution, lest the pace of change increase to the point of giving diminishing returns. The function of tradition is not the stoppage of growth but only the regulation of the speed of growth. Thus the conservative approach has its own function in the economy of human progress, provided it does not overreach itself. However, the pure conservative or modernist approaches tend to assume the two dimensional, either/or, logic of evaluation, according to which an object is either good or bad and should either be conserved or rejected. This type of blanket evaluation misses the complexity of the object judged. Evaluation must be preceded by an analysis of the elements and structure of the object in question and separate elements must be evaluated separately. All cultural traditions comprise separate elements of value and of disvalue, instead of being monolithic structures of either value or disvalue. The evolutionary approach ensures the blending of continuity and change. It criticizes and overcomes the elements of disvalue in the tradition while making the elements of value the nucleus of further growth.

Creativity and conservation should therefore dovetail into and supplement each other. Without creativity conservation leads to fossilization, while without conservation, creativity leads to irresponsible experimentation. While such adventures in the realm of art and literature may not be injurious, they could prove catastrophic in the realm of moral and social relationships. The new sex morality of Western Europe and America, according to which the game of sex may be played between any two willing parties without any mutual obligation arising there from, has played havoc with the spiritual growth of the contemporary Western man. It appears to me that the West is gradually realizing its fallacy and that a more balanced interpretation of sex is in the process of crystallization. Similarly, the limitations of different movements such as nationalism, capitalism, socialism, and scientism, etc., are being acknowledged. Humanity would have been spared countless tears, had the human judgment been more balanced and well informed. But man blunders, pays the penalty in the course of time, and forges ahead.

The revision of concepts is a continuing and self-correcting process. All attempted revisions are rooted in the concepts and values of the time and place of the integrating individual, though creative individuals are never merely reflections of their environment. No particular integration, whether made by an Ibn Sina or a Ghazzali, an Aquinas or a Kant, a Syed Ahmad or an Iqbal, can be accepted as final. The task of the systematic interpretation of the human situation is an unending collective task, at once the burden and the privilege of the human species rather than of any individual.

This conceptual evolution or reconstruction in the meaning of traditional symbols and images takes time. There may be said to be a 'conceptual lag' just as there is a cultural lag. The concept of conceptual lag makes us tolerant towards the tradition-oriented person. In this context the methodological approach of some Western philosophers is illuminating. They hold that philosophical or theological disputes arise because different persons select different features for emphasis within the same set of facts. Hence, the important thing is not the verbal formulation but rather the full awareness of the complexity of the set of facts. Provided this complexity is grasped, any formulation may be retained. This principle may be called the 'principle of formulational tolerance'. This together with the concept of conceptual lag should help our modernists in carrying out an authentic and fruitful dialogue with the traditionalists, as recommended above.

The principle of formulational tolerance is not an innovation in the cultural tradition of Islam, as is attested by the well-known story of *Moses and the Shepherd* in the *Masnawi* of Maulana Rum.[37] Earlier still, both Ghazzali and Ibn Rushd had said that truth must be communicated to suit the mental level of the hearer. This approach releases us from the monopolistic grip of traditional formulations and also the jargon of our own pet interpretative system.[38]

The concrete life situation of every person being unique, the concrete problems or tensions arising out of the different fields of human experience vary from case to case. The need, urgency, and range of field integration can, therefore, never be uniform for all persons. Where field tensions are not pronounced and an individual is happy and satisfied with his religious beliefs field integration is unnecessary. To make him aware of field tensions that have been registered by philosophers or other sophisticated intellects, but not by an average person, and then to help him overcome those tensions through field integration would be partly similar to raising the blood pressure of a healthy individual to a high degree, and then again bringing it down to normal through some therapy. Nevertheless, the generation of doubt in a satisfied individual is not pointless, since this encourages the conceptual or spiritual growth of individuals by increasing the area and depth of their awareness. This is the legacy of Socrates. The average believer, however, no matter what his religion, does not realize the need for the continuous search for new meanings of old concepts in the light of advancing human knowledge.

The cumulative growth in man's factual knowledge in the modern era has profoundly modified the basic conceptual framework of those who are aware of these developments. Now many such people just find it impossible to accept traditional interpretations. At the same time they do not see any point in repudiating or rejecting their cherished tradition with which they continue to feel a sense of emotional involvement and identification. They still draw inspiration from the tradition, but are not prepared to abdicate their own spiritual autonomy. It is these people who yearn for a new interpretation of basic religious concepts in the idiom of contemporary thought. This is not tantamount to making concessions or 'adjustments' for the sake of expediency or material gain, but reflects an awareness of the intellectual difficulties in the traditional thought or value system.

The quest for growth, must not, however, blind us to the power of the symbols and images of a tradition. These symbols must be retained and at the same time they must be reconstructed. If the symbols are discarded, the creative person isolates himself from the tradition and his new insights have no prestigious vessels to be poured into. If on the other hand the symbols are retained, it becomes very difficult to make them first absorb or assimilate and then convey the new ideas and values in question. The symbols cast their shadows and tend to obscure and distort the fresh stirrings of the human soul. Moreover, even if this difficulty be overcome there is another dilemma. If the symbols are retained in their traditional sense the reformer is heard and understood by the group, but the group does not move forward towards the vision of the leader. If the symbols are formally retained but their meaning or significance radically altered, he tends to suffer from a sense of intellectual dishonesty, and is also liable to be charged with hypocrisy by those who do not feel dissatisfied with the traditional meanings of the symbols in question. Every creative individual, therefore, has to solve this predicament. The fear of the charge of hypocrisy should not deprive him of the advantages of his membership of a living church or tradition. Provided he feels an emotional involvement with the tradition and genuinely finds many elements of value in the historical personalities and events of that tradition, he should go ahead with the task of reconstructing the tradition. The charge of hypocrisy cannot after all be treated as more discouraging or demoralizing than the charge of apostasy that was the order of the day in medieval times, nay, right up to our own.

The charge of hypocrisy will be valid only if the individual distorts his authentic meanings in order to get an audience. If the recommended changes in the meanings of the traditional symbols are fully and frankly acknowledged, employing those symbols for facilitating the genuine creative growth of the community can never be regarded as hypocrisy. Indeed this is the only way to further the cause of cultural evolution. The modifications in the traditional concepts and values should be viewed as fruits growing upon the tree of a living tradition rather than as alterations in an inherited inert brick and mortar structure for the sake of a better '*adjustment*' to life. This concept of growth, as distinguished from alteration, should dispel any lingering sense of disloyalty to the tradition.

# INDEX

## A

Abdali, Ahmad Shah, *121-122, 129*
Abduh, Muhammad, *176-177, 252-253*
Abdur Rahman III, *114, 261*
Abdus Salam, *115*
abstract,
- concepts, *162*
- values, *227*
Abu Bakr, Khalifa, *111, 155*
act of toleration, *96-97*
adultery, *191-198, 204-205, 229*
aesthetic,
- delight, *200, 226*
- taste, *45*
affluence, *24, 179, 240*
Afghani, Jamaluddin, *66, 252, 267*
Ahmadi Muslims, *53*
Akbar, emperor, *66, 118-120, 127, 161, 250-251*
alienation, *34, 57, 81, 179, 209*
Aligarh, *12, 49-50, 56-57, 66, 148, 176, 187, 215-216, 253, 257*
allegorical interpretation, *69*
American revolution, *133*
Amir Ali, *49, 125, 127, 240, 257*
amputation, *205-206, 208*
Angels, *58, 101, 207, 213, 219-220, 254-257*
Anglican Church, *125-126*
anthromorphic fallacy, *64*

apex creation, *207*
apostasy, *36, 68, 108-109, 200, 286*
appeasement, *88, 136-141*
Aquinas, Thomas, *79, 178, 284*
Arab,
- nationalism, *112*
- oil wealth, *152*
architecture, *58, 123*
Aristotle, *94, 131, 245-247, 260*
Arya Samaj, *183*
Asharites, *244-245*
Ashoke, emperor, *46, 76, 91, 124*
aspirations, *29, 72-73, 140, 152, 176*
astronomy, *58, 77, 150, 163, 270, 280*
Athar Ali, historian, *128*
Attar, Fariduddin, *73, 80, 127, 251*
Augustine, Saint, *92, 125*
Aurangzeb, emperor, *66, 76, 119-121, 127-128*
authentic,
- being, *27, 165*
- choice, *188*
authenticity, *16, 27, 29, 34, 39, 54, 65, 165, 198, 216, 229, 231-233, 260, 268, 272*
authoritarian, *24, 31, 41, 94, 132, 139, 141-142, 154*
Azad, Abul Kalam, *47-52, 56-57, 62, 66, 72, 148, 177, 257, 268-274, 278*

## B

Babar, emperor, *121-122*
Babylonia, *114, 178*
Baghdad, *93, 114-115, 188, 213*
Bahmani Kingdom, *120-121*
banking, *113, 178, 207*
Bartholomew, Saint, *95*
*Bengali Babus*, *67*
Bentham, Jeremy, *133, 153, 178, 231*
Bergson, Henry, *28, 238, 255, 260*
Berlin, Isiah, *155*
Bible, inerrancy of, *39*
Biblical stories, *64*
bigotry, *86, 96, 120, 230*
Bill of Rights, *133*
Biological,
- evolution, *21-22, 69, 155, 228, 238*
- reproduction, *167-168*
blasphemy, *116, 132, 148*
bonded labor, *160, 168*
*Brahmanism*, *59*
Brahmo Samaj, *183*
bribery, *158, 208*
British democracy, *59, 70*
brotherhood, *40, 70, 189, 240, 254, 267, 271, 278*
Bruno, Italian scientist, *95*
Buber, Martin, *28*
Buddha, Gautam, *37, 59, 76*
Buddhism, *12, 29, 46, 52, 59, 76, 113, 177, 179*
Bultmann, Rudolf, *59, 282*
Bury, J.B, historian, *124-125*
Byzantium, *94*

## C

Caliphate, *99, 111, 114*
Calvin, John, *94-95, 178, 261*
canon law, *40, 46, 108, 146, 178, 181-182, 185*
Capitalist, *132, 172, 174*
caste taboos, *91, 117*
casual sex, *192, 197-198*
Catholic Church, *39, 51, 95, 132, 282*
Certainty, existential, *124*
Chaos, *40, 82, 192*
Charles I, king, *96, 153*
chastity, *191-192, 227*
Chinese, *34-35, 58, 70, 122, 207*
Christian, militancy, *93*
Christianity, *12, 36, 39-41, 46, 51-52, 59, 76-77, 92-97, 108, 112-113, 125, 131-132, 161, 177, 185, 197, 238, 251, 260-263*
citizen vigilance, *137*
civil marriage, *98, 198*
clericalism, *32, 279*
code of conduct, *40, 47, 50, 68, 75, 77, 112, 176-177, 251, 260-263, 273, 275, 279*
colonial rule, *203*
common law marriage, *198*
communication, *16, 31, 49, 53, 72, 81, 88, 98, 185, 187, 236-237, 248*
communion, *193, 268*
Communism, *78, 141, 273, 280*
Compact of Omar, *111*
compassion, *17, 40, 82, 162, 167, 175, 200, 207, 209, 213*
competition, *71, 118*

composite culture, *123*
compound interest, *160*
Comte, *41*
conceptual,
- idolatry, *35*
- lag, *35, 284-285*
- model, *31, 58, 89, 163*
- pain killing, *31*
- picture, *44*
conscience, *42-45, 80, 94-97, 110, 117, 132, 185, 196, 223-224, 229-234, 270, 272*
conscientious objection, *69, 272*
conservative Muslim, *185*
conspiracy politics, *141*
Constitution, *43, 77, 95, 97-98, 126, 129, 147, 203, 261*
constructive compromise, *136, 139*
contextual analysis, *86*
continuity and change, *279, 284*
contraceptive revolution, *193, 199*
Copernican theory, *56, 275*
Cordova, *114*
Corporation, *97, 125, 173, 266*
corruption, *141, 170*
cost of,
- production, *171, 173-174*
- free capital, *169*
creation, *22-23, 28, 30, 51, 53, 58, 62-64, 78, 127, 193-194, 207, 220, 224-225, 230, 235, 237-239, 244-246, 255, 258-259, 275, 283*

creative fidelity, *29, 251, 283*
creativity of values, *25-26, 32, 261*
Cromwell, Oliver, *132, 153*
cross-fertilization, *33*
Crusades, *92, 125*
cultural,
- beliefs, *135, 143*
- emergent, *32-33*
- gestalt, *20, 29, 33, 228-229*
- islands, *72*
- reification, *89*
culture, *12, 15, 20, 26, 33, 45, 50, 58, 64, 68-70, 76, 89, 93-94, 113-115, 123, 128, 161, 207-208, 228, 230, 237, 243, 247-249, 267, 281-282*
customs, *20, 55, 57, 65, 120, 175, 193, 227*

# D

damnation in hell, *92*
Dara Shikoh, prince, *119-120*
Darwin, Charles, *39, 68, 77-78, 220-221, 238-241, 252-253, 259-260*
David, Prophet, *42, 114*
Day of Judgment, *53, 213*
deductive reasoning, *15, 44*
defection, *108-109*
defense mechanism, *33, 237, 242, 281*
Deism, *40, 277*
delegated authority, *136*
Democracy,
- alternatives to, *138, 141*

- as political expression of, *133*
- essence and forms of, *130, 137*
- evaluation of, *138, 267*
democratic,
- freedom, *142, 203*
- review, *44*
- egalitarianism, *117, 132, 147*
demon inside the ballot, *142*
Denominations, *47, 82, 98*
depth,
- response, *187*
- understanding, *209*
Descartes, Rene, *68, 79, 255, 262*
despair, *28, 185, 200, 233-234, 252*
Devil, *58, 153, 159*
*dharmashastras*, *122, 128, 179*
*dhimmis*, *110-113, 126*
Dilthey, German thinker, *96*
dimensional integration, *23, 27*
discrimination, *67, 87-88, 91, 97, 117, 119, 169, 179, 267*
Disloyalty, *32, 195, 277, 286*
Disraeli, Benjamin, *97*
distress loans, *161, 166, 167, 170-173, 178-180*
Divine,
- attributes, *53, 65, 244, 259, 269*
- sovereignty, *51, 66, 104, 130, 142-143, 273*
divorce, *147, 161, 159, 163, 197*
dogmas, *55, 57, 82-83, 93, 97*

double standards, *63, 199, 228*
dress, *46, 123, 126, 192, 220*

# E

Economic,
- fundamentalist, *51*
- gain, *71*
- independence, *199*
- mechanism, *170*
- rationality, *174-175*
- tool, *174*
education, *59, 183, 198, 205, 208, 261*
Egyptian, *58, 111-114, 153, 176-177, 207, 250, 252-253*
election expenditure, *139*
emotional distance, *98*
empathy, *89-90, 124*
empirically verifiable, *135, 221*
employment, *120, 123, 166*
Empty legalism, *118*
Enlightenment, *12, 27, 32, 40, 49, 96, 75-76, 132, 251, 279*
epidemic, *209, 220*
epoche, *164-165, 179*
equal rights of women, *185, 201*
ethics, *20, 116, 153, 188, 197, 206, 212, 236, 244, 255*
Ethnocentricity, *33, 78, 81, 212, 245, 281-282*
ethos, *24, 35, 128, 131-132, 161, 196, 198-200*
example of the Prophet, *56, 142, 145, 157, 160*
exclusive salvation, *16, 81, 92,*

*120, 200, 212*
**existential,**
- **insight,** *44*
- **interpretation,** *27-28, 221-225, 231, 236, 257, 264*
- **response,** *55, 79, 222*
**experimentation,** *30, 78-79, 284*
**extra-marital,** *191, 194-196*

## F

**factors of production,** *172*
**factual,**
- **information,** *143, 236*
- **knowledge,** *22, 44, 144, 224, 227, 235, 237, 258, 285*
**faith in the Unseen,** *44, 68, 200*
**family planning,** *185, 193, 199*
**fanaticism,** *97, 119, 125, 265*
**fatalism,** *64, 239*
**fatherhood of God,** *40*
**fear of freedom,** *45, 81, 148, 233, 237*
**fellowship of faiths,** *83, 254*
**feudal system,** *118*
**fidelity,** *29, 122, 192, 194, 199, 227, 251, 283*
**Five Points, Fundamentalism,** *39*
**forcible conversion,** *45*
**formulational pluralism,** *35*
**fornication,** *182, 204*
**forward-looking,** *12, 33, 77, 149*
**fossilization,** *30, 32, 284*
**Frederick, the Great,** *96*
**free enquiry,** *12-15, 40, 68-69, 95, 135, 149-150, 165, 185, 193,*
*283*
**freedom of,**
- **association,** *136*
- **conscience,** *42, 45, 94-95, 110, 185*
- **expression,** *136, 141*
**French Revolution,** *40, 95, 133, 251*
**Freud, Sigmund,** *41, 51, 68-69, 229, 231, 240-242*
**Fromm, Erich,** *45, 81, 148, 233*
**functional,**
- **innovations,** *140*
- **meaning,** *160*
- **secularism,** *66, 117-118, 123, 127*

## G

**Gabriel,** *60-62, 69, 80, 246, 259*
**gambling,** *168, 173, 240*
**Gandhi, Mahatma,** *55, 67*
**gender equality,** *15, 147, 199*
**Ghalib, Mirza, poet,** *43, 127*
**Ghori, Muhmmad, Sultan,** *121, 280-281*
**Gibb, H.A R.,** *126, 155, 282*
**Global society,** *98, 177, 186*
**Goethe,** *40, 76, 96*
**Gokhle, Balkrishna,** *67*
**good life,** *24, 33, 76, 144, 157, 162, 176, 189, 203, 227, 263, 271,*
**Gorbachov, Mikhail,** *152*
**Gospel,** *39, 64, 92, 104*
**Greek,** *33, 58, 64, 94, 122, 127, 130, 132, 207, 243, 246, 248*
**group snobbery,** *33, 282*

# H

**Hafiz, Persian poet,** *73, 127*
**Hallaj, Mansoor,** *115*
**Hambal, Imam,** *99, 115*
**heaven and hell,** *53, 254, 259*
**Hedonism,** *24, 234, 237*
**Hegel,** *23, 40, 76, 78, 96, 255*
**Hegemony,** *42, 76, 92, 141, 209*
**Heresy,** *68, 125*
**Heritage,** *30, 32, 69, 207, 255, 283*
**hermeneutic,** *143, 251, 254, 256*
**hierarchical,** *117, 130, 134*
**Hindu,**
- fundamentalism, *43, 177*
- liberalism, *43*
- response, *43*

**Hinduism,** *12, 29, 42-46, 49, 52, 60, 121, 131, 177, 185, 197, 280-282*
**Hindu-Muslim fraternity,** *66*
**Hitler, Adolph,** *96*
**Hitti, P.K.,** *126, 125-127*
**Holy Spirit,** *60-62*
**Human Development Index,** *175*
**Human,**
- needs, *72, 135, 221*
- rights, *15, 75, 98, 149, 199*
- welfare, *15, 41, 136, 147, 150, 175, 185, 209, 268*

**Humanism,** *16, 27, 56, 70-71, 93, 99, 105, 118, 132-133, 148-152, 176, 193, 195, 201, 209, 233, 250-251, 266, 271, 278*

**Humayun, emperor,** *122*
**Hume, David,** *40, 68, 76, 262*
**humility,** *48, 53, 88-90, 150, 189, 199-200, 207, 259*
**Husayn Shah, King,** *120*
**Husserl, Edmund,** *164-165, 179*

# I

**Ibn Sina,** *17, 31, 62, 73, 115, 245-248, 255, 284*
**idea of the Holy,** *40*
**ideals and interests,** *73, 151, 251, 266*
**idle money,** *166*
**idol worship,** *80, 91, 184-185*
**idolatry,** *35, 183-187*
**imperial interests,** *66, 71*
**India/Indian,** *12, 20, 32-35, 42-43, 47, 49-59, 66-67, 70-72, 77, 85, 87, 90-91, 98, 111, 113, 115-128, 137, 161, 177, 182, 207, 215-217, 249-252, 263, 272, 278-281*
**indoctrinate,** *89, 187*
**Indonesia,** *98, 113, 177, 252*
**infallibility,** *41, 60, 143*
**inheritance,** *46, 147, 157, 159, 161, 163, 179, 275*
**Inquisition,** *93*
**instinct,** *62, 197, 230, 241, 269-270*
**instrumental rules,** *17, 205-206, 213, 221, 227, 270*
**insurance,** *168, 173, 207, 262*
**integrity,** *31, 34, 36, 82, 90, 121, 183, 192, 196, 198, 226, 231*

# Index

**intellectual dishonesty,** *34, 242, 286*
**interest,** *40, 157-179*
**inter-marriage,** *181-190*
**intrinsic values,** *17, 205, 221, 226-227, 236, 241*
**Iqbal, Muhammad,** *46-57, 66, 71, 77, 140, 177, 253, 257-268, 271-276, 278, 284*
**Iranians,** *33, 47, 58, 68, 93, 99, 110-113, 118, 122, 126, 152, 161, 207, 227, 250*
**irenic,** *23, 248, 251*
*isht devata, 91*
**Islamic,**
- Naxalites, *52*
- economic system, *157-179*
- Economics, *129, 162, 175, 204*
- methodology, *150*
- political theory, *146*
- resurgence, *49, 149-150, 152, 157, 167, 176-177*

**Islamization,** *51, 150, 157, 177*

## J

**Jaafar Sadiq, Imam,** *99, 253*
**Jamaat e Islami,** *176*
**Jami, Persian poet,** *127, 251*
**Jesus,** *39, 76, 95, 101, 125, 232, 254, 257*
**Jews,** *54, 91-98, 102-106, 112-115, 125-126, 161, 178, 182, 184*
*jizya, 110, 118-121, 126, 161*
**judiciary, independence of,** *137*
**Julian, The Apostate,** *92*

**jurisdiction of religion,** *44-49, 57, 60, 65, 75, 77, 95-98, 118, 125, 177, 212, 261-262*

## K

**Kaaba,** *80, 111*
**Kabir, Sant,** *127*
**Kamal, Mustafa,** *203*
**Kant, Immanuel,** *22, 40, 68, 76, 79, 96, 226, 231, 248, 255, 258, 262, 284*
**Kierkegaard, Soren,** *69, 255*
**knowledge,** *15, 17, 21-23, 28, 41, 44, 58-59, 63, 68, 70, 90, 98, 135, 143-144, 150, 154, 158, 170, 207-208, 211-214, 223-227, 235, 237, 243-247, 251, 255, 258, 264, 268, 270, 278, 285*

## L

**Land of Islam,** *110, 112, 161-163, 204-205, 209*
**leadership,** *71, 76, 93, 172, 215*
**learned fools,** *141*
**legalism,** *34, 118, 247, 250*
**Lenin,** *174*
**liberal,** *19, 31, 39-54, 57, 60, 67-71, 74-76, 94-95, 114-115, 118, 120-121, 124-1256, 133, 148-152, 157, 161, 166, 175-179, 182, 191-197, 216, 240, 250-253, 257, 278, 283*
**life affirmation,** *24, 133, 239*
**Linguistic Analysis,** *34-35, 215*
**Locke, John,** *40, 66, 68, 76, 79, 87, 96, 255, 262*
**Lodi, Ibrahim,** *122*

**Logic,** *21-22, 27, 44-45, 58, 62, 78-79, 83, 87, 90, 109, 135, 142-143, 152, 161-163, 185, 188-189, 206, 223, 231, 234-237, 254-258, 268, 270, 279-280*
**love for God,** *213, 247*
**Luther, Martin,** *49, 94-96, 132, 178, 261*

# M

**Madani, Husain Ahmad,** *126*
**magic,** *21, 56, 64, 132, 243, 268*
**Magna Carta,** *133, 153*
**Malaviya, Madan Mohan,** *87*
**Malaysia,** *113, 216*
**mandate,** *134, 163, 263*
**market,**
- **forces,** *179*
- **price,** *173*

**marriage,** *46, 98, 111, 117, 147, 161, 163, 181-200, 227, 272*
**Marx, Karl,** *20, 22, 37, 41, 51, 68, 76, 78-79, 133, 151, 153, 174, 239-241*
**Materialist,** *40, 97, 125, 240*
**Mathematical truth,** *83, 135*
**Mawdudi, Abul Aala,** *46-52, 66, 68, 124, 179, 204, 273-274, 278*
**Mecca,** *51, 59, 76, 80, 111, 126, 145, 219-220*
**mechanics of revelation,** *53, 259*
**medieval, India,** *42, 77, 85, 115-117, 121, 123*
**Medina,** *46, 54, 76, 114, 126, 145*

**messianic hope,** *42*
**Metaphysical,** *21-22, 28, 44, 53, 100, 124, 175, 221-222, 233, 247, 259-260*
**methodology,** *44, 65, 144, 150, 234 249, 254*
**Mill. John Stuart,** *87, 136, 153, 178, 240, 267*
**Milton, John,** *96-97*
**miracles,** *39, 59-63, 69, 78, 143, 176, 235, 248, 254, 256-258*
**moderation,** *52, 71, 226*
**modernity,** *15-34, 48-49, 77, 149, 201, 211-216, 251, 279*
**monarchy,** *84, 146*
**Mongol invasion,** *93, 99, 248-249*
**monotheism,** *52, 59, 91-92, 184, 277-278*
**morality,** *23, 26, 28, 30, 44, 68, 73, 75, 80, 82, 88-90, 125, 131, 135, 188, 198, 212, 229, 233-234, 243, 247, 249, 264, 270*
**music,** *58, 61, 98, 120, 123, 127, 178, 185, 200, 207, 259*
**Muslim,**
- **hegemony,** *42*
- **identity,** *71*

**Muslims,** *11-13, 17, 42, 44-51, 53-56, 58, 67-74, 75-77, 81, 83, 85, 93, 108-123, 125-129, 144-149, 157, 161-162, 170, 173-175, 181-185, 199-200, 203, 205, 208, 211, 216, 221, 240-242, 245, 248-253, 257, 263, 265, 271-283*
**myths,** *57-62, 69, 91, 164, 175, 248*

# Index

## N

Nadir Shah, *121-122, 128*
Nanak, Guru, *12, 59*
natural,
- causation, *21, 78*
- science, *58, 60, 77-78, 82, 132, 193, 222, 234-235*
nature of God, *53, 247, 250, 258*
Nehru, Jawaharlal, *67, 126, 215*
Newton, Isaac, *77, 97, 238, 262*
Niebuhr, Reinhold, *28, 282*
Nihilism, *34, 212, 234, 264*
Nizam of Hyderabad, *121*
Nizami, K.A., *128*
nuclear, *34, 55-57, 73, 137, 228*

## O

Obedience, *40-41, 110, 132, 143, 159-160, 227, 259, 270, 273*
Omar, second Khalifa, *111, 114, 126-127, 145, 155, 161, 218*
opportunism, *32, 119, 279*
organic unity, *46, 50, 66, 71, 77, 94, 230, 254, 257, 263, 276*
orthogenetic, *148, 201, 256*
Ottoman empire, *203*
out-group, *57, 68, 82, 208, 276*
Owen, Robert, *174*

## P

pain and evil, *69, 230, 238, 268, 272*
painting, *58, 123, 185, 200, 228*
Pakistan, *51-53, 56, 71-72, 98, 127, 157-158, 216, 263, 275-278*
Palestine, *91, 115, 182*
Paley, William, *66, 68, 255*
Pande, Bishamber Nath, *128*
pan-Islamism, *66, 152, 267-268*
paradigm, *11-12, 16, 45, 47, 58, 63, 83-84, 122, 185, 201, 212-213*
partition of India, *43, 50, 67, 71*
party of,
- God, *52*
- the Devil, *52*
Parvez, Ghulam Ahmad, *179, 274-276*
peaceful conversion, *92*
Penology, *203-209*
people of the Book, *111-112, 126, 182, 184*
permissive approach, *40, 82, 191-192, 198-199, 251*
perplexity, *11, 90, 124*
Personal God, *35, 269*
petitionary prayer, *64, 241*
phenomenological analysis, *163*
Philosophy, *20, 45, 47, 51, 59, 67, 78-82, 95, 97, 153, 163, 171, 178, 207, 215-216, 228, 243-250, 254, 257, 267-268*
plural,
- interpretations, *45, 53-54, 100*
- societies, *47-48, 92, 250-251, 263, 275-276*
plurality, *40, 89-90, 98, 162, 189, 244*
poetry, *50, 56, 61, 71, 80, 127, 251, 258, 267-268*
polemics, *32, 79*

**politics,** *42-52, 65-72, 87-88, 114, 117, 124, 126, 135, 141, 144, 150-154, 157-158, 176, 209, 215, 229, 253, 270*
**polity,** *44, 48-49, 51, 66, 68, 99, 157, 162, 174, 203, 205, 260, 267, 274-279*
**polyandry,** *193-196*
**polymorphous equality,** *24-25*
**Pope,** *39-40, 49, 93-95, 131-132, 261*
**prejudice,** *42, 67, 72, 98, 110, 149, 189, 230, 264, 282*
**primitive,** *15, 78, 204-205, 208*
**printing of the Quran,** *185*
**procreation,** *193-196*
**profit,** *158, 160, 166-174, 178*
**prohibited degrees,** *163, 184*
**prohibition,** *45, 91, 157, 161, 164, 167-168, 174, 178-184*
**prophet, Muhammad,** *13, 17, 31, 36-37, 45-46, 52-54, 56, 59-65, 69-70, 76, 81, 91-92, 99-101, 109-114, 126, 128, 131, 142-146, 155, 157, 160-161, 182, 200, 205, 219-220, 245-246, 249, 251, 254, 256-261, 269-274*
**Protestants,** *40, 59, 75, 94-95, 98, 115, 125, 177-178, 238, 282*
**providence,** *28, 58, 97, 132, 239-240, 274*
**pseudo,**
- **miracles,** *63*
- **Muslims,** *116*
**punishment,** *46, 91, 93, 104, 130, 153, 160, 195, 199, 204-209, 220, 229, 244, 256, 258*

**puritan,** *98, 120, 199-201*
***purusharthas,*** *122*

## Q

**quest for value,** *73, 264, 281*
**quintessence of Islam,** *49*
**Quran,** *13, 16-17, 31, 36, 48-49, 53-54, 59-69, 81, 84-85, 99-113, 115, 127, 142-147, 154-155, 157-164, 166-169, 174-175, 178, 181-186, 191, 197-198, 200-201, 204-205, 207-208, 213-214, 220, 229-232, 241, 244-246, 249, 251-260, 268-276, 279*

## R

**Rabia Basri,** *188, 213*
**Rajputs,** *119, 121-122*
**rationalism,** *27, 34, 52, 246-255, 268, 273*
**rebellion,** *109, 131-132, 146*
**reductive theory,** *23, 171*
**Reformation,** *59, 75, 94, 132, 208, 241, 278*
**religious,**
- **complexion,** *71*
- **experience,** *26-28, 31, 237*
- **feeling,** *99, 187, 248*
- **fundamentalism,** *39-87, 98*
- **liberalism,** *41, 44, 49, 51-52, 70-71, 94, 118, 120, 124, 151*
- **modernity,** *19, 26-30, 34, 49*
**Renaissance,** *12, 19, 21, 24, 59, 76, 94, 126, 132, 251-252*
**revelation,** *28, 31, 44, 53-54, 60-62, 65, 69, 73, 75-76, 105-108,*

*142, 144, 155, 181, 219-220, 235, 245-246, 254-259, 269-270, 274, 277*
*riba*, *158, 160, 164, 168, 175*
**Rizvi, S.A.A.,** *127-128*
**romantic marriage,** *193-194*
**Rumi, Jalaluddin,** *17, 35, 64, 73, 80, 127, 260*

## S

**sacrosanct,** *46, 48, 143, 233, 266*
**sanatana dharma,** *91*
**Sanskrit,** *113, 120, 280*
**satanic,** *48, 151, 254*
**Schiller, Friedrich,** *40, 76, 96*
**Schimmel, Annemarie,** *155*
**Schleiermacher,** *68, 255*
**schools of jurisprudence,** *45, 99, 109*
**scientific,**
- attitude, *63-64, 240, 252*
- revolution, *49, 59, 79, 176, 251, 261-264*
- socialists, *76, 175*
**scope of religion,** *60, 65, 150*
**seal of the prophets,** *53*
**secular democracy,** *43-44, 51, 70, 75, 77, 128, 253, 279*
**secularism,** *32, 42, 44, 47, 66, 88, 117-118, 123-124, 127, 151, 211-212, 261, 263-264, 268, 272-273, 276-279*
**segregation,** *197-200*
**self,**
- alienation, *34, 81*
- conceit, *33, 282*
- corrective process, *135*
- expression, *88, 223*
**semantic confusion,** *163*
**sex morality,** *30, 19-201, 284*
**shariah,** *13, 46, 48-51, 65-68, 75, 80-81, 99, 108, 114, 116, 118-120, 127, 144-147, 150, 176-178, 181, 185, 204, 250-251, 263, 270-273, 279*
**Shibli, Allama,** *127, 257*
**Shivaji,** *122, 128*
**Sikhs,** *119, 121, 177, 183*
**slavery,** *91, 113, 147, 161*
**Smith, Adam,** *78, 178, 262*
**Social,**
- accident, *181*
- evils, *25, 163, 167, 234, 240*
- gradation, *123*
- justice, *25, 68, 158, 169, 261, 266, 272*
- organism, *172*
- science, *23, 31, 48, 59, 70, 75, 78, 82, 148-150, 162-163, 168, 174, 178, 193, 207, 238, 273*
**Socialism,** *25, 30, 129, 141, 157, 179, 263, 267, 272-276, 280, 284*
**Sociology,** *22, 29, 33-34, 47, 57, 78, 80, 128, 152, 206, 237, 239, 275, 281*
**Socrates,** *37, 95, 165, 280, 285*
**solidarity,** *71, 91, 114, 161*
**sovereignty of God,** *66, 142-143, 273*
**spiritual,**
- autonomy, *24-26, 41, 49, 133-134, 143-144, 149, 188, 231-233, 285*

- dimension, *41, 44, 176, 264*
- ecstasy, *118*
- suffering, *165*
- values, *69, 151, 186, 188-189*
spirituality, *16, 26-29, 34, 44, 49, 68, 99, 127, 151, 165, 209, 212-215, 229-230, 249, 270*
spouses, *183, 186*
status of non-Muslims, *110*
stoning unto death, *197, 200, 204-205, 229*
Sufi, *12, 35, 43, 49, 60, 64, 68, 80, 116, 118, 120, 127, 188, 213, 243, 246-251*
Sunni (Islam), *52, 65, 146, 157, 197, 201, 251*
Supernatural, *21, 39, 63-64, 78, 143, 245, 256*
Syed, Sir Syed Ahmad Khan, *12, 43, 47, 49, 50-52, 55-74, 148, 150, 176-177, 215*

## T

Tagore, Rabindra Nath, *12, 50, 55, 126, 282*
Taliban, *200*
Tarachand, Dr., historian, *128*
tensions, *11, 47, 131, 140, 165, 200, 228-230, 234, 237, 243-248, 276, 285*
Theocracy, *32, 177, 279*
Theodosius I, emperor, *92*
theory of,
- evolution, *39, 155, 228, 230, 238, 252*
- interest, *171*
- revelation, *62*

Tilak, Bal Gangadhar, *67*
Tillich, Paul, *28, 55, 229, 282*
tolerance, *13, 15, 32, 35, 40, 45, 54, 68, 83, 85-128, 133, 147, 149, 189, 193, 207, 240, 250, 254, 271, 285*
trade, *46, 117, 159, 171-172, 261*
tradition, *13, 17, 19-20, 25, 28-36, 40, 45-50, 55-63, 67, 70-72, 77, 80, 83-84, 88-92, 97, 99-100, 111-116, 124, 127, 147-149, 155, 165-166, 182-185, 188, 199-200, 204, 208-209, 212-215, 225, 228-240, 247-254, 259, 262, 267-274, 277-286*
Transcendental,
- belief, *53*
- truths, *205*
translation of the Quran, *181*
Tribalism, *78, 112*
Turkey, *115, 118, 203, 205, 263, 277-278*
Tyabji, Badruddin, *43, 49*
types of loans, *166-168*
tyranny, *42, 93, 128, 142, 223, 234*

## U

ulema, *43, 46, 48-49, 56-57, 116, 127, 148-149, 157, 161*
Unitarians, *95, 125*
unity of religion and state, *47, 52, 71, 77*
Upanishads, *120*
Usman, Khalifa, *111, 155*
usury, *157-163, 166-168, 173-175, 178-179*

**utopia,** *141, 154, 175-176, 199*

# V

**Vacuum,** *129, 233*
**value judgments,** *83, 86, 143, 164, 236*
**Vedic fundamentalism,** *52*
**veracity of Muhammad,** *53-54*
**Vijaynagar kingdom,** *120-121*
*vipasna,* *27*

# W

*wahi e jali,* **144**
*wahi e khafi,* *144, 155*
**Waliullah, Shah,** *56, 62, 127, 251, 253, 259*
**warrior caste,** *117, 122*
**Watt, Montgomery,** *126, 155*
**Western domination,** *129, 203*
**Westphalia, treaty of,** *96*
**Whitehead, Alfred North,** *28, 77, 224, 229*
**Word of God,** *13, 31, 49, 59, 61-66, 69-70, 99, 127, 145, 159-160, 186, 232, 245, 254-259, 277*
**Work of God,** *61-62, 66, 69, 254*
**World View,** *40, 47, 225, 229, 231, 235*

# Z

*zakat,* *110, 179, 219, 274*
**Zaynul Abidin, Sultan,** *120*
**zeitgeist,** *72-73*
**Zoroastrian,** *112-114, 126*

To learn more about the author - Jamal Khwaja, and his various works visit

# www.JamalKhwaja.com

Download free Digital Books, Lectures, Essays, browse links to related sites and much more...

Publishers website can be found at
# www.AlhamdPublishers.com

www.ingramcontent.com/pod-product-compliance
Lightning Source LLC
Chambersburg PA
CBHW030307080526
44584CB00012B/470